Sourdough bread is naturally ve[...] into extraordinary, delicious bre[...] bread-maker, and co-owner of the popular veg[...] with Natasha Tatton, has been baking and refining his recipes and techniques for naturally leavened sourdough for many years—including a wide array of boules, baguettes, loaves, flatbreads, buns, and pizza dough. As required, he uses plant-based alternatives in some savoury and sweet sourdoughs that would traditionally include dairy (butter, milk, or buttermilk) including panettone buns, hot cross buns, sticky buns, cinnamon buns, English muffins, brioche, and babka. Inside *BReD*, you'll find these perfected recipes to start your journey in bread-making; along with a detailed sourdough starter guide with step-by-step visuals on making and maintaining a sourdough starter, levain, mixing, shaping, and baking methods.

BReD is a complete plant-based book for bakers that goes beyond just making bread. Experienced bakers and novices alike can take their baking to the next level with gorgeous vegan baked goods from cakes, muffins, and scones to biscuits, cookies, and tarts. Passionate about a vegan lifestyle for the benefit of all people and the planet, the book also includes gluten-free recipes (bread and other baked goods), sourdough discard recipes to further zero-waste efforts, and an offering of dips, spreads, and accompaniments to complement the breads.

BReD

Sourdough Loaves,

Small Breads,

and Other Plant-Based Baking

ED TATTON

with Natasha Tatton

For my grandfather, John Dickie

PENGUIN

an imprint of Penguin Canada, a division of Penguin Random House Canada Limited

Canada • USA • UK • Ireland • Australia • New Zealand • India • South Africa • China

First published 2023

www.penguinrandomhouse.ca

Library and Archives Canada Cataloguing in Publication

Title: BReD : sourdough loaves, small breads, and other plant-based baking /
Ed Tatton with Natasha Tatton.
Names: Tatton, Ed, author. | Tatton, Natasha, author.
Description: Includes index.
Identifiers: Canadiana (print) 20220410283 | Canadiana (ebook) 20220410291 |
ISBN 9780735244443 (hardcover) | ISBN 9780735244450 (EPUB)
Subjects: LCSH: Cooking (Sourdough) | LCSH: Sourdough bread. | LCSH: Vegan cooking. |
LCGFT: Cookbooks.
Classification: LCC TX770.S66 T37 2023 | DDC 641.81/5—dc23

Cover and interior design by Terri Nimmo
Food and prop styling by Ed and Natasha Tatton
Photography by Janis Nicolay
Photos on pages vii, 7, 22, 52, 79, and 358 by Darby Magill

Printed in China

10 9 8 7 6 5 4 3 2 1

Penguin
Random House
PENGUIN CANADA

Contents

introduction

Traditional techniques from a time when everything was made from scratch in the family kitchen will be forever revered, and those recipes are part of our cultural heritage. Holding true to the roots of what our grandmothers achieved, we strive to make delicious foods to share and enjoy with our loved ones. But what we generally assume about how we have eaten for years is not actually so.

Food is always evolving. The foods that most of us have available to us now were not available to our ancestors. Curry is one of the UK's best-loved dishes, but it was introduced to Britain only in the 1800s. Tomatoes may be integral to Italian cuisine these days but were introduced from the Americas around 1530. The way we produce food is also in a state of flux, evolving with scientific breakthroughs and technology. A farm today looks unrecognizable from a farm a couple of centuries ago. Animal agriculture has become so industrialized that we have completely lost any sense that other sentient beings have any feelings or rights at all.

As we are experiencing a great shift in climate, resource dependency, technology, and ultimately mental well-being, might we not shift to a higher level of consciousness where we live our lives in a way that respects sentient beings and causes the least possible amount of suffering? Recipes from a time gone by are not serving us in the modern world in the way they did for our ancestors.

Although many books have been written about baking, and the market is saturated with vegan cookbooks, we ourselves have not found much literature that bridges the gap between traditional baking and vegan eating. This book is a nod to where we have come from and a bridge to where we all need to go. Our hope is that you will fall in love with our recipes and be inspired to keep on baking and eating vegan.

HOW IT ALL BEGAN FOR US

Originally from Kent in England, I have always worked in fine-dining kitchens around the world and have been making sourdough since 2008. I always knew that I wanted to be a chef, and there are many old photographs of me as a chubby child mixing cakes with my mother in our kitchen. As soon as I turned sixteen, I left school and began studying at culinary college and working part-time in an upmarket bistro. During this time, I met Natasha, who was going to university and working as a waitress and barmaid to supplement her student loan. As soon as my studies were over, I went on to work as a chef de partie in the Michelin-starred Read's Restaurant, in Faversham, which held its star for twenty years. I worked on various sections, such as larder, garmache, and pastry. After gaining over a year's experience at Read's, Natasha and I headed around the world on a working holiday to Australia and New Zealand.

When we returned home we moved to Bristol, where I really developed my bread-making skills at a prestigious French/British bistro called Bell's Diner. Under the guidance of executive chef Chris Wicks, we made sourdough, poolish baguettes, and focaccia to pair with the à la carte menu. I worked there for a few years and was then transferred to nearby Berwick Lodge, a boutique hotel, to become head chef. I continued to bake bread.

All the years of studying British and French fine cuisine and working in high-end eateries has instilled a passion for sourcing the best quality local ingredients and for changing with the seasons. This equates to growing food in a garden, using an indoor cultivation unit to sprout seeds and grow microgreens, building relationships with local farmers and producers, and foraging for mushrooms, fruits, and herbs instead of relying on the conventional food-distribution channels, which tend to be exploitative and environmentally damaging. Long before I went vegan, as head chef at Berwick Lodge, I would rescue battery hens who were still laying eggs but not enough to provide a profit for the egg industry. Throughout my career I have had a respect for animals and looking after them as well as possible, but as I learnt more about animal agriculture, I wanted less and less to do with it.

Natasha and I came to Canada in 2013 to snowboard for a season, and I worked as sous chef at Alta Bistro in Whistler. While taking some shoulder-season leave and working on Vancouver Island vegetable farms and vineyards in the summer of 2014, I started a sourdough culture. I have happy memories of us going from farm to farm carrying a large canvas bag containing the starter, a small digital scale, and various flours and seeds, asking the farmers if they had a fridge I could keep the mother ferment in, and the amusement on their faces at this farm worker travelling with a live culture, us riding rusty bikes around and delivering rustic loaves to the farmers' families and baking bread in all sorts of ovens, including a homemade outdoor pizza oven and in an ancient trailer that was stuck in a 1970s time warp. I eventually took my starter back with me to Alta Bistro and implemented a bread program for the restaurant.

Also in 2014, Natasha and I started to practise yoga at a studio called Loka Yoga with Tina James, an Ashtanga-certified teacher. To show our gratitude for all her teachings, I would gift Tina a loaf of bread, which would fill the studio with the aromas of fresh baking and make all the students salivate during their yoga classes. Soon, all the yoga students were asking if they could get a loaf of bread, and when I was in a headstand one day, the idea of renting Alta Bistro's kitchen once a week to bake for friends was born.

Everything was organized through Facebook back then. I created a business page, took orders by Messenger, and people paid cash. They could reorder for the following week, and I would note it all down in a brown notebook, but it was basically all done on trust. I didn't know if I would be able to sell thirty loaves the first time I rented that kitchen, but I did, and before I knew it I had maximized production to a consistent 150 loaves in two small ovens in different kitchens, and I was turning people away because I couldn't meet demand. The community were loud and clear: I needed to open my own bakery.

During all of this, Natasha had become a little frustrated by the lack of impact she felt she was making sitting on the board of directors for a local environmental group, and she wanted to do something far more hands on, engaging the community and saving animals and the environment. She had started to dream about opening a vegan café. Once we put our heads together, the concept of a vegan sourdough bakery was born. We sold our house in the UK, risked our life's savings, and threw ourselves into this amazing adventure of vegan baking and sourdough.

VEGAN INFLUENCES

There has never been a better time to go vegan, as more products are available and more people are championing the movement than we know of. It always amazes us when we discover another famous vegan who has been waving the flag for years without us hearing about it. I guess we spend too much time in the kitchen to follow them all!

One of the first names that left a big impression on us was Matthew Kenney. Prior to opening the Whistler bakery, I went to Los Angeles to get some experience in some of its distinguished sourdough bakeries, and while I was working there, I sought out a vegan fine-dining restaurant called Plant Food + Wine. It was completely revolutionary—I had only ever known fine-dining menus to showcase an abundance of meat and seafood and had no idea of the potential of plant-based cuisine. I was utterly blown away by what I was eating. Natasha and I later took Matthew's online cookery course and had so much fun fermenting nut cheeses, churning ice creams, and a lot more.

Doug Evans is an old-school vegan, lovable, young-at-heart former Silicon Valley entrepreneur who has an infectious enthusiasm for sprouting seeds. He inspired us to take up sprouting as a full-time hobby when we heard him interviewed by Rich Roll on *The Rich Roll Podcast*. Rich himself is a plant-based pioneer in endurance athletics and has been on our radar since the beginning of our vegan journey. He has been interviewed in many documentaries not only on nutrition but also on vegan parenting. He is solid proof that you can be healthy and perform well on plants alone, and you can successfully bring up kids on a vegan diet too.

Erin Ireland is kind of a big deal here in British Columbia. She began her career as an omnivorous food journalist and blogger, with a grassroots bakery business, To Die For. Then she eventually became a vegan and rebranded her wholesale bakery as To Live For, which makes strictly vegan products, and none of her customers noticed when her products went vegan! When I was still the sous chef at Alta Bistro, I designed a three-course vegan menu when the yoga festival Wanderlust was in town. Erin came in and ate, then wrote a very generous piece about it online. That is how I discovered this local vegan icon. I was so honoured to see my vegan food mentioned by a food critic! Erin has since visited our bakery numerous times, usually with her vegan kids in tow, and has always been very supportive of us. We are equally excited to see Erin branch out into a retail bakery with her husband. The vegan business world is not dog-eat-dog like many other industries; we are all on the same mission to create a vegan world and want to lift each other up to do so.

Richard Makin, also known as School Night Vegan, is a former ice-cream truck owner turned food stylist, recipe developer, and food editor specializing in animal-free dishes. He has a wealth of knowledge regarding all sorts of vegan food and has built his own test kitchen in his house where he conducts vegan food experiments. Richard has been so generous sharing his research on vegan baking, such as egg substitutes, and we are constantly inspired by all the delicious dishes he creates.

VEGAN, THE NEW NORMAL

The word *vegan* can conjure negative connotations of angry animal activists or fussy eaters, so the term *plant-based* is perhaps more approachable. Unfortunately, not everything labelled as plant-based or veggie is free of animal products and there are not any laws in any country we know of that define and regulate these labels in the same way that "gluten-free" is, for example.

Veganism is a fairly new concept in that the word *vegan* was created in 1944 and was only recently adopted into the mainstream. Its nuance is still very misunderstood today, particularly when it comes to ingredients, such as honey or backyard chicken eggs. It's encouraging to see corporations jumping on the bandwagon, offering so-called plant-based options, and veganism is a hugely popular trend on social media. But we believe it is a growing movement here to stay and not just a passing dietary zeitgeist.

A token vegan option is usually available in any average eatery amongst the usual exploitative meat, dairy, and seafood, but there is a vast amount of cross-contamination and mistakes get made by staff all the time. If you can make something just as good or even better with vegan ingredients, why not eliminate its animal-based counterpart and cut out harming animals and potentially other humans too? There shouldn't just be vegan *options* in restaurants—vegan should be the new normal. Why should vegans have to label our foods when we are the ones causing the least amount of harm?

Most of us do not give a second thought to the fact that we drink cow's milk, designed by nature to feed a calf and not humans. Cows are impregnated most of their short lives. A dairy cow may naturally live to the age of twenty but is usually slaughtered at six years, after birthing two or three calves. Today, dairy cows typically produce ten times more milk per year than they did two hundred years ago. To extract the milk of a cow, it is necessary to remove the calf from the mother. It never occurs to many vegetarians who choose not to eat meat that the baby cow is nearly always killed immediately after birth if they are male, and a good portion of female calves are also destroyed.

When we really think about it, in the natural order no other animal imprisons another species to impregnate them or kills their babies to steal their lactation fluids. We use euphemisms such as "normal milk" or "regular milk" that highlight our conditioning to this incredibly unnatural diet. We seem to accept that this is the natural order of things but it may be the case that prehistoric populations were not able to stomach raw cow's milk at all but did so at times of food scarcity, risking potentially deadly bouts of diarrhea to stay alive, and even today it is estimated that 70 percent of the world's population are lactose intolerant. When the research suggests that a quarter of Americans are lactose intolerant, we must ask why dairy is touted as being a healthful food as part of a balanced diet by the government dietary guidelines. Most people have no idea that we even have this intolerance, as we are completely out of touch not only with our environment and animal relatives but even with our own bodies. Could this be a contributing factor in the mental and physical health crises we are facing?

There is overwhelming research into the connections between animal-based diets and chronic diseases such as heart disease and type 2 diabetes, its role in creating breeding grounds for pandemic viruses, its generation of greenhouse gases and the toxicity of excrement entering the water system, its land and water use, and the list goes on and on.

I have reversed my own heart disease complications by switching to a vegan diet. In my mid-twenties, I had a stent fitted in my aorta and was prescribed drugs every day for the rest of my life. After adopting a vegan diet devoid of all animal products, I came off those medicines within weeks. When I go for my check-ups, the doctors tell me to stick with whatever I am doing because it is working.

Living a vegan life means considering your footprint on the earth and its resources. Clothing, transport, homewares, stationery, personal products, almost everything we use can be made from ingredients or processes that unnecessarily exploit other sentient beings. Any type of vegetable farming causes the death of many insects, but livestock eat a lot more plant matter than humans. Producing grain feed for animals is a waste of resources when we could feed so many more people with the same number of crops. How can we mass-produce meat, dairy, and eggs for the privileged few when a billion people are hungry?

There are many reasons people eat a vegan diet, such as religion, allergies, or intolerances, or they want to be healthier, or they want to live a compassionate lifestyle that reduces the suffering done to animals, the planet, and the environment. It is more than just a diet, though.

Veganism is ultimately a lifestyle philosophy that advocates living compassionately and causing the least possible amount of suffering. It's an ideal, and not at all completely achievable, but we believe that we should endeavour to work towards a happier and compassionate lifestyle even amid adversity. It's the right thing to do, morally. Many people try a vegan diet for health reasons but most of the ones that keep it up do so for the animals.

Expecting anyone to put their hands up and say "I'm vegan" is not the goal of this book, though. We are sharing our recipes to make it easier for everyone to participate in a vegan world, to demonstrate that eggs, butter, cream, and all of that is unnecessary, and maybe not even as tasty as plants can be. Not everyone needs to understand the precepts of veganism to follow it, because if they try something amazing, they will want to eat it again and again, whatever their world view may be, wherever their moral compass is at. Think about how much horses were used until cars came along. The use of horses for transport was not eradicated out of any sense of ethics but because engines are better than equestrian means in so many ways. This is the result we hope to achieve by sharing recipes from our bakery and home kitchen.

Sourdough bread itself is inherently vegan in that is consists of flour, water, and salt. To add anything beyond this (such as baker's yeast) is often regarded almost as sacrilege by many artisan sourdough bakers. We share this deep passion and appreciation for naturally leavened sourdough, but we also see no reason why we cannot also honour our ancestors' other baking traditions without exploiting animals to do so. In our experience, artisanal sourdough bakeries cater very little for vegans, with their heavy emphasis on butter, eggs, and cream and a stubborn attitude of "This is how we have always made it, and if you don't like it, tough!"

Here is our guide to cruelty-free substitutes.

- *Eggs:* There is no one-to-one conversion from a chicken egg to a vegan substitute. Eggs have many properties, such as the leavening effect of whipped egg whites and the excellent emulsifying effect of egg yolks. When considering an egg substitute, you need to consider what function the egg has in what you are making.

  To bind ingredients together, you can use vegetable starches such as potato starch or cornstarch. These have emulsifier properties, as do flaxseeds, chia seeds, and psyllium husk.

  Flaxseed, also known as linseed, acts as a binder, emulsifier, and leavener. It is super high in omega-3 essential fatty acids and is also high in protein and fibre, so when it is activated with water, it turns into a gel, which glues everything together and keeps the finished product moist—just as a whole egg would. A large chicken's egg weighs 50 to 55g, so use a 1:4 ratio of flaxseed to water in weight, or a 1:3 ratio in volume. 10g ground flaxseed mixed with 40 to 45g water or plant milk is equivalent to about 1 tablespoon of finely ground flaxseed (made in a food processor) mixed with 3 tablespoons of water. Allow the mixture to sit for 10 minutes before mixing it into the batter. Brown flaxseeds will darken your baked goods. If you don't want this to happen, use golden flaxseeds. You can buy ground flax, but grinding the seeds in a small blender ensures freshness.

  Although flax is mild in flavour, some people find it has an aftertaste and choose psyllium husk instead, though it is a little harder to find and more expensive. Psyllium husk generally comes as a powder, so you don't have to grind it up, and it is very fine, so 1 teaspoon is enough to replace one whole egg. The liquid content of the recipe will need to be increased with a little extra plant milk or water.

  Chia seeds can also be used as a substitute for eggs. Per egg, 1 tablespoon of chia seeds can be mixed with 3 tablespoons of boiling water and left to sit for 5 minutes to create a viscous binding agent with a neutral flavour.

Vegan baking has long used applesauce and mashed banana as egg replacers. A soft, moist structure can be achieved from the pectin in applesauce, which acts as a binder and traps oxygen. Bananas also provide a moist alternative to egg, but their flavour can be noticeable in the finished product.

The commercially available Bob's Red Mill Egg Replacer is easy to use and caters to most dietary needs. It contains the following binding starches: potato starch, tapioca powder, baking soda, and psyllium husk. These all help keep the baked goods moist and structured. The ratio is 1 tablespoon of powder with 2 tablespoons of water.

Although we are more focused on using whole food egg substitutes such as flax in our bakery, we have also had some fun with vegan liquid egg replacers made from legumes that can be used like whole beaten eggs in recipes at home, such as in our Meyer lemon tart. One brand widely available across North America is JUST Egg, which is a stabilizer, emulsifier, and binder. It doesn't taste at all like the mung beans it's made from, and in fact tastes very similar to real eggs, especially in an omelette. A quarter cup of JUST Egg is about the equivalent of one large chicken's egg, with the same quantity of calories and fat, but less saturated fat and none of the cholesterol.

A magical egg white substitute is aquafaba, from the Latin *aqua* (water) and *faba* (bean). It's the liquid from a can of chickpeas—or if you cooked the chickpeas yourself, reduce the cooking liquid by half. Aquafaba can be used to make meringues and won't have any of the chickpea flavour. The trick to perfect aquafaba meringue is not using an oven but a dehydrator, as the temperature can be kept consistent. Aquafaba lasts for ages in the freezer and can be thawed in the fridge overnight to be used the following day. The colder it is, the more likely it is to act like egg whites. You don't need to throw that bean water away ever again!

For an egg wash on pastry, we have found that soy milk (which has a high lecithin content) and a little maple syrup (for sweetness) and neutral oil of choice can work well. Brush it on and you can get a little shine on your tarts! You may find that using vegan butter in a recipe might give a natural shine anyway and no glaze is necessary. Sometimes, vegan baking involves just taking something away without missing out. For pizza crust and burger buns, which might have an egg wash for seeds to stick to, we just use water. The seeds stick to the dough just as well, without any need for egg.

- *Butter:* Traditionally, many margarines were automatically vegan, but they were heavy and greasy, with an unpalatable flavour, and were seen as inferior to butter made from mammalian milk. Thanks to many plant activists, such as Miyoko Schinner, there are more and more vegetable-based butters out there, ever-improving in quality and practicality, tasting and performing as well as any animal-based counterpart. Miyoko's is a vegan brand from California that makes an incredible oat butter and cashew butters, which brown like cow's butter. It is rather pricey and can be difficult to find, depending on where you are in the world. Miyoko's also donates to animal sanctuaries, so it gets extra vegan points!

  Some plant-based butters contain palm oil, though. Palm oil has excellent culinary properties, but there are ethical concerns around using it, as its popularity has caused mass deforestation and the displacement of wild animals in countries such as Indonesia. We source palm oil-based butters that are sourced in an environmentally and socially responsible way, such as Earth Balance.

  For viennoiserie pastries, the Danish brand Naturli' has a plant butter made with an organic blend of canola (rapeseed), coconut, shea butter, and almond. It contains 75 percent fat and has a mild taste of almond, making it perfect for laminated pastries like croissants.

  Vegan butter is relatively easy to make at home in a blender as long as you add soy or sunflower lecithin. Lecithin is considered a health food or medicine, used in the treatment of many disorders, such as Alzheimer's. Not all oils can be used when it comes to making butter. Olive oil and avocado oil, which are typically used for stovetop cooking, maintain a liquid form, so they are not ideal for making solid butter, but they can replace melted butter in recipes.

  Before adding fat to a recipe, consider its structure. Using liquid oil in a pastry dough would result in a very disappointing puddle of oil when baked. Coconut oil is smooth, rich, and creamy, is semi-solid at room temperature like lard, and has a low smoke point like butter. Vegan butter, in comparison, has a firmer structure at room temperature.

  Organic extra-virgin coconut oil is what we use in our cinnamon buns because it has a delicious buttery flavour. Always check that the brand you are using is ethical; some companies use monkeys to harvest coconuts.

  Using a nut butter such as peanut or almond in place of dairy butter will occasionally work. Peanut butter is a source of saturated fats and protein, but its taste will be noticeable, unlike a more nuanced fat like vegan butter or coconut oil. It works great in our peanut butter blondies, but we wouldn't try making shortcrust pastry with it!

- *Milk:* You can generally use any plant milk in place of dairy milk. We prefer an unsweetened, neutral-tasting milk that is conducive to the texture needed in the baked good. Store-bought milks tend to be more neutral in flavour than fresh or homemade versions. Milks labelled "original" usually contain added sugar.

  We like to use local ingredients, and Earth's Own is a Vancouver brand that uses non-GMO Canadian gluten-free oats, so it ticks all the boxes for us.

  Coconut milk is probably the most pungent of all the plant milks. The canned variety is a great replacement for whole milk, but it can curdle if it is cooked too long at a high temperature.

  Almond milk's versatility allows for it to be used for both savoury and sweet dishes. Its flavour may dissipate once baked. Some people are sensitive to some of the bitter compounds in almonds.

  Soy milk is more neutral, with a thicker texture. It is a substitute for whole milk as it has a high protein content, with starches that gelatinize, and it has a thick, creamy texture. Protein helps to maintain structure and consistency in baked goods, as well as aid browning to give baked goods a nice finish.

  Rice, flax, hemp, and almond milks are on the thinner side, so they are good for replacing skim, reduced-fat, and low-fat milk. Rice has a mild flavour, while that of flax and hemp is more distinctive.

- *Buttermilk:* Buttermilk adds fat and acidity to a recipe. Apple cider, lemon juice, or distilled white vinegar mixed with plant-based milk mimics the interaction of buttermilk. Stir 1 tablespoon of lemon juice into 1 cup of soy milk and let it sit for a minute until it curdles. Use a high-protein plant milk, such as soy, hemp, or oat milk, as they will curdle. If you want your "buttermilk" a bit thicker, put it in the blender with some lecithin and maybe some lemon zest.

- *Cream:* Tofu blended with soy milk has a similar protein content to dairy milk and creates the same rich texture that fat adds to dairy cream, in a cheesecake, for instance. Our local Earth's Own brand has a range of creams that can be used in cooking.

  Cashew cream has a fairly neutral taste and is very easy to make. Blend 1 cup of soaked and drained cashews with ¾ cup of water until smooth for a versatile heavy cream substitute that complements everything.

At our bakery, we make an incredible full-fat coconut whip that we add to drinks and desserts. The trick is to completely chill a can of coconut milk in the fridge and then scoop out the denser top layer, saving the watery liquid left in the can for other uses. We then mix the thick fat with vanilla extract and a little maple syrup. It is important to use cans of coconut milk that contain just coconut and water because added emulsifiers can stop the fat and water particles from separating. Pure coconut cream is a little harder to find but saves the bother of separating the fat from the liquid.

A plant milk such as soy or almond blended or whisked with a neutral oil at a ratio of 2 parts non-dairy milk to 1 part oil can replicate the richness of heavy cream. For savoury baking, olive oil can work well too, as long as you consider the olive flavour may persist after baking.

- *Sugar:* Not many people know that sugar is sometimes processed with bone char from livestock to whiten it, although it does not remain in the sugar itself after the refining process. Look for certified vegan sugar or certified organic, which prohibits bone char as a filtration tool. Sugar made from beets or coconut do not use bone char either. It also depends on where you live: Australian sugar has not been processed with bone char since the 1990s but instead is processed with granular activated carbon that is derived from coal. However, bone char remains a common processing agent in US sugar whitening. In Canada, Rogers is a major sugar producer, and products with the code starting with "22" do not contain bone char, while products with the code starting with "10" are likely to contain bone char. Sugar sold under the same company's Lantic brand is free of bone char. Redpath sugar is also free of bone char.

- *Chocolate:* Dark chocolate is commonly thought to be vegan and yet it often contains milk, sometimes accidentally because it is often processed on the same equipment as milk chocolate. When baking for people who are strictly vegan, it is critical to read food labels. A 2021 law passed in the UK dubbed "Natasha's Law" requires labels to state which of fourteen allergens, including milk, the product contains. If the dark chocolate is processed in a dairy facility, the label must state that it contains milk. This brings us one step closer to a vegan world, as there is now pressure on food producers to make vegan products in vegan-certified factories.

Note on Using a Digital Scale: I cannot emphasize enough how important it is to use a digital scale rather than cups in both bread baking and baking in general, vegan or not. A digital scale will help you to bake to a consistent quality much more than cups will. Not only does weighing speed up the measuring process, but it also reduces the dishwashing load, and that's a win for everybody! We have included cup volumes as a guide, but use them at your own risk and do not expect the same result every time.

The main problem with using cups is that people measure differently: one person will spoon-and-level, others will dig into the flour bag with the cup, while others will leave heaps in the cup. It also doesn't help that there is little standardization for measuring cups and spoons. Furthermore, powdery ingredients such as flours vary in coarseness and density, so each cupful will have a different weight. The result is inconsistent texture, moisture, and/or flavour.

If you are going to attempt to follow the recipe in cups rather than weight, it is a good idea to fluff the flour with a fork before measuring. This will prevent it compacting and thus gaining a few grams, which can negatively affect a bake.

STRIVING FOR ZERO FOOD WASTE

In our bakery we aim to sell out of bread and baked goods every day so we do not have to throw food out. This is certainly going against the grain, when we see how much our competitors have left at closing time, and unfortunately it does mean that latecomers may miss out. These customers may not return, which is obviously a risk that not many bakeries want to take, but we are passionate about not wasting food and on educating the public on the implications of their convenience in terms of food waste.

Food waste is both a social and an environmental challenge: bread waste at the retail level is anywhere from 10 to 30 percent, depending on the establishment. When we consider that approximately 10 percent of humanity is malnourished, nexus thinking indicates we do not need more land to feed a growing population: we need to repurpose food or donate it.

Monitoring the previous weeks' sales and those from the same day a year before allows us to forecast sales and keep our wastage down. On quiet days, we will often stay open an extra hour to sell all our bread and maybe even offer some deals or discounts. We look ahead to public holidays and events when we are likely to be busier and encourage customers to place orders online so we can predict what will be sold and make no more than that.

In the event of products being left on the shelves at the end of the day, we might upcycle them into bread pudding (see the "Zero-Waste" chapter for

a recipe, as well as how to use up sourdough discard), or we will donate bread to the local food bank. We will sometimes deliver unsold treats to our local emergency services, who always appreciate the sugar pick-me-up! It feels good to serve our community in these ways, which counteracts any loss in sales.

Our recipes make big loaves, around 1kg, as this tends to produce a better crumb than a small loaf that is all crust and no substance. If you are concerned about not getting through our large loaves, we suggest you cut them in half, slice and freeze one half and eat the fresh half now. This way, you don't waste good bread. Freezing it on the day of baking preserves a loaf at its best.

GLUTEN

Gluten has become somewhat of a dirty word lately, since so many people are noticing adverse reactions in their digestive tracts and fatigue after consuming products containing gluten, and so they do their best to avoid gluten often without even understanding what it is.

Gluten is a family of hundreds of glycoproteins found in wheat, rye, barley, and oats, plus all their hybrid varieties, such as glutenin and gliadin, which are found in wheat. Gliadin is found in the endosperm, or inner layer, of the grain and is therefore more concentrated in white flours, from which the bran and germ have been sifted out. Gliadin is responsible for most of the adverse effects people complain about, as it contains peptide sequences known as epitopes, which are highly resistant to gastric, pancreatic, and intestinal proteolytic digestion. Oats have glycoproteins too, called avenins, barley's gluten proteins are called hordeins, and rye's are called secalins. People have varying degrees of tolerances to these glycoproteins.

Only about 1 percent of the population are clinically diagnosed with celiac disease, an autoimmune disorder that treats glycoproteins as foreign invaders and attacks the lining of the gut, but many more people believe they have gluten sensitivities.

We have started to see an ever-increasing number of people noticing digestive problems after eating the food they call bread. But we also notice many people are surprised that their symptoms vanish when they consume naturally leavened sourdough made with whole-grain flours, perhaps since these contain less gliadin than sifted white flour, and the fermentation helps break down the gluten before it enters the digestive tract.

Many consumers have been conditioned to enjoy light, fluffy aerated bread, and you cannot achieve this amount of oven spring without white flour. A 100 percent whole-grain loaf will be heavier and denser than a regular loaf of white bread and may not suit everybody's palate, but that is the kind of bread our ancestors ate for centuries, long before the Industrial Revolution turned bread on its head. A commercial yeasted dough process may produce a loaf ready to eat within a couple of hours, whereas a naturally leavened sourdough loaf takes forty-eight to seventy-two hours from start to finish. It is no wonder that mass production has favoured the quicker and more convenient way of producing bread! But this has come at the cost of flavour, the environment and soil quality, and our nutrition and health.

TYPES OF FLOUR

In the UK and Europe, bakers are spoilt for choice when it comes to sourcing good quality flours. Canada's prairies also produce an enormous number of grains, but there is more concern about pesticides and genetically modified crops. Modern wheat farming involves spraying petrochemicals, synthetic fertilizers, and carcinogenic herbicides, some of which have been known to contaminate neighbouring organic farms. Knowing where your grain comes from, which farms and where they are, will help you find a good quality flour that is free of dangerous sprays. It is important to make bread that is both beneficial for our own health and that of the planet: the two are inextricably linked. You cannot spray a chemical to kill life on a plant and then deem that plant safe to eat, especially not when you consider the large quantities of wheat in the standard diet.

Ninety-five percent of the world's wheat is a variety called common wheat, which has been cultivated to produce a softer and looser papery husk, called chaff, that covers the grain. This makes it easier to thresh common wheat clean. As well, with their lighter husk, the seeds do not fall off the plant before harvesting. In short, common wheat is well suited to mechanized agriculture and processing. The remaining 5 percent of global wheat is mainly durum wheat, which is primarily used for pasta production.

Common wheat can be categorized into hard and soft varieties, winter and spring varieties, and red and white varieties, with various combinations of these differentiations. Winter wheat is planted in autumn and harvested in the spring, whereas spring wheat is planted in the spring and harvested in the late summer or early autumn. For this reason, the short growing season in Canada lends itself to hard red spring wheat, which is ideal for making artisanal bread. Red wheat has a higher percentage of protein than white wheat, as well as being more flavoursome, making it excellent in bread.

All-purpose flour is usually composed of 80 percent hard red wheat and 20 percent soft red wheat. Similarly, bread flour is generally made of hard red spring wheat. A strong white bread flour should contain 12 to 14 percent protein, though you can usually substitute all-purpose flour. When starting out to make bread, if the result is not perfect straight away, persevere and tweak the recipe, using the same flour, until you get a loaf you're happy with. There are so many factors that determine a good bake that you should master one flour before conquering the next.

The following ancient grains are crops that were eaten for centuries before the common wheat variety came about during the Industrial Revolution.

- *Einkorn:* Its name means "single grain" and it is referred to as "man's first wheat" or "mother wheat." It has been cultivated since 7500 BCE, the Neolithic period, but it fell out of favour and was almost extinct by the 1960s because it is inherently difficult to machine. Einkorn kernels can withstand threshing, so it needs to be hulled instead. Fewer people with sensitivities react to einkorn because it has a stickier and less pliable gluten structure.

- *Emmer:* A hybrid of einkorn and an unidentified wild grass, emmer was the staple wheat of pharaonic Egypt.

- *Barley:* It was first cultivated around 10,000 years ago in Eurasia and has remained widely used because of its ability to grow at high altitude and latitude.

- *Oats:* Their use has been noted as far back as 7000 BCE in China. Oats were introduced to the UK mainly as livestock feed by the Romans, who looked down on the Scots for eating them.

- *Rye:* Thought to have been cultivated since 6500 BCE in southwestern Asia, rye is well suited to cold climates. It never really lost popularity in northern Europe, and rye bread is a staple in Scandinavia today.

- *Buckwheat:* This is not a wheat at all, or even a grass. It's a seed, which is gluten-free, first cultivated in Asia around 6000 BCE and one of the earliest crops introduced to North America by Europeans.

- *Spelt:* It has been cultivated since 5000 BCE and is known as "ancient wheat" or "dinkel wheat."

- *Kamut:* Its berries were apparently discovered in Tutankhamun's tomb, and kamut was dubbed "King Tut wheat" when it was first sold in the US in the 1990s, although it originates from over 4000 years ago.

These heritage grains grow deep roots that penetrate the soil to extract nutrients, and they are grown without the weedkiller glyphosate, otherwise known as Roundup or Vision. The use of such non-selective herbicides depletes soil quality and therefore reduces the nutritional value of the grains themselves, while also being catastrophic for the ecology of the land. Healthy soil is packed with nutrients that in turn feed our microbiome. These ancient grains contain antinutrients called phytates, but soaking and sprouting deactivate these components and result in increased bioavailability of nutrients like zinc and iron. They also have lower levels of gliadin and higher levels of glutenin, which means more people can eat these without digestive upset.

Stone-grinding flour, rather than roller-milling, exposes the grains to minimal heat, thus preserving their nutrients and flavour. The home baker can store wheat berries and mill them just before baking, using a tabletop mill such as the KoMo Fidibus. By outward appearance, there may not be a significant difference, but you will definitely notice a difference in flavour between a bread baked with freshly ground flour and one with old flour. Fermentation is much more active with fresher flours. We recommend using organic flour, locally sourced and as freshly milled as possible, for all our recipes.

LIES OF THE FOOD INDUSTRY

The food manufacturing industry has seen the renewed popularity of sourdough bread and is packaging loaves that contain baker's yeast as sourdough. Movements such as the Real Bread Campaign in the UK are raising awareness in the public and lobbying the government to regulate the labelling of bread so that only bread made without yeast and additives may be called sourdough. They have even adopted the term *sourfaux* for the yeasted sourdough imitation.

Other tricks that the food industry has mastered include dying white bread a brown colour to make regular fast-yeasted sifted flour loaves look like healthy whole-grain ones and adding sugar to brown bread so that it stays softer for longer and doesn't stale as fast as a true whole-grain loaf would. Most supermarkets bake frozen loaves that may be up to a year old before reaching the in-house bakery and pass them off as "freshly baked" while pumping the smell of baking bread at the entrance to their stores.

It's difficult for most shoppers to see through the illusion of words on food labels. If you cannot make your own bread, look for your local artisanal baker and ask questions about the yeast they use, if it is baker's yeast or naturally leavened; how long they ferment the dough; where they source their grains from and which ones they use; and how often they buy flour and if they mill any themselves.

TOOLS AND EQUIPMENT

At the bakery, we bake our loaves in a gas-powered steam pipe deck oven. Although natural gas is indeed a finite resource and there is pressure to move to other technology, there is little development in eco-friendly commercial deck ovens that produce the same result. That said, we do not recommend using a gas oven for home baking because the heat is not evenly dispersed.

For most of our small baked items, we use a convection combination oven, which is an electric oven that is fan-assisted, keeping the temperature consistent top and bottom, with the option to inject steam to control humidity.

All the recipes in this book are written for a convection oven, so if you are using a standard electric oven you may need to increase the temperature by 25 to 30°F (15 to 17°C) to achieve the same result. Electric ovens have heat elements at the top and bottom, so the heat is more focused there and the temperature you bake at needs to be higher than in a convection oven.

Below is a list of tools and equipment you will need to make the recipes in this book.

- Baking dish, ovenproof ceramic or cast iron (13 × 9 inches/33 × 23cm)
- Baking sheets (two 18 × 13-inch/46 × 33cm and one 13 × 9-inch/33 × 23cm)
- Box grater
- Baking stone or baking steel: Aluminum baking sheets are susceptible to hot spots in a home oven and quickly lose their heat when the door is opened. A preheated baking stone will mimic a big bakery oven in that it ensures even heat distribution, and the high temperature of the stone's porous surface extracts moisture from the outside of the dough, yielding a crackly, crunchy, crispy crust with a light interior. I use a baking steel at home, as it conducts more than twenty times the heat of a brick oven or baking stone.
- Bread bin or linen bag: For storing bread.
- Bread knife, serrated
- Cake tin (two 9-inch/23cm square)
- Cast-iron cloche-style bread pan, such as the Challenger Bread Pan or the 3.2-quart Lodge Combo Cooker: These are essentially upside-down Dutch ovens. Both are great for baking bread because the steam from the dough cannot escape, which ensures a soft crust and good oven spring, while the metal holds heat well so the dough has a long cool-down. You will only ever need to buy one of these pans in your life, as they are so sturdy. The temperature of the dough is maintained in this bread-specific pan until it is time to remove the lid and allow the crust to caramelize. A cast-iron

casserole pot such as the 7.25-quart Le Creuset Dutch oven also works, but you need to take care not to burn yourself when dropping dough into the preheated pan.

- Citrus juicer
- Chef's knife
- Cooling racks
- Crumpet rings, non-stick (3.5 × 1.25 inches/9 × 3cm)
- Cutting board: We prefer wood, since it doesn't dull knives.
- Digital scales: A set of digital scales is a must. Baking is a precise science, and I cannot guarantee your measurement of a cup of flour equals mine.
- Doughnut pan, such as the Wilton Standard 6-ring (12 × 8 inches/ 30 × 20cm)
- Flexible plastic dough scraper: Used to remove dough from bowls.
- Food processor
- High-speed blender
- Kitchen towels and linen couche: Used to support baguettes while they rise, as well as for bagels and English muffins to maintain the dough's shape and dry surface. A thin skin can form and that helps create a chewy crust. Alternatively, the baguette dough can be placed on a clean kitchen towel, but the baguettes will probably spread a little with no sides to hold them up.
- Lame: This is French for "handle," and with replaceable razor blades attached to it, you can score bread more accurately and create more intricate patterns than with a sharp knife. The lame holds the blade at an ideal angle, making it more precise.
- Loaf tins, 1 lb/450g such as 9 × 5 × 3 inches (23 × 12 × 8cm) and smaller 8½ × 4½ × 2½ inches (22 × 11 × 6cm)
- Madeleine tin
- Metal bench knife (dough scraper or blade): Used to divide the dough, lift it off the bench, and assist with shaping.
- Microplane (zester)
- Mixing bowls: I recommend small, medium, and large thick stainless steel or ceramic bowls.
- Muffin tins (extra-large and large 6-cup tins; regular 12-cup tin)
- Oven mitts (thick)
- Parchment paper
- Pastry brush
- Pastry cutter, round (3 inches/8cm)
- Piping bag (canvas), with various sizes of plain tips
- Popover tins (or deep muffin tins)
- Pullman loaf tin, 1lb (9 × 5 × 4 inches/23 × 12 × 10cm)

- Proofing baskets (bannetons), round and oval: I prefer wicker ones (which need linen liners) to cane bannetons because they tend to be sturdier and breathable.
- Rolling pin
- Saucepans, multiple sizes
- Sieve, fine-mesh
- Silicone baking mats
- Skillet, cast-iron (10 inches/25cm)
- Skillet, non-stick (10 or 12 inches/25 or 30cm)
- Spray bottles: One with water to spray dough, and one with oil to grease tins with.
- Springform cake pans (two 9-inch/23cm)
- Spoons, wooden and metal
- Stand mixer: I recommend either KitchenAid or Kenwood.
- Tart ring or tart pan with removable bottom (10 inches/25cm)
- Thermometers: (1) probe thermometer, such as Thermapen, for checking the internal temperature of loaves, (2) regular thermometer to check the temperature of the room and water, and (3) candy (sugar) thermometer.
- Timer: Used to monitor stages of making sourdough, such as the timings of stretch-and-folds.
- Waffle iron
- Whisk
- Wire-mesh spider: Used for removing doughnuts from the fryer.

OPTIONAL

- Baguette board
- Dehydrator
- Pasta machine
- Pizza peel
- Sprouting jars (half-gallon/2L)
- Stroopwafel iron

sourdough
starter guide

WHAT IS SOURDOUGH?

Ultimately, sourdough bread is made with three ingredients: flour, water, and salt. There is no baker's yeast or other additives, but only natural cultures to make it rise. When flour is mixed with water, left in a warm (72 to 75°F/22 to 24°C), draft-free place, and fed every day with fresh water and flour for at least ten days, many wondrous processes take place: a marriage of wild yeasts with lactic acid bacteria that are naturally occurring in grains, in the air, and on our hands.

The wild yeasts produce most of the carbon dioxide (CO_2) that is trapped by the gluten structure of the dough, which is what makes the big holes in the crumb. An active starter will produce a light and airy loaf if given enough time.

Lactic acid bacteria produce organic acids such as acetic and lactic acids. The amount of these is different from starter to starter and, along with the flour type, room and dough temperature, and length of fermentation, will result in various flavours and textures in the baked loaf.

Some sourdough aficionados can go deep into the science of the various enzymes and sugars, but knowing the microbial science in minute detail does not necessarily help you make better bread. To master the art of bread making, you must make bread often and experiment with all the variables. There are all sorts of gadgets on the market for bakers to use too, but the equipment a baker has is also secondary to the mastery of fermentation required to manage a sourdough starter.

HOW TO MAKE A SOURDOUGH STARTER

Follow the basic recipe below to help you grow a sourdough starter. For the first three days, flour and water are added to a jar. Do not discard any of the starter during this period. Each day, the starter will gain weight, and on day 4 we begin to discard the excess.

DAY 1

50g warm water (75 to 78°F/24 to 26°C)
30g stone-ground whole-grain rye flour

Pour the warm water into a small bowl. Add the rye flour. Using a clean hand, mix the flour and water together to form a paste. Carefully transfer the mixture to a clean 500mL (2-cup) glass jar. Cover with a loose-fitting lid slightly askew to allow airflow. Let the paste sit in a warm (72 to 75°F/22 to 24°C), draft-free place for 24 hours. (Placing the jar of starter in a bowl will catch any overspill if the starter gets very active.)

DAY 2

Check the jar to see if there is any activity in the way of growth and smell. If the ferment has domed a little and smells slightly sour, this is a good sign, and it is time for the next feed. If it looks like nothing has happened and the flour still smells grassy, leave the starter for another 12 to 24 hours before moving on.

50g warm water (75 to 78°F/24 to 26°C)
30g stone-ground whole-grain rye flour

Add the warm water and rye flour to the starter in the jar and mix together with a small spatula. Avoid getting the mixture up the sides of the jar, where it will dry out. Dampening a sheet of paper towel and wiping inside the jar a little will also prevent dryness from occurring. Cover with a loose-fitting lid slightly askew. Allow to ferment in a warm (72 to 75°F/22 to 24°C), draft-free place for another 24 hours.

DAY 3

By day 3 there should be more activity in appearance and aromas. The mixture should have doubled in size, have a few more bubbles, and smell a little like beer with some acidity or sourness like yogurt. If you cannot notice any activity at this point, then wait another 12 hours before continuing with the feed schedule.

50g warm water (75 to 78°F/24 to 26°C)
30g stone-ground whole-grain rye flour

Add the water and rye flour to the starter in the jar and mix together with a small spatula. Avoid getting the mixture up the sides of the jar, where it will dry out. Dampening a sheet of paper towel and wiping inside the jar a little will also prevent dryness. Cover with a loose-fitting lid slightly askew. Allow to ferment in a warm (72 to 75°F/22 to 24°C), draft-free place for another 24 hours.

DAY 4

On day 4, there should have been further fermentation and the mixture should have some fermentation bubbles on the top and sides, and a sour smell similar to yogurt. As time goes on, you may notice the bubbles get larger. The starter is building strength, active micro-organisms are multiplying, and the culture can be fed with a higher ratio of flour and water than before. This means removing some of the starter and adding it to flour and water.

50g sourdough starter
80g warm water (75 to 78°F/24 to 26°C)
50g stone-ground whole-grain rye flour

Place the 50g of sourdough starter in a small bowl. Add the water and rye flour and mix together. Discard the excess sourdough starter (approximately 190g) and thoroughly clean and dry the jar. Pour the refreshed starter into the jar, cover with a loose-fitting lid slightly askew, and leave it to ferment in a warm (72 to 75°F/ 22 to 24°C), draft-free place for another 24 hours.

DAY 5

The starter should be quite active on day 5, doubled or even tripled in size, have more bubbles than the previous days with a noticeably stronger smell. If the starter is still a little slower than this, it may be because of a cooler environment, so repeat day 4 one more time before moving on to the new feed and maintaining your starter (see below).

HOW TO MAINTAIN A SOURDOUGH STARTER

Consistency is key when making sourdough, but there are so many factors and variants that require a baker's close attention. Keeping timings throughout the process, the length of autolyse, mixer timings, time gaps between the stretch-and-folds, and being exact with weights (using digital scales) and temperatures (using a digital probe thermometer) at every stage of making sourdough is essential.

Follow the 12-hour feed recipe on page 28 for building a starter. Once a starter has formed, the best formula to keep it healthy and active is the one that suits your schedule. Find a balance that allows you to bake when you want. Discarding starter is unavoidable, but keeping this to a minimum helps reduce food waste (see the "Zero-Waste" chapter for discard recipes, page 305).

Sourdough starters are very happy when stored at room temperature but will need to be fed twice a day. Alternatively, starters can be just as happy in the fridge and fed once a day or even once a week. Storing in a fridge, and hence reducing feedings, reduces discarding, but you must refresh the starter following the 12-hour feed recipe a few times before making bread.

INOCULATION

Inoculation is the amount of sourdough starter compared to the total weight of flour. The ratio controls the speed of fermentation. The more starter you add (pre-fermented flour), the faster the starter will ferment. Likewise, the less starter you add, the slower the starter will ferment.

FEEDING SCHEDULES

If you are not baking every few days, store the sourdough starter in the fridge and refresh it with flour and water at least once a week.

A day or two before you plan to make bread, remove the starter from the fridge and allow it to sit at room temperature for 2 hours. Then follow the 12-hour feed recipe (page 28) to increase the activity. If there is some liquid on the top of the starter, don't worry. This totally natural liquid, called hooch, is the alcohol given off during the wild yeasts' slow fermentation. Hooch is not a problem, but it does indicate that the starter needs to be fed.

Mix the liquid back into the starter and refresh the starter using the 12-hour feed recipe for 1 to 2 days. The starter will be more active and produce better bread if it is fed three or four times ahead of building the levain. It should be doubled in size, with a slightly sweet and sour aroma like natural yogurt.

When refreshing sourdough starter for the 12-hour feed recipe, there will be approximately 200g discard, which can be used in the zero-waste recipes or composted.

If you want a pure 100 percent wheat-free rye starter, feed it only rye flour, using the same quantities given for the wheat flour.

12-HOUR FEED RECIPE

25g sourdough starter (25% inoculation)
100g warm water (75 to 78°F/24 to 26°C) (100% hydration)
50g stone-ground whole wheat or whole-grain rye flour
50g bread flour (or whole-grain rye flour if making a pure 100% rye starter)

Using your hand, mix together the sourdough starter, water, whole wheat flour, and bread flour in a medium bowl. Use a plastic scraper to scrape all the starter into a clean 750mL (3-cup) glass jar. Cover with a loose-fitting lid slightly askew and leave it at room temperature for 12 hours. There will be no discard from this recipe.

SOURDOUGH LEVAIN

When the sourdough starter has been fed and developed to the quantity required to make bread, it is called *levain* or *leaven*. A levain is fed slightly differently from a starter, and all the levain is used in the bread to make it rise. The levain can be altered and adjusted to suit your schedule, the flour you want to use, the style of bread, the flavour, and so on.

The starter is always fed and maintained with the same ratios and timings to keep it consistent. When I say ratios, the percentages are compared to each other. For example, 25 percent inoculation can be 25g starter to 100g flour, or 2.5kg starter to 10kg flour, while the 100 percent water/hydration remains constant.

The levain recipe below makes enough for two loaves (1kg each), so if you want to make more bread, simply double or triple the recipe. Half the recipe if you just want to make one loaf at a time.

DAY 1: FEED THE SOURDOUGH STARTER TWICE—AT 7 A.M. AND 7 P.M.

STARTER

25g sourdough starter
50g stone-ground whole wheat or whole-grain rye flour
50g bread flour
100g warm water (75 to 78°F/24 to 26°C)

Using your hand, mix together the sourdough starter, whole wheat flour, bread flour, and warm water in a medium bowl. Use a spatula to scrape all the starter into a clean 1L (4-cup) glass jar or transparent container. Cover with a loose-fitting lid slightly askew. Allow it to ferment at room temperature for 12 hours.

This will give you 225g of sourdough starter in total. You will need 50g of this to make the levain and 25g to refresh the starter, both of which are fed separately at 7 a.m. the following day. The remaining 150g starter is discard, which can be used in the zero-waste recipes.

DAY 2, 7 A.M.: PREPARE THE SOURDOUGH LEVAIN
(MAKES ENOUGH FOR TWO 1KG LOAVES)

Feed the active starter early in the morning (by 7 a.m.) the day you plan to mix the dough so that it is active and tripled in volume in 4 to 6 hours.

LEVAIN

Option 1—ready in 4 to 6 hours

50g active sourdough starter (50% inoculation)
100g warm water (75 to 78°F/24 to 26°C) (100% hydration)
50g stone-ground whole wheat flour
50g bread flour

Using your hand, mix together the active starter, water, whole wheat flour, and bread flour in a medium bowl. Use a spatula to scrape all the levain into a clean 1L (4-cup) glass jar or transparent container and cover with a loose-fitting lid slightly askew. Draw a line or place a rubber band around the container to mark the top of the levain. This will indicate when the levain has doubled or tripled in size. Allow it to ferment in a warm (72 to 75°F/22 to 24°C), draft-free place. Depending on the season and temperature, the levain should be ripe and ready to use in 4 to 6 hours.

OR

Option 2—ready in 8 to 10 hours

Prepare the levain with a less active starter—approximately 10 percent inoculation (10g) calculated to the total weight of flours—the night before (by 10 p.m.) so it's ready in the morning, 8 to 10 hours later. In this recipe, there are two options for the amount of sourdough starter you use, depending on the room temperature. It's good to test both and see what works best. For a colder room temperature, you might need as much as 20g starter, but this also depends on how active the starter is to begin with.

continued . . .

10g to 20g active sourdough starter (10% to 20% inoculation)
100g warm water (75 to 78°F/24 to 26°C) (100% hydration)
50g stone-ground whole wheat or whole-grain rye flour
50g bread flour

Using your hand, mix together the active starter, water, whole wheat flour, and bread flour in a medium bowl. Use a spatula to scrape all the levain into a clean 1L (4-cup) glass jar or transparent container and cover with a loose-fitting lid slightly askew. Draw a line or place a rubber band around the container to mark the top of the levain. This will indicate when the levain has doubled or tripled in size. Allow it to ferment in a warm (72 to 75°F/22 to 24°C), draft-free place. Depending on the season and temperature, the levain should be ripe and ready to use in 8 to 10 hours.

DAY 2, 7 A.M.: FEED THE STARTER

Feed the starter as usual with the ingredients below, allowing the starter to ferment for at least 8 hours before storing it in the fridge, or leave it at room temperature and continue refreshing it every 12 hours.

25g sourdough starter
50g stone-ground whole wheat or whole-grain rye flour
50g bread flour
100g warm water (75 to 78°F/24 to 26°C)

IS THE SOURDOUGH LEVAIN READY?

Begin the autolyse mix (flour and water) about 1 hour before the levain has peaked. This is best judged by its appearance, smell, and taste. The levain should have at least doubled or tripled in volume from its original size and be domed with some nice bubbles and activity on the top and sides. It should have a pleasant fruity aroma and a flavour like lightly fermented yogurt. If the levain still has a strong taste of flour like a pancake batter, it will need to ferment a little longer. Keep an eye on the levain to judge the right time to add it to the dough. Let the levain peak and use it before it drops or sinks, but you can still use it if it has dropped. You could also wait for it to regain its original height in 1 to 2 hours, but it will develop a sourer flavour.

AUTOLYSE

This very important, simple, yet very effective process is the first step to making great sourdough bread. Autolyse (or autolysis) is a term used for the mixing of flour and water to form a shaggy dough, which allows the flour to absorb the water slowly before any additional yeasts are added. This helps develop the gluten in the dough and, in turn, allows for easier shaping and better flavour and texture.

This step only takes a couple of minutes. Don't be tempted to knead the dough—just mix it until there are no dry patches of flour. Lightly cover the bowl with a kitchen towel or loose-fitting lid and set it aside in a warm (72 to 75°F/22 to 24°C), draft-free place for at least 20 minutes and up to 2 hours before moving on to the mixing stage.

MIXING AND KNEADING

When bakers talk about percentages, they are calculated in the same way as the inoculation ratio. The water, levain, and salt are divided by the total weight of the flour. For example:

800g water to 1kg flour is 80% hydration
25g salt to 1kg flour is 2.5%

Ingredient	Quantity	Baker's Percentage
Water	800g	80% hydration
Flour	1kg	100%
Levain	200g	20%
Salt	25g	2.5%

I highly recommend mixing most of the breads in this book by hand. Mixing by hand helps you learn how dough feels and changes throughout the kneading process as gluten develops. Enriched sweeter doughs are often mixed for longer, and a stand mixer is very helpful for these, though not essential. If you are mixing larger quantities—more than double the amounts used in the recipe—use a stand mixer fitted with the dough hook. Small mixers can be used for all the bread recipes in this book, but be careful not to overmix the dough, as this can drastically increase its temperature. Start with water that's a few degrees cooler than what's called for, mix for only a few minutes at a time, and allow rest periods between mixing.

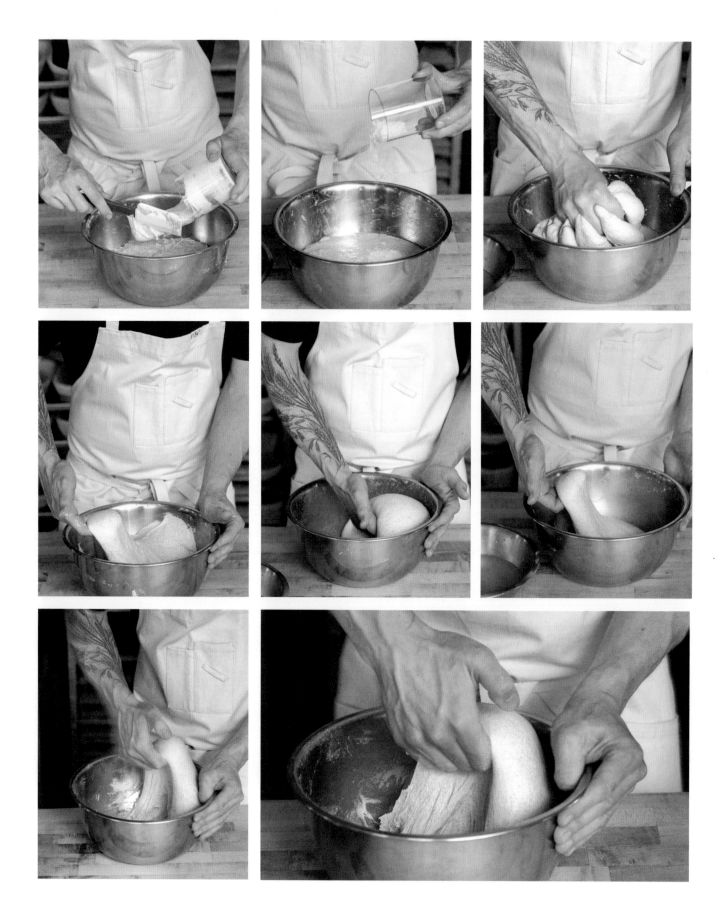

When mixing by hand, I like to use the Rubaud method, which was developed by the late Gérard Rubaud and popularized by Trevor Wilson, who trained with Rubaud. It's the most effective and efficient way to knead an extensible higher-hydration dough, inspired by commercial diving arm mixers that are very gentle and minimize heat generated by friction in the mixing stage. It is also a lot cleaner and leaves a lot less dough on your hands.

The Rubaud kneading technique is quite simple: Hold the bowl with one hand to keep it steady. Cup your other hand like a scoop and lift one edge of the dough straight up, stretching it slightly, and then let it fall back onto itself. Turn the bowl and repeat this action. This technique will need to be done for a few minutes with some rest periods to allow the dough to relax. See the Country Sourdough (page 55) for guidance on timings for mixing and resting.

BASSINAGE

There is great satisfaction in slicing freshly baked sourdough and unveiling an open crumb. One way of achieving this open crumb is by holding back 5 to 10 percent of the water called for in the recipe and adding it incrementally during mixing, or just at the end. This technique is called *bassinage*. The exact percentage will depend on the choice of flour: lower-protein flours require less water, and the opposite is true of higher-protein flours.

To illustrate, if the recipe requires 800g of water and you are opting for a 10 percent bassinage, then you would initially mix in 720g, leave the dough to tighten and relax, then mix in the remaining 80g before the bulk fermentation. The dough will be drier during the kneading stage, and this will strengthen the bonds within the gluten structure and improve its elasticity. When the bassinage is added, this free water will be trapped in the matrix and will create a more open cell structure. Bassinage does take a bit more time and patience, and it is a bit more of a challenge to knead, but worth it if you want to make attractive bread.

BULK FERMENTATION AND FOLDING

The bulk fermentation stage helps to build additional strength and flavour. It is a crucial part of making sourdough and it should not be rushed. This stage starts when the kneaded dough is transferred to a lightly oiled container or bowl and ends when the dough is pre-shaped. Using a clear container or glass bowl means you can see the dough and is recommended if you are new to bread making. Keeping the dough in a warm (72 to 75°F/22 to 24°C), draft-free place will help it to bulk ferment in 3 to 4 hours. It's a good idea to taste the dough at various points throughout the bulk fermentation stage to learn how the flavour of the dough changes.

STRETCH-AND-FOLDS AND COIL FOLD

Stretch-and-fold is exactly how it sounds. Once the kneaded dough has been in its container for approximately 30 minutes, it will have relaxed and probably look quite flat with maybe a few bubbles. You need to fold the dough to build strength in it, otherwise the baked bread will be flat.

1. Pour some warm water into a container or bowl big enough to wet one hand.

2. Hold the dough container with one hand and with your wet hand, push your fingers down between the dough and the side of the container and grab the underside of the dough from the bottom. Lift it up until you feel it stretching, but not tearing, and fold it over towards the opposite side of the container. Turn the container slightly and repeat the stretch-and-fold action four or five more times, until you feel the dough becoming tighter and rounded on the sides.

3. This is a good time to check the temperature of the dough with a digital probe thermometer. The ideal dough temperature is 78 to 82°F (24 to 27°C). Cover the dough with the kitchen towel or loose-fitting lid and return it to a warm (72 to 75°F/22 to 24°C), draft-free place to rest between stretch-and-folds. Set a timer for another 30 minutes.

4. Repeat the stretch-and-fold step another three or four times, leaving 30 minutes between each set (also known as turns). As the dough starts to ferment and build more strength with each set of folds, you will notice it growing in volume and activity, with fermentation bubbles and aromas. The dough should also be doming, rather than sitting flat.

5. Once you have bulk fermented the dough for 2 to 3 hours and have performed the last set of stretch-and-folds and the final 30-minute rest, finish the bulk fermentation stage with a gentle coil fold. This helps tuck in all the sides of the dough for the last resting period.

   To do a coil fold, wet both your hands with warm water. With your hands at 9 o'clock and 3 o'clock, gently lift the dough a few inches until it has stretched as far as it will go, then allow it to fall back under itself, leaving a smooth top side. Repeat this coil fold once or twice more, turning the bowl each time, until the top of the dough is smooth and slightly domed. Cover the dough with a kitchen towel or loose-fitting lid and allow it to rest for another 30 to 40 minutes. By the end of the bulk fermentation, the dough should have increased in volume by 40 to 50 percent.

PRE-SHAPING LOAVES

Once the dough has gone through the bulk fermentation stage and has rested, it's time to divide and pre-shape it. The best way to remove the dough from the container or bowl is to place the container on its side and with a wet flexible plastic scraper, gently ease the dough out onto an unfloured work surface.

Allow the dough to relax for a minute, then use a bench knife to cut the dough in half. Check the weight on the scale to ensure it is equally divided; most loaf recipes in this book are for two 1kg loaves. Starting at 3 o'clock and working your way back to 12 o'clock, angle the bench knife at slightly under 45 degrees and push it in a smooth counter-clockwise arch motion, while tucking the dough under itself with your other dampened hand, to form it into a reasonably tight round ball with a smooth rounded top. If the dough is a little sticky, lightly wet your hand to help form the shape.

Place each pre-shaped ball of dough on the work surface with a few inches between them.

BENCH RESTING

Bench resting helps the gluten relax before the final shaping. If you omit this step, the dough will tear as you force it into shape.

After the pre-shaping stage, allow the dough to rest on your work surface (bench) for 30 to 45 minutes, depending how tightly you pre-shaped the dough.

The dough should relax outwards, though you don't want a totally flat dough. If the dough starts to dry out, lightly cover it with a damp kitchen towel.

If the dough is flattening a lot and tapering at the edges, this is a sign of not enough kneading or folding earlier in the process. If this is the case, try a little extra stitching at the shaping stage and once again when the dough is in the baskets. Alternatively, shape the dough and place it in loaf tins for extra support.

FINAL SHAPING

Shaping the dough builds extra tension throughout the bread, builds structure, and assists with a beautiful oven spring, which is the expansion of dough that occurs in the first 10 minutes of baking when the last burst of trapped CO_2 heats up and expands the loaf to its full potential, forming an airy crumb and a balanced shape.

SHAPING AND BASKET 50:50 FLOUR BLEND

500g bread flour
500g brown rice flour

Prepare the proofing baskets first so they are ready once the dough is shaped. Mix the bread flour and brown rice flour in a large bowl. Dust newer proofing baskets with a liberal amount of the flour mixture, as there's nothing worse than sourdough sticking to the baskets when it comes time to bake. After the baskets are used a few times, they will become more seasoned, like a cast-iron pan, and you'll be able to judge how much flour to use. Transfer the remaining flour blend to an airtight container to be used for shaping other breads in the future.

SHAPING A BOULE (ROUND)

1. Lightly flour the proofing baskets with the 50:50 flour blend (page 36).

2. To shape the loaves, lightly flour the tops of the pre-shaped rounds. Slide the bench knife under one of the rounds, lifting it off the work surface and gently flipping it over onto its floured side. The bottom is now facing up.

3. Lift the left side of the dough and fold it to the middle. Repeat with the right side so it slightly overlaps the middle. Gently turn the dough 90 degrees and repeat the previous steps. You should have a square shape.

4. Now lift the bottom right-hand corner, stretch it to the middle, and gently press so it sticks. Repeat the same movement with the top left corner and then the two remaining corners. Once all the corners are folded in, carefully roll the shaped dough over so the seam is on the bottom. Pull the dough back towards you a few times, rotating the dough to form a tight boule shape.

5. Using the bench knife, carefully lift the dough and place it to the side. Repeat the process with the second pre-shaped ball. Allow both shaped loaves to rest for a minute on the work surface so that the seams seal.

6. Carefully slide the bench knife under one shaped boule, lift it off the bench, and gently flip it upside down so the smooth top surface is now in the bottom of the floured proofing basket and the seam side is up. Repeat this process with the second loaf.

    If there are seeds or flakes to be added to the surface, place them on a small baking sheet or in a large bowl, then mist the top of the shaped boules with water, lift the boule, placing the damp top side in the seeds or flakes, then transfer the dough to the proofing baskets as directed above.

7. Allow both the shaped loaves to rest again for a few minutes. If the dough still looks quite slack, lift an outer edge to the middle. As the dough is still wet from resting on the work surface, it should stick. Turn the basket and repeat until the boule looks tighter. This is called basket stitching, and it helps to create a nice oven spring.

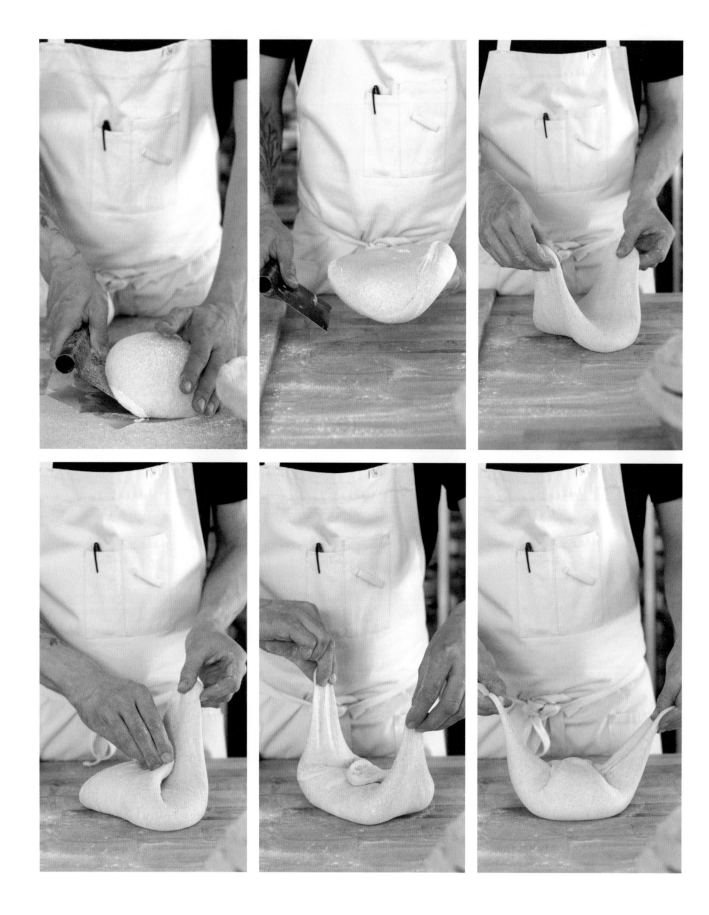

SHAPING A BÂTARD (OVAL)

1. Lightly flour the proofing baskets with the 50:50 flour blend (page 36).

2. To shape the loaves, lightly flour the tops of the pre-shaped rounds. Slide the bench knife under one of the rounds, lifting it off the work surface and gently flipping it over onto its floured side. The bottom is now facing up.

3. Ever so slightly tease the bottom and top of the dough outwards to reform the dough round into a more rectangular shape with a short side facing you, keeping the dough loose without stretching it. Fold the bottom third away from you to cover one-third of the dough. Fold the top third towards the middle so the edges overlap and form a seam.

4. Rotate the dough 90 degrees so that a short side is in front of you again. Starting from the top edge, roll the dough towards you while pushing down along the seam with your fingers to create surface tension. Continue rolling until the dough reaches the bottom edge and the seam is underneath.

5. Using the bench knife, carefully lift the dough and place it to the side. Repeat the process with the second round of dough. Allow both doughs to rest seam side down for a minute so that the seams seal.

6. Pinch the ends of the dough to seal the loaves. Lightly flour the tops of the dough with the flour blend if the dough feels a little wet on top.
   If there are seeds or flakes to be added to the surface, place them on a small baking sheet or in a large bowl, then mist the top of the shaped boules with water, lift the boule, placing the damp top side in the seeds or flakes, then transfer the dough to the proofing baskets as directed above.

7. Using the bench knife, gently pick up both long sides of one loaf and gently turn it so that the smooth side is in your hands and the seam is facing up. Gently fold one side over the other as though you are closing a book so the seam is now inside the folded loaf, and place the loaf in the floured basket. Repeat this process with the second loaf. If the seam is opening, starting at one end of the loaf, and working to the opposite end, gently pinch a piece of dough from one side and pull it to the middle. Repeat this motion on the other side so you are following a shoelace pattern, bringing the dough from the sides to the middle and alternating from left to right (stitching).

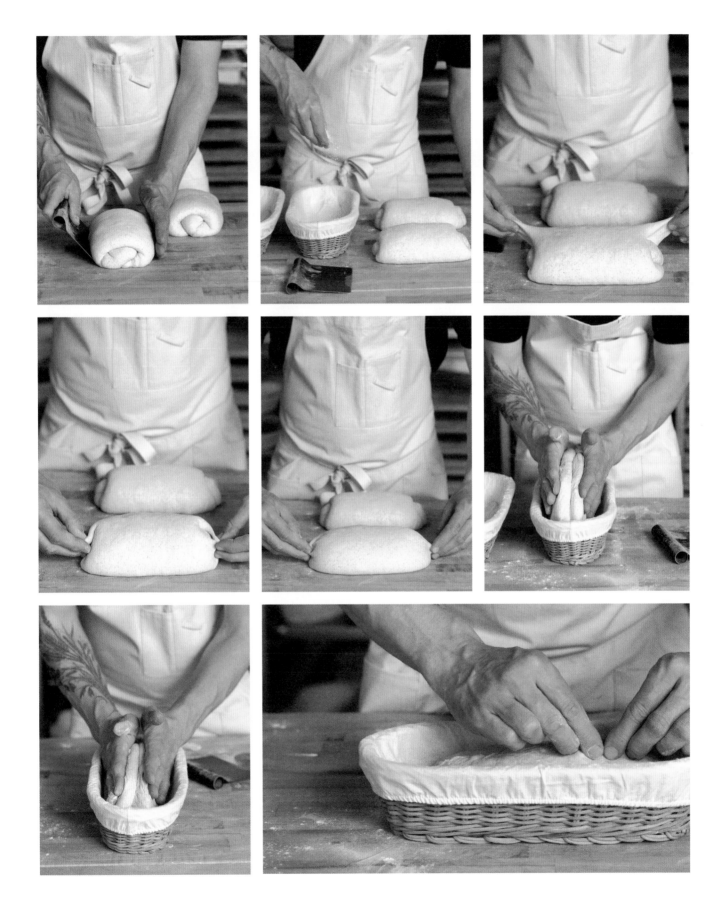

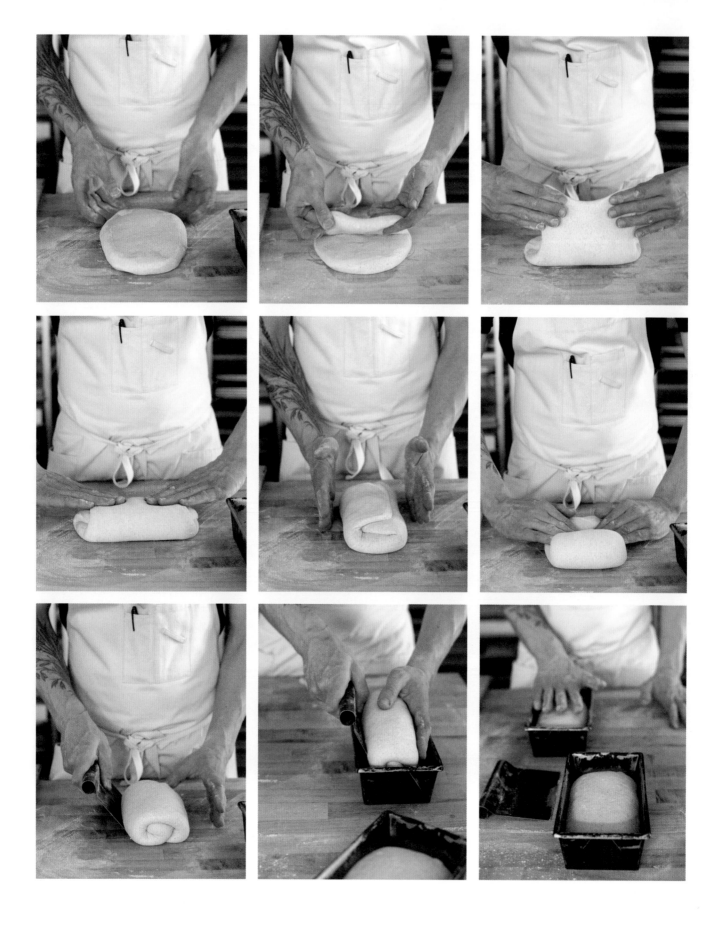

SHAPING A TIN (PAN) LOAF

1. Spray the loaf tins lightly with a neutral oil such as vegetable or sunflower oil.

2. Follow steps 2 through 5 in Shaping a Bâtard (page 41).

3. Once the dough is shaped, lightly dust each loaf with flour. Use the bench knife to pick up each loaf.

   If there are seeds or flakes to be added to the surface, place them on a small baking sheet or in a large bowl, then mist the top of the shaped boules with water, lift the boule, placing the damp top side in the seeds or flakes, then transfer the dough to the tin with the seam on the bottom and in the middle. This is the "spine" (backbone) and will help the bread proof and bake evenly.

PROOFING AND BAKING

ROOM-TEMPERATURE BASKET PROOF

Once the loaves are shaped and in the proofing baskets or loaf tins, allow them to proof at room temperature (72°F/22°C) until they are domed and, when pressed, they bounce back slowly, leaving a slight indentation.

The length of time the bread should proof at room temperature will depend on how much the dough increased in volume during the bulk fermentation stage. You may want to start by leaving the loaves out on the counter for 20 to 45 minutes, but some loaves need to sit out for 1½ to 2 hours before being placed in the fridge. I find loaves with more whole grains or inclusions, like fruit and nuts or seeds, like some extra time. If the dough is extremely active, then you can place the loaves straight into the fridge. Be careful not to push the basket proofing too long, as the dough can overproof. Press the dough gently with your finger to determine if it is properly proofed and ready for the overnight cold proof. If the dough *slowly* springs back, it is properly proofed. If the dough *immediately* springs back, then it is probably underproofed and needs more time. If the indentation remains, then the dough is overproofed and may rise too much when baked or the ear may be cracked. Despite its appearance, the loaf should still be edible even if it is not perfectly proofed. The ability to recognize how far along the fermentation is will come with experience and seeing what works in your environment.

OVERNIGHT COLD PROOF

When the loaves are ready, cover with a loose-fitting lid or plate, and transfer them to the fridge. Refrigerating the loaves allows the dough to continue to develop, improves the flavour, improves the caramelization on the crust, and helps the grain be more digestible.

It is best to place the loaves on the top shelf, as this tends to be slightly warmer than the bottom shelf. Leave the loaves in the fridge to cold proof for at least 12 hours, but 16 to 18 hours is best.

The ideal fridge temperature for bread dough is 45 to 47°F (7 to 8°C), which is a little higher than normal for a home fridge, so it is best to give the loaves a long, slow proof. Some professional bakeries have a separate fridge that is used only for cold proofing bread. Because we don't have space at our bakery for this, we cold proof at around 40 to 42°F (4 to 6°C) with great results.

BAKING EQUIPMENT

There are a couple of options for what to bake your bread in that are very effective.

For the home baker, I recommend using a preheated 3.2-quart cast-iron cloche-style bread pan, such as the Challenger Bread Pan or the Lodge Combo Cooker. These are essentially upside-down Dutch ovens, with a shallow base for the bread to sit on and a domed top to allow plenty of space for the bread to grow during baking. It is easy to place the bread on the base, and the lid prevents the steam from escaping, ensuring a soft crust and a pleasing oven spring. The lid is removed partway through the bake to ensure a crisp, caramelized crust. The cast iron holds heat well so the dough has a long cool-down, which slows the retrogradation process. In turn, the bread will stale more slowly. It is important to learn about seasoning anything made of cast iron to ensure longevity and prevent rust.

The second option is to preheat a heavy cast-iron baking steel or a baking stone, with an additional baking sheet on the bottom rack. Once the bread has been scored and slid onto the baking steel or stone, pour boiling hot water into the baking sheet to create steam in the oven. Use caution: the water will bubble and splutter, so stand back with your arm fully stretched out to avoid burning yourself. You can use colder water, but it will likely spit more than hot water. Ice cubes work better as you can throw them in the oven quickly and close the door. With this method, it is easier to bake two loaves at the same time. Most home ovens are designed to vent steam out. This is not too much of an issue, but if you see a lot of steam escaping, then the Dutch oven is going to be a better choice.

If you are baking one loaf at a time, simply leave the other loaf in the fridge while baking the first one.

SCORING

Scoring is a simple action that is done just before baking to allow the bread to expand, which helps to produce a light, open crumb. A razor blade attached to a small handle called a lame is used to quickly score a thin cut on the surface of the bread. This is the baker's signature and can be extremely decorative or just one simple swipe. The latter is usually preferable, since the more the bread is messed with, the more it will deflate. For best results, score at a 45-degree angle, quickly and confidently. This will get easier with practice and is also easier if you have developed good surface tension during the shaping stage.

With a boule loaf, scoring a simple 3-inch (8cm) square on top helps with oven spring and keeping the shape uniform as the loaf bakes.

If scoring a bâtard or a tin loaf, position the loaf so a short end is facing you. In one motion, score the bread with one crescent-moon shape, about ¼ inch (5mm) deep.

BAKING BREAD

It's important to read *all* the steps for each baking method before beginning to bake.

Baking sourdough straight from the fridge makes scoring and oven spring more achievable. Take both loaves out of the fridge if they are to be baked at the same time. If you are baking one loaf at a time, leave the second loaf in the fridge until the first one is done.

If a Dutch oven–style cast-iron bread pan is being used, follow this method:

1. Cut 2 pieces of parchment paper to fit inside the pan; set these aside. Remove the top rack from the oven and put the pan, with its lid, on the middle rack. Preheat the oven to 475°F (240°C) so that the pan heats up along with the oven. Set a timer for 1 hour.

2. When the timer goes, prepare the lame and place it close by in a safe spot. Remove the bread from the fridge.

3. Carefully remove the preheated pan from the oven using thick oven gloves or a kitchen towel and place it on the stovetop. Remove the lid, setting it next to the base.

4. Drop the parchment paper onto the base, being careful not to touch the very hot pan.

5. Gently turn the proofing basket upside down so that the shaped loaf rolls out onto the parchment paper, seam side down.

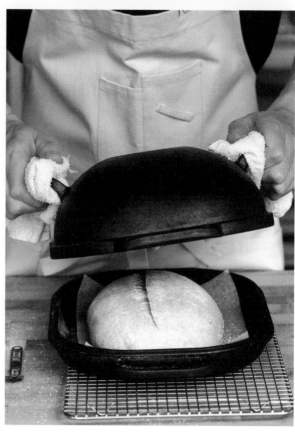

6. Using the lame, score the loaf with a quick and efficient action. You can add a single ice cube to the pan base to provide a little extra steam that will help create a glossy, crunchy crust, but this isn't essential as the dough in the sealed pan will give off its own steam. Cover the base with the lid and immediately place the pan back in the oven and close the door.

7. Bake the bread with the lid on for 20 minutes.

8. Using oven gloves, take the pan out of the oven and remove its lid. Return the base with the loaf to the oven. If you are baking two loaves in succession, return the lid to the oven so that it maintains heat for the second loaf's bake. Reduce the heat to 410°F (210°C). Continue baking the bread until it is a beautiful dark golden brown all over, 25 to 30 minutes.

9. Transfer the baked loaf to a cooling rack and allow to cool for at least 1 hour before slicing. If you are baking a second loaf, increase the oven temperature to 475°F (240°C) and place the cast-iron pan back in the oven to preheat for at least 15 minutes before repeating the process.

If baking on a baking stone or steel, follow this method:

1. Place the stone or steel on the middle rack of the oven and a baking sheet on the lower rack. Preheat the oven to 475°F (240°C) and set a timer for 1 hour.

2. When the timer goes off, bring a kettle of water to a boil.

3. While waiting for the water to boil, remove the bread from the fridge.

4. Sprinkle a little cornmeal or semolina flour over the top of the loaves. When the loaves are flipped out of the proofing baskets, this cornmeal top will become the bottom and will prevent sticking while creating a desirable texture on the bottom crust.

5. Carefully remove the baking stone or steel using thick oven gloves or a kitchen towel and place it on the stovetop.

6. One at a time, gently turn the loaves out of the proofing baskets and onto the stone or steel so they are parallel to each other with a couple of inches between them to allow the heat to circulate and the bread to expand.

7. Using the lame, quickly score each loaf. Carefully transfer the baking stone or steel back into the oven.

8. Very carefully, at arm's length, pour about 1 cup of boiling water into the preheated baking sheet, then immediately close the oven door.

9. Bake the bread for 20 minutes.

10. Reduce the oven temperature to 410°F (210°C). Rotate the loaves front to back for more of an even colour if needed, then continue baking until the bread is dark golden brown, 25 to 30 minutes.

11. Transfer the baked loaves to a cooling rack and allow to cool for at least 1 hour before slicing.

STORING BREAD

We do not use any plastic packaging at our bakery. Wrapping a loaf in a plastic bag does not allow the bread to breathe and keeps moisture in, creating the perfect conditions for mould. However, exposing the bread to too much air will cause it to stale quickly. Therefore, it is best to store bread in a bread box, drawer, or linen bag at a cool room temperature, up to 68°F (20°C). Do not store it in the fridge as this dries it out. Cutting an artisanal loaf into slices ahead of time will cause it to stale, so keep the loaf whole and slice it as needed. We find our bread lasts for 3 to 4 days if stored correctly, but it also freezes well if you are worried about not getting through a whole loaf. Once the loaf has cooled completely, slice it, place a piece of wax paper between each slice to prevent them from sticking, and store in a resealable plastic bag in the freezer for up to 1 month. Toast just the amount needed from frozen. (Keep the pieces of wax paper in the freezer when not in use so they don't go mouldy.)

Sourdough Loaves

Country Sourdough

Makes two 1kg loaves

This is our everyday sourdough formula at the bakery that we tweak and modify depending on the flour, sourdough starter, temperature, humidity, quantity, and inclusions. There are so many factors to consider when making sourdough, but don't feel intimidated, it's just bread! The best advice I can give to a new bread baker is to make this simple recipe ten to twenty times before moving on to other recipes. Build your confidence and master this recipe before adding more whole grains or other additions. This will give you experience in how your flour feels and behaves. Write everything down in a little notepad: the date, flour brand, temperature of water, dough temperature after mixing and before pre-shaping, oven temperature, and bake times, and add notes about the oven spring, texture, crumb, flavour, and crust of the finished loaf.

Levain

    1 batch Levain (page 29)

Dough

    800g warm water (75 to 78°F/24 to 26°C)
        (80% hydration)
    750g bread flour
    200g stone-ground whole wheat flour
    50g stone-ground whole-grain rye flour
    200g active levain
    5g fine sea salt

Prepare the levain

1. Prepare the levain as directed on pages 29 to 30 in the Sourdough Starter Guide. Feed the active starter early in the morning (by 7 a.m.) the day you plan to mix the dough so that it is active and tripled in size after 4 to 6 hours. Alternatively, prepare the levain with a less active starter—approximately 10 percent inoculation (10g) calculated to the total weight of flours—the night before (by 10 p.m.) so it's ready in the morning, 8 to 10 hours later.

Autolyse and mix

2. This dough is easily mixed by hand in a large bowl or with a stand mixer fitted with the dough hook on low speed. Pour the warm water into the bowl. Add the bread flour, whole wheat flour, and rye flour and mix until a shaggy dough forms with no dry patches, 2 to 3 minutes. Cover the dough with a kitchen towel or loose-fittling lid and let rest in a warm (72 to 75°F/22 to 24°C), draft-free place for 1 hour (autolyse).

3. After the resting period, add the active levain to the dough and mix for 1 to 2 minutes. Cover the bowl and let sit for 10 minutes.

4. Add the salt and knead the dough using the Rubaud method as directed on page 33 (see photos on page 32) until it is smoother in appearance, feels more active, and has a little more elasticity, 5 to 6 minutes. (If using a stand mixer, knead the dough on medium-low speed.) Cover the bowl and let the dough relax for another 10 minutes.

5. Knead the dough a final time at a faster speed to fully develop the gluten and stretch it a little more. (If using a stand mixer, knead on medium speed for 2 minutes.) The dough should pull away from the sides of the bowl.

Bulk ferment

6. Place the dough in a lightly oiled bowl or container that is four times the size of the dough and cover with

continued . . .

a loose-fitting lid or kitchen towel. Place the dough in a warm (72 to 75°F/22 to 24°C), draft-free place. A constant temperature will ensure a consistent fermentation. Set a timer for 30 minutes.

7. When the timer goes off, perform the first set of stretch-and-folds as directed on pages 33 to 34. Again, set the timer for 30 minutes. Repeat the set of stretch-and-folds another three or four times over a 2-hour period, depending on how the dough feels (for a total of 3 hours of timed stretch-and-folds). Once the dough feels tighter, is doming, and has good strength, perform a gentle coil fold as directed on page 34. Cover the dough and allow it to rest for 30 to 40 minutes, until you can see some fermentation bubbles and the dough has increased in volume by approximately 40 percent.

Pre-shape and bench rest

8. Gently remove the dough from the container and allow it to relax on an unfloured work surface for a minute. Using a bench knife, cut the dough into 2 equal pieces (1kg each). Working with 1 piece at a time, gently pre-shape the dough into a round ball. Cover the dough with a thin kitchen towel to prevent the top drying out.

Allow the dough to bench rest until it has spread about an inch (2.5cm) in diameter and looks more relaxed, at least 30 minutes and up to 1 hour. (Follow the directions on pages 34 to 36; see photos on page 36.)

Final shape and overnight cold proof

9. Prepare 2 proofing baskets (for bâtards or boules) as directed on pages 36 to 37 or 1kg loaf tins as directed on page 45.

10. Shape the loaves into bâtards, boules, or tin loaves as directed on pages 37 to 45. Allow the loaves to sit at room temperature until increased in volume by approximately 20 percent, 30 to 60 minutes. This time will vary depending on how active the dough is.

11. Cover the loaves with a loose-fitting lid or plate and place them in the fridge to cold proof overnight, 16 to 18 hours.

Bake

12. The following day, score and bake the loaves as directed on pages 47 to 51.

13. See Storing Bread (page 51).

50% Whole-Grain Country Sourdough

Makes two 1kg loaves

This recipe is a great introduction to adding more healthy and nutritious flours to your bread. Increasing the whole-grain percentage may require the addition of more water, depending on the freshness of the flour and grade that it has been milled at. If the flour is quite coarse and very fresh, you may find a little extra warm water (bassinage; see page 33) is required. This can be added towards the end of the mixing stage. At this point, up to 10 percent (80g) extra water can be added, which is best mixed in quickly before removing the dough from the bowl. I recommend first adding 5 percent (40g) bassinage, then increasing if needed.

Levain

    1 batch Levain (page 29)

Dough

    800g warm water (75 to 78°F/24 to 26°C)
      (80% hydration)
    500g bread flour
    450g stone-ground whole wheat flour
    50g stone-ground whole-grain rye flour
    200g active levain
    25g fine sea salt

Prepare the levain

1. Prepare the levain as directed on pages 29 to 30 in the Sourdough Starter Guide. Feed the active starter early in the morning (by 7 a.m.) the day you plan to mix the dough so that it is active and tripled in size after 4 to 6 hours. Alternatively, prepare the levain with a less active starter—10 to 15 percent inoculation (10 to 15g) calculated to the total weight of flours—the night before (by 10 p.m.) so it's ready in the morning, 8 to 10 hours later.

Autolyse and mix

2. This dough is easily mixed by hand in a large bowl or with a stand mixer fitted with the dough hook on low speed. Pour the warm water into the bowl. Add the bread flour, whole wheat flour, and rye flour and mix until a shaggy dough forms with no dry patches, 2 to 3 minutes. Cover the dough with a kitchen towel or loose-fitting lid and let rest in a warm (72 to 75°F/22 to 24°C), draft-free place for 1 hour (autolyse).

3. After the resting period, add the active levain to the dough and mix for 1 to 2 minutes. Cover the bowl and let sit for 10 minutes.

4. Add the salt and knead the dough using the Rubaud method as directed on page 33 (see photos on page 32) until it is smoother in appearance, feels more active, and has a little more elasticity, 5 to 6 minutes. (If using a stand mixer, knead the dough on medium-low speed.) Cover the bowl and let the dough relax for another 10 minutes.

5. Knead the dough a final time at a faster speed to fully develop the gluten and stretch it a little more. (If using a stand mixer, knead on medium speed for 2 to 3 minutes.) The dough should pull away from the sides of the bowl. Add an additional 40g to 80g of warm water (75 to 78°F/ 24 to 26°C) (bassinage) if the dough still feels tight. The amount will vary depending on the freshness of the flour and absorption rate. (Test the recipe with and without the bassinage and see what hydration works for your flour.)

continued . . .

Bulk ferment

6. Place the dough in a lightly oiled bowl or container that is four times the size of the dough and cover with a loose-fitting lid or kitchen towel. Place the dough in a warm (72 to 75°F/22 to 24°C), draft-free place. A constant temperature will ensure a consistent fermentation. Set a timer for 30 minutes.

7. When the timer goes off, perform the first set of stretch-and-folds as directed on pages 33 to 34. Again, set the timer for 30 minutes. Repeat the set of stretch-and-folds another three or four times over a 2-hour period, depending on how the dough feels (for a total of 3 hours of timed stretch-and-folds). Once the dough feels tighter, is doming, and has good strength, perform a couple of sets of coil folds as directed on page 34. Cover the dough and allow it to rest for 30 to 40 minutes, until you can see some fermentation bubbles and the dough has increased in volume by approximately 40 percent.

Pre-shape and bench rest

8. Gently remove the dough from the container and allow it to relax on an unfloured work surface for a minute. Using a bench knife, cut the dough into 2 equal pieces (1kg each). Working with 1 piece at a time, gently pre-shape the dough into a round ball. Cover the dough with a thin kitchen towel to prevent the top drying out. Allow the dough to bench rest until it has spread about an inch (2.5cm) in diameter and looks more relaxed, at least 30 minutes and up to 1 hour. (Follow the directions on pages 34 to 36; see photos on page 36.)

Final shape and overnight cold proof

9. Prepare 2 proofing baskets (for bâtards or boules) as directed on pages 36 to 37 or 1kg loaf tins as directed on page 45.

10. Shape the loaves into bâtards, boules, or tin loaves as directed on pages 37 to 45. Allow the loaves to sit at room temperature until increased in volume by approximately 20 percent, 30 to 60 minutes. This time will vary depending on how active the dough is. Cover the loaves with a loose-fitting lid or plate and place them in the fridge to cold proof overnight, 16 to 18 hours.

Bake

11. The following day, score and bake the loaves as directed on pages 47 to 51.

12. See Storing Bread (page 51).

100% Whole Wheat Sourdough

Makes two 1kg loaves

A few years ago, I came across a research study by Dan Buettner about Blue Zones in the world. The people who live in these zones are some of the healthiest and longest-lived in the world. The five Blue Zones around the world are Okinawa, Japan; Nicoya, Costa Rica; Loma Linda, California; Ikaria, Greece; and Sardinia, Italy. A lot of the residents eat a primarily plant-based diet (about 95 percent), which includes fruits, grains, and legumes. But the part that really got my attention was that a lot of the Blue Zone communities eat whole-grain sourdough bread! Whole-grain loaves are what I truly love to make, bake, and eat.

To make this sourdough truly 100 percent whole-grain, feed the starter for a few days with only whole wheat flour. It should develop a sweeter flavour profile.

The first few times you make this recipe, bake the loaves in tins. This will get you used to how the dough feels and behaves at different stages of fermentation, helping build your confidence.

Whole Wheat Levain

25g active starter (25% inoculation; see page 27)
100g warm water (75 to 78°F/24 to 26°C)
   (100% hydration)
50g stone-ground whole-grain red spring wheat flour
50g stone-ground whole-grain hard white wheat flour

Dough

820g warm water (75 to 78°F/24 to 26°C)
   (82% hydration; 40 to 80g extra if needed)
800g stone-ground whole-grain red spring
   wheat flour
200g stone-ground whole-grain hard white
   wheat flour
200g active whole wheat levain
25g fine sea salt

Prepare the whole wheat levain

1. Prepare the whole wheat levain for this recipe following the method in the levain recipe as directed on pages 29 to 30 in the Sourdough Starter Guide. Feed the active starter early in the morning (by 7 a.m.) the day you plan to mix the dough so that it is active and tripled in size after 4 to 6 hours. Alternatively, prepare the levain with a less active starter—approximately 10 percent inoculation (10g) calculated to the total weight of flours—the night before (by 10 p.m.) so it's ready in the morning, 8 to 10 hours later.

Autolyse and mix

2. This dough is easily mixed by hand in a large bowl or with a stand mixer fitted with the dough hook on low speed. Pour the warm water into the bowl. Add the red spring wheat flour and white wheat flour and mix until a shaggy dough forms with no dry patches, 2 to 3 minutes. Cover the dough with a kitchen towel or loose-fitting lid and let rest in a warm (72 to 75°F/22 to 24°C), draft-free place for 1 hour (autolyse).

3. After the resting period, add the active whole wheat levain to the dough and mix for 1 to 2 minutes. Cover the bowl and let sit for 10 minutes.

4. Add the salt and knead the dough using the Rubaud method as directed on page 33 (see photos on page 32) until it is smoother in appearance, feels more active, and has a little more elasticity, 5 to 6 minutes. (If using a stand mixer, knead the dough on medium speed.) Cover the bowl and let the dough relax for another 10 minutes.

5. Knead the dough a final time at a faster speed to fully develop the gluten and stretch it a little more. (If using a stand mixer, knead on medium-high speed for 2 minutes.) The dough should pull away from the sides of the bowl.

continued . . .

Bulk ferment

6. Place the dough in a lightly oiled bowl or container that is four times the size of the dough and cover with a loose-fitting lid or kitchen towel. Place the dough in a warm (72 to 75°F/22 to 24°C), draft-free place. A constant temperature will ensure a consistent fermentation. Set a timer for 30 minutes.

7. When the timer goes off, perform the first set of stretch-and-folds as directed on pages 33 to 34. Again, set the timer for 30 minutes. Repeat the set of stretch-and-folds another two or three times over a 2-hour period, depending on how the dough feels (for a total of 3 hours of timed stretch-and-folds). Once the dough feels tighter and is doming and has good strength, perform a couple of sets of coil folds as directed on page 34. Cover the dough and allow it to rest for 30 to 60 minutes, until you can see some fermentation bubbles and the dough has increased in volume by approximately 40 percent.

Pre-shape and bench rest

8. Gently remove the dough from the container and allow it to relax on an unfloured work surface for a minute. Using a bench knife, cut the dough into 2 equal pieces (1kg each). Working with 1 piece at a time, gently pre-shape the dough into a round ball. Cover the dough with a thin kitchen towel to prevent the top drying out. Allow the dough to bench rest until it has spread about an inch (2.5cm) in diameter and looks more relaxed, at least 30 minutes and up to 1 hour. (Follow the directions on pages 34 to 36; see photos on page 36.)

Final shape and overnight cold proof

9. Prepare two 1kg loaf tins as directed on page 45 or proofing baskets (for bâtards or boules) as directed on pages 36 to 37.

10. Shape the loaves into tin loaves, bâtards, or boules as directed on pages 37 to 45. Allow the loaves to sit at room temperature until increased in volume by approximately 20 percent, 30 to 60 minutes. This time will vary depending on how active the dough is. Cover the loaves with a loose-fitting lid or plate and place them in the fridge to cold proof overnight, 16 to 18 hours.

Bake

11. The following day, score and bake the loaves as directed on pages 47 to 51.

12. See Storing Bread (page 51).

Toasted Sunflower and Flaxseed Sourdough

Makes two 1kg boules

Toasting and soaking the seeds before mixing them into the dough means they won't absorb water from the dough. It also adds lots of flavour and makes them more digestible. This bread is lovely shaped as a boule and rolled in additional sunflower and flaxseeds. The seeds in the dough add extra texture to the crumb, and the ones on the outside elevate the crust further.

Flaxseed is a wonderful seed, and 40 percent of the world's flax is grown in Canada. Flaxseeds are rich in vitamins and minerals and have many health benefits, being high in fibre, omega-3, omega-6, and omega-9 fatty acids, 18 percent protein, and low in cholesterol, so they are great to eat as part of a healthy diet.

Levain

    1 batch Levain (page 29)

Inclusions

    75g sunflower seeds
    75g flaxseeds
    150g boiling water

Dough

    630g warm water (75 to 78°F/24 to 26°C)
        (73% hydration)
    520g bread flour
    180g stone-ground whole wheat flour
    80g stone-ground whole-grain spelt flour
    80g stone-ground whole-grain rye flour
    160g active levain
    20g fine sea salt

Seed Mix (for rolling)

    150g sunflower seeds
    150g flaxseeds

Prepare the levain

1. Prepare the levain as directed on pages 29 to 30 in the Sourdough Starter Guide. Feed the active starter early in the morning (by 7 a.m.) the day you plan to mix the dough so that it is active and tripled in size after 4 to 6 hours. Alternatively, prepare the levain with a less active starter—10 to 15 percent inoculation (10 to 15g) calculated to the total weight of flours—the night before (by 10 p.m.) so it's ready in the morning, 8 to 10 hours later.

Prepare the inclusions

2. Prepare the seeds a couple of hours before beginning the dough. Preheat the oven to 350°F (175°C).

3. Scatter the 75g sunflower seeds and 75g flaxseeds on a small baking sheet and lightly toast them in the oven until they are light golden brown, 5 minutes, stirring halfway through. Set aside to cool.

4. Place the cooled seeds in a medium bowl. Pour over the boiling water and stir. Let the seeds soak until the water has been absorbed and the seeds are completely cooled, 2 hours.

Autolyse and mix

5. This dough is easily mixed by hand in a large bowl or with a stand mixer fitted with the dough hook on medium speed. Pour the warm water into the bowl. Add the bread flour, whole wheat flour, spelt flour, and rye flour and mix until a shaggy dough forms with no dry patches, 2 to 3 minutes. Cover the dough with a kitchen towel or loose-fitting lid and let rest in a warm (72 to 75°F/22 to 24°C), draft-free place for 1 hour (autolyse).

6. After the resting period, add the active levain to the dough and mix for 1 to 2 minutes. Cover the bowl and let sit for 10 minutes.

7. Add the salt and knead the dough using the Rubaud method as directed on page 33 (see photos on page 32) until the dough is smoother in appearance, feels more

continued . . .

active, and has a little more elasticity, 5 to 6 minutes. (If using a stand mixer, knead the dough on medium speed.) Cover the bowl and let the dough relax for another 10 minutes.

8. Knead the dough a final time at a faster speed to fully develop the gluten and stretch it a little more. (If using a stand mixer, knead on medium-high speed for 2 to 3 minutes.) The dough should pull away from the sides of the bowl.

9. Add the soaked seeds and knead them into the dough for 1 minute.

Bulk ferment

10. Place the dough in a lightly oiled bowl or container that is four times the size of the dough and cover with a loose-fitting lid or kitchen towel. Place the dough in a warm (72 to 75°F/22 to 24°C), draft-free place. A constant temperature will ensure a consistent fermentation. Set a timer for 30 minutes.

11. When the timer goes off, perform the first set of stretch-and-folds as directed on pages 33 to 34. Again, set the timer for 30 minutes. Repeat the set of stretch-and-folds another two or three times over a 2-hour period, depending on how the dough feels (for a total of 3 hours of timed stretch-and-folds). Once the dough feels tighter and is doming, perform a couple of sets of coil folds as directed on page 34. Cover the dough and allow it to rest for 30 to 60 minutes, until you can see some fermentation bubbles and the dough has increased in volume by approximately 40 percent.

Pre-shape and bench rest

12. Gently remove the dough from the container and allow it to relax on an unfloured work surface for a minute. Using a bench knife, cut the dough into 2 equal pieces (1kg each). Working with 1 piece at a time, gently pre-shape the dough into a round ball. Cover the dough with a thin kitchen towel to prevent the top drying out. Allow the dough to bench rest until it has spread about an inch (2.5cm) in diameter and looks more relaxed, at least 30 minutes and up to 1 hour. (Follow the directions on pages 34 to 36; see photos on page 36.)

Final shape and overnight cold proof

13. Prepare 2 round proofing baskets as directed on pages 36 to 37.

14. Shape the loaves into boules as directed on pages 37 to 39.

15. For the seed mix, combine the 150g sunflower seeds and 150g flaxseeds in a large bowl or on a small baking sheet. Dampen a kitchen towel and lay it on the work surface. Holding the shaped dough seam side up, roll the smooth top side onto the damp towel and then immediately roll it in the seeds. Transfer the dough to the proofing basket with the seeds on the bottom. (Alternatively, mist the top of the dough with water, then use a bench knife to lift the dough from the bench and flip it over into the seed mix.) Repeat for the second loaf.

16. Allow the loaves to sit in a warm (72 to 75°F/ 22 to 24°C), draft-free place until increased in volume by approximately 20 percent, 30 to 60 minutes. The time will vary depending on how active the dough is.

17. Cover the loaves with a loose-fitting lid or plate and place them in the fridge to cold proof overnight, 16 to 18 hours.

Bake

18. The following day, score and bake the loaves as directed on pages 47 to 51.

19. See Storing Bread (page 51). Because of the extra hydration (90 percent), from the soaked seeds, this sourdough will stay soft for a few extra days.

Mega Multi-Seed Sourdough

Makes two 1kg loaves

The Mega Multi-Seed Sourdough was named by one of our regular customers who said they had never had a light sourdough that had so much flavour and so many seeds! When creating recipes for the bakery, I find it's best to not be parsimonious with additions such as seeds, nuts, dried fruits, spices, sprouts, or chocolate. Why not be generous if the bread is going to taste so much better? It's always a disappointment if you look forward to eating a treat filled with something only to find it doesn't have enough filling inside.

   This bread is lovely shaped as a bâtard or boule, then rolled in additional mixed seeds. The toasted and soaked blend of seeds adds a wonderful peanut butter aroma and taste to the crumb. Rolling the shaped loaves in the same blend of raw seeds allows the seeds to soften while the dough ferments overnight and then toast perfectly while the bread is baking. This way there are toasted seeds both inside and on the outside of the loaf, which is the aim of the game.

Levain

   1 batch Levain (page 29)

Seed Mix (for inclusions and rolling)

   50g sunflower seeds

   50g flaxseeds

   50g pumpkin seeds

   50g sesame seeds

   50g poppy seeds

   50g millet

   150g boiling water

Dough

   630g warm water (75 to 78°F/24 to 26°C)
      (73% hydration)

   520g bread flour

   180g stone-ground whole wheat flour

   80g stone-ground whole-grain spelt flour

   80g stone-ground whole-grain rye flour

   160g active levain

   20g fine sea salt

Prepare the levain

1. Prepare the levain as directed on pages 29 to 30 in the Sourdough Starter Guide. Feed the active starter early in the morning (by 7 a.m.) the day you plan to mix the dough so that it is active and tripled in size after 4 to 6 hours. Alternatively, prepare the levain with a less active starter—approximately 10 percent inoculation (10g) calculated to the total weight of flours—the night before (by 10 p.m.) so it's ready in the morning, 8 to 10 hours later.

Prepare the inclusions

2. Prepare the seeds a couple of hours before beginning the dough. Preheat the oven to 350°F (175°C).

3. In a medium bowl, mix the sunflower seeds, flaxseeds, pumpkin seeds, sesame seeds, poppy seeds, and millet. Transfer half of the seed mixture (150g) to an airtight container and reserve for the outside of the dough. Spread the remaining half of the seed mixture (150g) on a small baking sheet and lightly toast them in the oven until golden brown, 5 minutes, stirring halfway through. Set aside to cool.

4. Place the cooled seeds in a small bowl. Pour over the boiling water and stir. Let the seeds soak until the water has been absorbed and the seeds are completely cooled, 2 to 3 hours.

Autolyse and mix

5. This dough is easily mixed by hand in a large bowl or with a stand mixer fitted with the dough hook on

continued . . .

medium speed. Pour the warm water into the bowl. Add the bread flour, whole wheat flour, spelt flour, and rye flour and mix together until a shaggy dough forms with no dry patches, 2 to 3 minutes. Cover the dough with a kitchen towel or loose-fitting lid and let rest in a warm (72 to 75°F/22 to 24°C), draft-free place for 1 hour (autolyse).

6. After the resting period, add the active levain to the dough and mix for 1 to 2 minutes. Cover the bowl and let sit for 10 minutes.

7. Add the salt and knead the dough using the Rubaud method as directed on page 33 (see photos on page 32) until it is smoother in appearance, feels more active, and has a little more elasticity, 5 to 6 minutes. (If using a stand mixer, knead the dough on medium-low speed.) Cover the bowl and let the dough relax for another 10 minutes.

8. Knead the dough a final time at a faster speed to fully develop the gluten and stretch it a little more. (If using a stand mixer, knead on medium speed for 2 minutes.) The dough should pull away from the sides of the bowl.

9. Add the soaked seeds and knead them into the dough for 1 minute.

Bulk ferment

10. Place the dough in a lightly oiled bowl or container that is four times the size of the dough and cover with a loose-fitting lid or kitchen towel. Place the dough in a warm (72 to 75°F/22 to 24°C), draft-free place. A constant temperature will ensure a consistent fermentation (see page 33). Set a timer for 30 minutes.

11. When the timer goes off, perform the first set of stretch-and-folds as directed on pages pages 33 to 34. Again, set the timer for 30 minutes. Repeat the set of stretch-and-folds another two or three times over a 2-hour period, depending on how the dough feels (for a total of 3 hours of timed stretch-and-folds). Once the dough feels tighter and is doming, perform a couple of sets of coil folds as directed on page 34. Cover the dough and allow it to rest for 30 to 60 minutes, until you can see some fermentation bubbles and the dough has increased in volume by approximately 40 percent.

Pre-shape and bench rest

12. Gently remove the dough from the container and allow it to relax on an unfloured work surface for a minute. Using a bench knife, cut the dough into 2 equal pieces (1kg each). Working with 1 piece at a time, gently pre-shape the dough into a round ball. Cover the dough with a thin kitchen towel to prevent the top drying out. Allow the dough to bench rest until it has spread about an inch (2.5cm) in diameter and looks more relaxed, at least 30 minutes and up to 1 hour. (Follow the directions on pages 34 to 36; see photos on page 36.)

Final shape and overnight cold proof

13. Prepare 2 proofing baskets (for boules or bâtards) as directed on pages 36 to 37.

14. Shape the loaves into boules or bâtards as directed on pages 37 to 43.

15. Place the reserved 150g seed mixture in a large bowl or on a small baking sheet. Dampen a kitchen towel and lay it on the work surface. Holding the shaped dough seam side up, roll the smooth top side onto the damp kitchen towel and then immediately roll it in the seeds. Transfer the dough to the proofing basket with the seeds on the bottom. (Alternatively, mist the top of the dough with water, then use a bench knife to lift the dough from the bench and flip it over into the seed mix.) Repeat with the second loaf.

16. Allow the loaves to rest in a warm (72 to 75°F/ 22 to 24°C), draft-free place until increased in volume by approximately 20 percent, 30 to 60 minutes. This time will vary depending on how active the dough is.

17. Cover the loaves with a loose-fitting lid or plate and place them in the fridge to cold proof overnight, 16 to 18 hours.

Bake

18. The following day, score and bake the loaves as directed on pages 47 to 51.

19. See Storing Bread (page 51). Because of the extra hydration from the soaked seeds (90 percent), this sourdough will stay soft for a few extra days.

Porridge Sourdough

Makes two 1kg loaves

There's something special about cooking porridge—it's so simple yet so delicious and comforting. Most people make porridge with oats, but it can also be made with other flaked grains, such as spelt or barley. Adding porridge to a sourdough adds another level of texture and flavour. The initial dough is 70 percent hydration, but the porridge bumps that up to 96 percent. The extra moisture prolongs the bread's shelf life.

Gently cook the flakes with the ratio of 1:3 water, which swells the flakes and softens the starches. For extra flavour, the flakes can be lightly toasted in the oven before cooking. Experiment with different flakes and maybe add some seeds too.

Levain

1 batch Levain (page 29)

Porridge

75g oat, barley, rye, or spelt flakes
225g water

Dough

600g warm water (75 to 78°F/24 to 26°C)
  (70% hydration)
500g bread flour
260g stone-ground whole wheat flour
100g stone-ground whole-grain rye flour
170g active levain
20g fine sea salt

250g oat, barley, rye, or spelt flakes, for rolling

Prepare the levain

1. Prepare the levain as directed on pages 29 to 30 in the Sourdough Starter Guide. Feed the active starter early in the morning (by 7 a.m.) the day you plan to mix the dough so that it is active and tripled in size after 4 to 6 hours. Alternatively, prepare the levain with a less active starter—approximately 10 percent inoculation (10g) calculated to the total weight of flours—the night before (by 10 p.m.) so it's ready in the morning, 8 to 10 hours later.

Prepare the porridge

2. In a medium saucepan, combine the 75g grain flakes and water and gently cook over low heat, stirring occasionally to prevent burning, until soft and creamy, 10 minutes. Some flakes, like rye and spelt, benefit from being covered during cooking. Transfer the porridge to a small bowl and cool to room temperature before starting to mix the dough.

Autolyse and mix

3. This dough is easily mixed by hand in a large bowl or with a stand mixer fitted with the dough hook on medium speed. Pour the warm water into the bowl. Add the bread flour, whole wheat flour, and rye flour and mix together until a shaggy dough forms with no dry patches, 2 to 3 minutes. Cover the dough with a kitchen towel or loose-fitting lid and let rest in a warm (72 to 75°F/ 22 to 24°C), draft-free place for 1 hour (autolyse).

4. After the resting period, add the active levain to the dough and mix for 1 to 2 minutes. Cover the bowl and let sit for 10 minutes.

5. Add the salt and knead the dough using the Rubaud method as directed on page 33 (see photos on page 32) until it is smoother in appearance, feels more active, and has a little more elasticity, 5 to 6 minutes. (If using a stand mixer, knead the dough on medium speed.) Cover the bowl and let the dough relax for another 10 minutes.

continued . . .

6. Knead the dough a final time at a faster speed to fully develop the gluten and stretch it a little more. (If using a stand mixer, knead on medium-high speed for 2 minutes.) The dough should pull away from the sides of the bowl.

Bulk ferment

7. Place the dough in a lightly oiled bowl or container that is four times the size of the dough and cover with a loose-fitting lid or kitchen towel. Place the dough in a warm (72 to 75°F/22 to 24°C), draft-free place. A constant temperature will ensure a consistent fermentation (see page 33). Set a timer for 30 minutes.

8. When the timer goes off, perform the first set of stretch-and-folds as directed on pages 33 to 34. After the first set of stretch-and-folds, break the porridge into coin-size pieces and scatter it all over the top of the dough. The porridge doesn't need to be fully mixed in just yet, as during the folding it will be evenly dispersed. Again, set the timer for 30 minutes. Repeat the set of stretch-and-folds another two or three times over a 2-hour period, depending on how the dough feels (for a total of 3 hours of timed stretch-and-folds). Once the dough feels tighter and is doming, perform a couple of sets of coil folds as directed on page 34. Cover the dough and allow it to rest for 30 to 60 minutes, until you can see some fermentation bubbles and the dough has increased in volume by approximately 40 percent.

Pre-shape and bench rest

9. Gently remove the dough from the container and allow it to relax on an unfloured work surface for a minute. Using a bench knife, cut the dough into 2 equal pieces (1kg each). Working with 1 piece at a time, gently pre-shape the dough into a round ball as directed. Cover the dough with a thin kitchen towel to prevent the top drying out. Allow the dough to bench rest until it has spread about an inch (2.5cm) in diameter and looks more relaxed, at least 30 minutes and up to 1 hour. (Follow the directions on pages 34 to 36; see photos on page 36.)

Final shape and overnight cold proof

10. Prepare 2 proofing baskets (for boules or bâtards) as directed on pages 36 to 37.

11. Shape the loaves into boules or bâtards as directed on pages 37 to 43.

12. Place the 250g raw grain flakes in a large bowl or on a small baking sheet. Dampen a kitchen towel and lay it on the work surface. Holding the shaped dough seam side up, roll the smooth top side onto the damp towel and then immediately roll it in the flakes. Transfer the dough to the proofing basket with the flakes on the bottom. (Alternatively, mist the top of the dough with water, then use a bench knife to lift the dough from the bench and flip it over into the flakes.) Repeat for the second loaf.

13. Allow the loaves to rest in a warm (72 to 75°F/ 22 to 24°C), draft-free place until increased in volume by approximately 20 percent, 30 to 60 minutes. This time will vary depending on how active the dough is.

14. Cover the loaves with a loose-fitting lid or plate and place them in the fridge to cold proof overnight, 16 to 18 hours.

Bake

15. The following day, score and bake the loaves as directed on pages 47 to 51.

16. See Storing Bread (page 51). Because of the extra hydration from the porridge, this sourdough will stay soft for a few extra days.

Sprouted Buckwheat with 10% Whole-Grain Buckwheat Flour

Makes two 1kg loaves

While sprouts from grocery stores are a highly perishable and expensive commodity, buying the seeds in bulk and sprouting them at home not only guarantees freshness but is also far more economical.

Sprouting unlocks huge amounts of vitamins and minerals, up to fifty times more than we get from the mature vegetable counterpart. Our passion really took off after listening to the sprout pioneer Doug Evans, and author of *The Sprout Book*, talk on *The Rich Roll Podcast*, emphasizing the nutritional benefits, food security, and accessibility of sprouts.

Sprouting couldn't be easier: simply soak the seeds, grains, legumes, or nuts overnight until they are softened, then drain and let the magic begin. It usually takes three or four days for the shoots to appear, with a rinse and drain every 8 hours. This bread is lovely shaped as a tin loaf or boule and rolled in additional cracked buckwheat groats.

Inclusions

150g raw buckwheat groats (300g sprouted weight)

Levain

1 batch Levain (page 29)

Dough

750g warm water (75 to 78°F/24 to 26°C)
  (75% hydration)
600g bread flour
200g stone-ground whole wheat flour
100g stone-ground whole-grain buckwheat flour
100g stone-ground whole-grain rye flour
200g active levain
25g fine sea salt

100g raw buckwheat groats, for rolling

Days 1 to 3: Sprout the buckwheat groats

1. Thoroughly wash the 150g buckwheat groats in a fine-mesh sieve under cold running water. Place the groats in a half-gallon (2L) sprouting jar. Fill the jar with cold filtered water, cover with a mesh lid or piece of muslin cloth secured with a rubber band, and soak the groats for at least 6 hours and preferably overnight. Drain the water through the lid and rinse the groats with some fresh cold filtered water. Drain again and place the jar upside down and tilted at a 45-degree angle in a bowl or on a drying rack. Every 8 to 12 hours, fill the jar with fresh cold filtered water, swirl it gently to wash the groats, then drain the water and return the jar to drain upside down at a 45-degree angle. Repeat this process every 8 to 12 hours for 3 to 4 days, until the buckwheat groats are sprouted and have a tail approximately ½ inch (1cm) long.

Day 3/4: Prepare the levain

2. When the sprouts are ready, prepare the levain as directed on pages 29 to 30 in the Sourdough Starter Guide. Feed the active starter early in the morning (by 7 a.m.) the day you plan to mix the dough so that it is active and tripled in size after 4 to 6 hours. Alternatively, prepare the levain with a less active starter—approximately 10 percent inoculation (10g) calculated to the total weight of flours—the night before (by 10 p.m.) so it's ready in the morning, 8 to 10 hours later.

Autolyse and mix

3. This dough is easily mixed by hand in a large bowl or with a stand mixer fitted with the dough hook on medium speed. Pour the warm water into the bowl. Add the bread flour, whole wheat flour, buckwheat flour, and rye flour and mix until a shaggy dough forms with no dry patches, 2 to 3 minutes. Cover the dough with a kitchen

continued . . .

towel or loose-fitting lid and let rest in a warm (72 to 75°F/22 to 24°C), draft-free place for 1 hour (autolyse).

4. After the resting period, add the active levain to the dough and mix for 1 to 2 minutes. Cover the bowl and let sit for 10 minutes.

5. Add the salt and knead the dough using the Rubaud method as directed on page 33 (see photos on page 32) until the dough is smoother in appearance, feels more active, and has a little more elasticity, 5 to 6 minutes. (If using a stand mixer, knead the dough on medium-low speed.) Cover the bowl and let the dough relax for another 10 minutes.

6. Knead the dough a final time at a faster speed to fully develop the gluten and stretch it a little more. (If using a stand mixer, knead on medium speed for 2 minutes.) The dough should pull away from the sides of the bowl.

Bulk ferment

7. Place the dough in a lightly oiled bowl or container that is four times the size of the dough and cover with a loose-fitting lid or kitchen towel. Place the dough in a warm (72 to 75°F/22 to 24°C), draft-free place. A constant temperature will ensure a consistent fermentation. Set a timer for 30 minutes.

8. When the timer goes off, perform the first set of stretch-and-folds as directed on pages 33 to 34. Scatter the sprouts over the top of the dough—the sprouts don't need to be fully mixed in just yet, as during the folding they will be evenly dispersed. Again, set the timer for 30 minutes. Repeat the set of stretch-and-folds another two or three times over a 2-hour period, depending on how the dough feels (for a total of 3 hours of timed stretch-and-folds). Once the dough feels tighter and is doming, perform a couple of sets of coil folds as directed on page 34. Cover the dough and allow it to rest for 30 to 60 minutes, until you can see some fermentation bubbles and the dough has increased in volume by approximately 40 percent.

Pre-shape and bench rest

9. Gently remove the dough from the container and allow it to relax on an unfloured work surface for a minute.

Using a bench knife, cut the dough into 2 equal pieces (1kg each). Working with 1 piece at a time, gently pre-shape the dough into a round ball as directed. Cover the dough with a thin kitchen towel to prevent the top drying out. Allow the dough to bench rest until it has spread about an inch (2.5cm) in diameter and looks more relaxed, at least 30 minutes and up to 1 hour. (Follow the directions on pages 34 to 36; see photos on page 36.)

Final shape and overnight cold proof

10. Prepare two 1kg loaf tins as directed on page 45 or round proofing baskets (for boules) as directed on pages 36 to 37.

11. Shape the loaves into tin loaves as directed on page 45 or boules as directed on pages 37 to 39.

12. Place the 100g raw buckwheat groats in a food processor and pulse until they have broken up a little. Scatter the cracked groats on a small baking sheet. Dampen a kitchen towel and lay it on the work surface. Holding the shaped dough seam side up, roll the smooth top side onto the damp towel and then immediately roll it in the cracked groats. Transfer the dough to the tin with the groats on the top or to the proofing basket with the groats on the bottom. (Alternatively, mist the top of the dough with water, then use a bench knife to lift the dough from the bench and flip it over into the groats.) Repeat with the second loaf.

13. Allow the loaves to rest in a warm (72 to 75°F/ 22 to 24°C), draft-free place until increased in volume by approximately 20 percent, 30 to 60 minutes. This time will vary depending on how active the dough is.

14. Cover the loaves with a loose-fitting lid or plate and place them in the fridge to cold proof overnight, 16 to 18 hours.

Bake

15. The following day, score and bake the loaves as directed on pages 47 to 51.

16. See Storing Bread (page 51). Because of the extra hydration from the sprouts, this sourdough will stay soft for a few extra days.

Sprouted Rye with 20% Whole-Grain Rye Flour

Makes two 1kg loaves

Rye is one of my favourite grains because of what it brings to baking in the way of flavour, texture, and earthy colour with blue and green hues. It's quite different to work with compared to other grains due to the low gluten content. I find that 20 percent whole-grain rye flour is the perfect amount to add that will still ensure an open crumb and light texture. Sprouted rye berries elevate this bread's maltiness and bring a great chewy texture. Make extra rye berry sprouts because they are a great addition to salads or a garnish for root vegetable soups.

As an alternative to rolling the dough in cracked rye berries, you can lightly dust the loaves with stone-ground rye flour just before baking.

Inclusions

150g raw rye berries (300g sprouted weight)

Levain

100g warm water (75 to 78°F/24 to 26°C)
 (100% hydration)
50g stone-ground whole-grain rye flour
50g bread flour
25g active starter (25% inoculation; see page 27)

Dough

750g warm water (75 to 78°F/24 to 26°C)
 (75% hydration)
600g bread flour
200g stone-ground whole wheat flour
200g stone-ground whole-grain rye flour
200g active levain
25g fine sea salt

100g whole raw rye berries, for rolling (optional;
 see headnote)

Day 1 to 3: Sprout the rye berries

1. Thoroughly wash the 150g rye berries in a fine-mesh sieve under cold running water. Place the berries in a couple of half-gallon (2L) sprouting jars. Fill the jars with cold filtered water, cover with mesh lids or a piece of muslin cloth secured with a rubber band, and soak the berries for 24 hours, refreshing the water after 12 hours. Drain the water through the lid and rinse the berries with some fresh filtered cold water. Drain again and place the jars upside down and tilted at a 45-degree angle in a bowl or on a drying rack. Every 8 to 12 hours, fill the jars with fresh filtered cold water, shake them gently to wash the rye berries, then drain the water and return the jars to drain upside down at a 45-degree angle. Repeat this process every 8 to 12 hours for 3 to 4 days, until the rye berries are sprouted and have a tail approximately ½ inch (1cm) long.

Day 4: Prepare the levain

2. When the sprouts are ready, prepare the levain for this recipe following the method in the levain recipe as directed on pages 29 to 30 in the Sourdough Starter Guide. Feed the active starter early in the morning (by 7 a.m.) the day you plan to mix the dough so that it is active and tripled in size after 4 to 6 hours. Alternatively, prepare the levain with a less active starter—approximately 10 percent inoculation (10g) calculated to the total weight of flours—the night before (by 10 p.m.) so it's ready in the morning, 8 to 10 hours later.

Autolyse and mix

3. Pour the warm water into a large bowl. Add the bread flour, whole wheat flour, and rye flour and mix by hand until a shaggy dough forms with no dry patches, 2 to 3 minutes. Cover the dough with a kitchen towel or loose-fitting lid and let rest in a warm (72 to 75°F/ 22 to 24°C), draft-free place for 1 hour (autolyse).

4. After the resting period, add the active levain to the dough and mix for 1 to 2 minutes. Cover the bowl and let sit for 10 minutes.

5. Add the salt and knead the dough using the Rubaud method as directed on page 33 (see photos on page 32) until it is smoother in appearance, feels more active, and has a little more elasticity, 5 to 6 minutes. Cover the bowl and let the dough relax for another 10 minutes.

6. Knead the dough a final time at a faster speed to fully develop the gluten and stretch it a little more. The dough should pull away from the sides of the bowl.

Bulk ferment

7. Place the dough in a lightly oiled bowl or container that is four times the size of the dough and cover with a loose-fitting lid or kitchen towel. Place the dough in a warm (72 to 75°F/22 to 24°C), draft-free place. A constant temperature will ensure a consistent fermentation. Set a timer for 30 minutes.

8. When the timer goes off, perform the first set of stretch-and-folds as directed on pages 33 to 34. Scatter the sprouts over the top of the dough—the sprouts don't need to be fully mixed in just yet, as during the folding they will be evenly dispersed. Again, set the timer for 30 minutes. Then repeat the set of stretch-and-folds another two or three times over a 2-hour period, depending on how the dough feels (for a total of 3 hours of timed stretch-and-folds). Once the dough feels tighter and is doming, perform a couple of sets of coil folds as directed on page 34. Cover the dough and allow it to rest for 30 to 60 minutes, until you can see some fermentation bubbles and the dough has increased in volume by approximately 40 percent.

Pre-shape and bench rest

9. Gently remove the dough from the container and allow it to relax on an unfloured work surface for a minute. Using a bench knife, cut the dough into 2 equal pieces (1kg each). Working with 1 piece at a time, gently pre-shape the dough into a round ball. Cover the dough with a thin kitchen towel to prevent the top drying out. Allow the dough to bench rest until it has spread about an inch (2.5cm) in diameter and looks more relaxed, at least 30 minutes and up to 1 hour. (Follow the directions on pages 34 to 36; see photos on page 36.)

Final shape and overnight cold proof

10. Prepare two 1kg loaf tins as directed on page 45 or round proofing baskets (for boules) as directed on pages 36 to 37.

11. Shape the loaves into tin loaves as directed on page 45 or boules as directed on pages 37 to 39.

12. If rolling in cracked rye berries, run the 100g whole berries through a flour mill on the coarse to medium setting, or pulse in a high-speed blender. Spread the cracked rye berries on a small baking sheet. Dampen a kitchen towel and lay it on the work surface. Holding the shaped dough seam side up, roll the smooth top side onto the damp towel and then immediately roll it in the cracked rye berries. Transfer the dough seam side down to the tin or seam side up to the proofing basket. (Alternatively, mist the top of the dough with water, then use a bench knife to lift the dough from the bench and flip it over into the rye berries.) Repeat with the second loaf.

13. Allow the loaves to rest in a warm (72 to 75°F/ 22 to 24°C), draft-free place until increased in volume by approximately 20 percent, 30 to 60 minutes. This time will vary depending on how active the dough is.

14. Cover the loaves with a loose-fitting lid or plate and place them in the fridge to cold proof overnight, 16 to 18 hours.

Bake

15. The following day, score and bake the loaves as directed on pages 47 to 51.

16. See Storing Bread (page 51). Because of the extra hydration from the sprouts, this sourdough will stay soft for a few extra days.

Sesame and Brown Rice Miso Sourdough

Makes two 1kg boules

This sourdough is multi-layered and complex in flavour and textures. Miso paste is pre-fermented, and adds a savoury note to the dough. The deep caramelization of the toasted sesame crust adds delicious umami flavour, and the tangzhong (see Note) creates an unbelievable softness and extends shelf life.

note: *Tangzhong is an Asian technique often used in milk bread. It involves cooking flour and water or milk to create a viscous paste that acts as a substitute for animal-based binding ingredients such as eggs. In a tangzhong paste, the flour's starches are gelatinized, so they can absorb twice as much liquid. Knead the dough first and then add the tangzhong near the end of the kneading stage. The resulting dough is wetter, and the bread stays soft for longer too. The first few times you make this dough, bake it in a tin until you get used to handling a higher hydration dough.*

Levain

1 batch Levain (page 29)

Tangzhong

190g water

20g toasted sesame oil

65g bread flour or all-purpose flour

Dough

650g warm water (75 to 78°F/24 to 26°C) (75% hydration)

600g bread flour

220g whole wheat flour

45g stone-ground whole-grain spelt flour

175g active levain

20g fine sea salt

50g black sesame seeds

40g brown rice miso paste

100g white sesame seeds, for rolling

Prepare the levain

1. Prepare the levain as directed on pages 29 to 30 in the Sourdough Starter Guide. Feed the active starter early in the morning (by 7 a.m.) the day you plan to mix the dough so that it is active and tripled in size after 4 to 6 hours. Alternatively, prepare the levain with a less active starter—approximately 10 percent inoculation (10g) calculated to the total weight of flours—the night before (by 10 p.m.) so it's ready in the morning, 8 to 10 hours later.

Make the tangzhong

2. One hour before making the dough, make the tangzhong. In a small saucepan, bring the water to a simmer, then add the sesame oil and whisk in the bread flour. Cook the tangzhong for 2 to 3 minutes over low heat, whisking constantly, until thick and smooth. You may find it gets so thick that you need to switch from a whisk to a spatula. Transfer the tangzhong to a small container, cover with a loose-fitting lid, and set aside to cool.

Autolyse and mix

3. This dough is easily mixed by hand in a large bowl or with a stand mixer fitted with the dough hook on medium speed. Pour the warm water into the bowl. Add the bread flour, whole wheat flour, and spelt flour and mix until a shaggy dough forms with no dry patches, 2 to 3 minutes. Cover the dough with a kitchen towel or loose-fitting lid and let rest in a warm (72 to 75°F/ 22 to 24°C), draft-free place for 1 hour (autolyse).

4. After the resting period, add the active levain to the dough and mix for 1 to 2 minutes. Cover the bowl and let sit for 10 minutes.

5. Add the salt and knead the dough for 5 to 6 minutes using the Rubaud method as directed on page 33 (see photos on page 32) until the dough is smoother in appearance, feels more active, and has a little more elasticity, 5 to 6 minutes. (If using a stand mixer, knead

continued . . .

the dough on medium speed.) Cover the bowl and let the dough relax for another 10 minutes.

6. Knead the dough a final time at a faster speed to fully develop the gluten and stretch it a little more. (If using a stand mixer, knead on medium-high speed.) The dough should pull away from the sides of the bowl.

7. Add the cooled tangzhong, black sesame seeds, and miso and knead for 1 more minute, until just combined.

Bulk ferment

8. Place the dough in a lightly oiled bowl or container that is four times the size of the dough and cover with a loose-fitting lid or kitchen towel. Place the dough in a warm (72 to 75°F/22 to 24°C), draft-free place. A constant temperature will ensure a consistent fermentation. Set a timer for 30 minutes.

9. When the timer goes off, perform the first set of stretch-and-folds as directed on pages 33 to 34. Again, set the timer for 30 minutes. Repeat the set of stretch-and-folds another two or three times over a 2-hour period, depending on how the dough feels (for a total of 3 hours of timed stretch-and-folds). Once the dough feels tighter and is doming, perform a couple of sets of coil folds as directed on page 34. Cover the dough and allow it to rest for 30 to 60 minutes, until you can see some fermentation bubbles and the dough has increased in volume by approximately 40 percent.

Pre-shape and bench rest

10. Gently remove the dough from the container and allow it to relax on an unfloured work surface for a minute. Using a bench knife, cut the dough into 2 equal pieces (1kg each). Working with 1 piece at a time, gently pre-shape the dough into a round ball. Cover the dough with a thin kitchen towel to prevent the top drying out. Allow the dough to bench rest until it has spread about an inch (2.5cm) in diameter and looks more relaxed, at least 30 minutes and up to 1 hour. (Follow the directions on pages 34 to 36; see photos on page 36.)

Final shape and overnight cold proof

11. Prepare 2 round proofing baskets (for boules) as directed on pages 36 to 37.

12. Shape the loaves into boules as directed on pages 37 to 39.

13. Place the white sesame seeds in a large bowl. Dampen a kitchen towel and lay it on the work surface. Holding the shaped dough seam side up, roll the smooth top side onto the damp towel and then immediately roll it in the seeds. Transfer the dough to the proofing basket. (Alternatively, mist the top of the dough with water, then use a bench knife to lift the dough from the bench and flip it over into the seeds.) Repeat for the second loaf.

14. Allow the loaves to rest in a warm (72 to 75°F/22 to 24°C), draft-free place until increased in volume by approximately 20 percent, 30 to 60 minutes.

15. Cover the loaves with a loose-fitting lid or plate and place them in the fridge to cold proof overnight, 16 to 18 hours.

Bake

16. The following day, score and bake the loaves as directed on pages 47 to 51.

17. See Storing Bread (page 51).

Marinated Olive, Garlic, Cornmeal Porridge, and Herb Sourdough

Makes two 1kg loaves

Adding water to a starch causes it to swell, as in the case of a porridge, and the technical name for this process is starch gelatinization. Adding porridge to dough as it is being stretched and folded makes for a very soft and spongy texture. Porridge-based breads have a slightly denser crumb and keep soft a bit longer than other loaves. Marinated olives bring a depth of flavour and add a natural salty element that elevates the fresh herbs and roasted garlic.

Levain

1 batch Levain (page 29)

Inclusions

1 large head of garlic

65g coarse cornmeal

200g water

Zest and juice of 1 lemon

250g mixed pitted marinated olives, roughly chopped

5g fresh rosemary, finely chopped

5g fresh thyme, finely chopped

Dough

600g warm water (75 to 78°F/24 to 26°C) (75% hydration)

550g bread flour

200g stone-ground whole wheat flour

45g stone-ground whole-grain rye flour

160g active levain

16g fine sea salt

Prepare the levain

1. Prepare the levain as directed on pages 29 to 30 in the Sourdough Starter Guide. Feed the active starter early in the morning (by 7 a.m.) the day you plan to mix the dough so that it is active and tripled in size after 4 to 6 hours. Alternatively, prepare the levain with a less active starter—approximately 10 percent inoculation (10g) calculated to the total weight of flours—the night before (by 10 p.m.) so it's ready in the morning, 8 to 10 hours later.

Prepare the inclusions

2. Preheat the oven to 350°F (175°C).

3. Wrap the head of garlic in foil and bake in a small ovenproof dish until soft, 1 hour. Set aside to cool.

4. Meanwhile, scatter the cornmeal on a small baking sheet and toast alongside the garlic until golden brown, 10 minutes. Set it aside to cool.

5. To make the cornmeal porridge, in a medium saucepan, combine the water, lemon zest and juice, and the toasted cornmeal. Cover and cook, stirring frequently with a wooden spoon or spatula, over medium-low heat until soft and the water has been absorbed, about 10 minutes. Transfer the cornmeal porridge to a small bowl, cover, and set aside to cool for at least 1 hour before adding it to the dough.

Autolyse and mix

6. This dough is easily mixed by hand in a large bowl or with a stand mixer fitted with the dough hook on medium speed. Pour the warm water into the bowl. Add the bread flour, whole wheat flour, and rye flour and mix together until a shaggy dough forms with no dry patches, 2 to 3 minutes. Cover the dough with a kitchen towel or loose-fitting lid and let rest in a warm (72 to 75°F/ 22 to 24°C), draft-free place for 1 hour (autolyse).

continued . . .

7. After the resting period, add the active levain to the dough and mix for 1 to 2 minutes. Cover the bowl and let sit for 10 minutes.

8. Add the salt and knead the dough using the Rubaud method as directed on page 33 (see photos on page 32) until it is smoother in appearance, feels more active, and has a little more elasticity, 5 to 6 minutes. (If using a stand mixer, knead the dough on medium speed.) Cover the bowl and let the dough relax for another 10 minutes.

9. Knead the dough a final time at a faster speed to fully develop the gluten and stretch it a little more. (If using a stand mixer, knead on medium-high speed.) The dough should pull away from the sides of the bowl.

10. Add the cooled cornmeal porridge to the dough and continue to knead for 1 more minute until just combined.

Bulk ferment

11. Place the dough in a lightly oiled bowl or container that is four times the size of the dough and cover with a loose-fitting lid or kitchen towel. Place the dough in a warm (72 to 75°F/22 to 24°C), draft-free place. A constant temperature will ensure a consistent fermentation. Set a timer for 30 minutes.

12. Meanwhile, cut the baked garlic in half crosswise and squeeze out all the soft cloves into a medium bowl. Add the olives, rosemary, and thyme and stir.

13. When the timer goes off, evenly scatter half the garlic, olives, and herbs over the top of the dough and begin the first set of stretch-and-folds as directed on pages 33 to 34. Once the dough has been stretched a few times, and the inclusions are starting to mix through the dough, add the remaining garlic, olives, and herbs. Complete the first set of stretch-and-folds.

14. Again, set the timer for 30 minutes. Repeat the set of stretch-and-folds another two or three times over a 2-hour period, depending on how the dough feels (for a total of 3 hours of timed stretch-and-folds). Once the dough feels tighter and is doming, perform a couple of sets of coil folds as directed on page 34. Cover the dough and allow it to rest for 30 to 60 minutes, until you can see some fermentation bubbles and the dough has increased in volume by approximately 40 percent.

Pre-shape and bench rest

15. Gently remove the dough from the container and allow it to relax on an unfloured work surface for a minute. Using a bench knife, cut the dough into 2 equal pieces (1kg each). Working with 1 piece at a time, gently pre-shape the dough into a round ball. Cover the dough with a thin kitchen towel to prevent the top drying out. Allow the dough to bench rest until it has spread about an inch (2.5cm) in diameter and looks more relaxed, at least 30 minutes and up to 1 hour. (Follow the directions on pages 34 to 36; see photos on page 36.)

Final shape and overnight cold proof

16. Prepare 2 proofing baskets (for boules or bâtards) as directed on pages 36 to 37 or 1kg loaf tins as directed on page 45.

17. Shape the loaves into boules, bâtards, or tin loaves as directed on page 37 to 45. Allow the loaves to sit at room temperature until increased in volume by approximately 20 percent, 30 to 60 minutes. This time will vary depending on how active the dough is.

18. Cover the loaves with a loose-fitting lid or plate and place them in the fridge to cold proof overnight, 16 to 18 hours.

Bake

19. The following day, score and bake the loaves as directed on pages 47 to 51.

20. See Storing Bread (page 51).

Stout and Potato Sourdough

Makes two 1kg loaves

I first made this sourdough to celebrate St. Patrick's Day. Potatoes and Ireland are inextricably linked, no doubt because of the tragic potato famine of 1845–52. Though stout originated from London's porter beers, it was the Irish who added pale and black malts to their dark ales, which later became more commonly known as stout.

Not only do I greatly appreciate the humble potato, but I also relish the combined bitterness of acrid malt and strong hops that are characteristic of stout, and I am so grateful that Guinness veganized their recipe! (Isinglass, made from fish bladders, was previously used in the filtration process.) The combination of the earthy potato and malty stout brings a complex flavour to this bread, underpinned by a soft, hearty texture.

As with all sourdough, it's essential to plan ahead. The potatoes need to be cooked and cooled before you can start the dough. It's best to cook the potatoes the day you make the sourdough, though, so they keep their beautiful flavour and texture.

Levain

1 batch Levain (page 29)

Inclusions

425g small waxy potatoes (such as German Butterball, Maris Piper, or Yukon Gold)

Dough

225g stout
525g warm water (75 to 78°F/24 to 26°C) (75% hydration)
700g bread flour
200g stone-ground whole wheat flour
100g stone-ground whole-grain rye flour
200g active levain
25g fine sea salt

Prepare the levain

1. Prepare the levain as directed on pages 29 to 30 in the Sourdough Starter Guide. Feed the active starter early in the morning (by 7 a.m.) the day you plan to mix the dough so that it is active and tripled in size after 4 to 6 hours. Alternatively, prepare the levain with a less active starter—approximately 10 percent inoculation (10g) calculated to the total weight of flours—the night before (by 10 p.m.) so it's ready in the morning, 8 to 10 hours later.

Cook the potatoes

2. Wash the potatoes thoroughly, leaving the skin on for extra flavour and nutrition. Cut the potatoes into approximately 1-inch (2.5cm) pieces. Place the potatoes in a medium saucepan, cover with water, lightly season with salt, and bring to a boil. Once boiling, reduce the heat and simmer the potatoes until tender. Drain the potatoes and allow them to cool to room temperature.

Autolyse and mix

3. This dough is easily mixed by hand in a large bowl or with a stand mixer fitted with the dough hook on medium speed. Pour the stout and warm water into the bowl. Add the bread flour, whole wheat flour, and rye flour and mix together until a shaggy dough forms with no dry patches, 2 to 3 minutes. Cover the dough with a kitchen towel or loose-fitting lid and let rest in a warm (72 to 75°F/ 22 to 24°C), draft-free place for 1 hour (autolyse).

4. After the resting period, add the active levain to the dough and mix for 1 to 2 minutes. Cover the bowl and let sit for 10 minutes.

5. Add the salt and knead the dough using the Rubaud method as directed on page 33 (see photos on page 32) until it is smoother in appearance, feels more active, and has a little more elasticity, 5 to 6 minutes. (If using a stand mixer, knead the dough on medium speed.) The

continued . . .

dough should pull away from the sides of the bowl. Let the dough rest for a couple of minutes.

6. Crush the cooled potatoes into small pieces and scatter them over the top of the dough. Gently fold the dough over and around the potatoes to mix them in a little. Don't worry about fully incorporating them just yet, as the stretch-and-folds will help.

Bulk ferment

7. Place the dough in a lightly oiled bowl or container that is four times the size of the dough and cover with a loose-fitting lid or kitchen towel. Place the dough in a warm (72 to 75°F/22 to 24°C), draft-free place. A constant temperature will ensure a consistent fermentation. Set a timer for 30 minutes.

8. When the timer goes off, perform the first set of stretch-and-folds as directed on pages 33 to 34. Again, set the timer for 30 minutes. Repeat the set of stretch-and-folds another two or three times over a 2-hour period, depending on how the dough feels (for a total of 3 hours of timed stretch-and-folds). Once the dough feels tighter and is doming, perform a couple of sets of coil folds as directed on page 34. Cover the dough and allow it to rest for 30 to 60 minutes, until you can see some fermentation bubbles and the dough has increased in volume by approximately 40 percent.

Pre-shape and bench rest

9. Gently remove the dough from the container and allow it to relax on an unfloured work surface for a minute. Using a bench knife, cut the dough into 2 equal pieces (1kg each). Working with 1 piece at a time, gently pre-shape the dough into a round ball. Cover the dough with a thin kitchen towel to prevent the top drying out. Allow the dough to bench rest until it has spread about an inch (2.5cm) in diameter and looks more relaxed, at least 30 minutes and up to 1 hour. (Follow the directions on pages 34 to 36; see photos on page 36.)

Final shape and overnight cold proof

10. Prepare 2 proofing baskets (for boules or bâtards) as directed on pages 36 to 37.

11. Shape the loaves into boules or bâtards as directed on pages 37 to 43. Allow the loaves to rest in a warm (72 to 75°F/22 to 24°C), draft-free place until increased in volume by approximately 20 percent, 30 to 60 minutes.

12. Cover the loaves with a loose-fitting lid or plate and place them in the fridge to cold proof overnight, 16 to 18 hours.

Bake

13. The following day, score and bake the loaves as directed on pags 47 to 51.

14. See Storing Bread (page 51).

The Boreal Forest Loaf

Makes two 1kg loaves

This distinctive sourdough celebrates the forest and all it gives us. The boreal forest is a vast ecosystem that rings the world's northern hemisphere. Sixty percent of Canada is covered in the boreal forest, with eight varied ecozones but all with a characteristic flora and fauna. Most of the trees are coniferous, particularly black spruce, white spruce, lodgepole pine, jack pine, red cedar, white birch, and Douglas fir.

Like a moving meditation, foraging in the forest engages all our senses, making it one of our favourite hobbies. When searching for leaves, shoots, blossoms, roots, berries, bark, and mushrooms, your mind is focused. Foraging combines the benefits of breathing incredibly fresh air with being active and agile.

If you cannot find your own morels, as they are rather expensive to buy, feel free to use other dried varieties, such as porcini or shiitakes.

note: *Bark flour can be found online and imported from Scandinavia or extracted from a tree that may be cut down soon. Harvesting a tree's bark will damage it permanently so bear that in mind. Toast the bark pieces on a baking sheet in the oven at 350°F (175°C) for 30 to 45 minutes, depending on the size of the chunks. Let the bark cool, then grind in a food processor into a powder.*

Levain

1 batch Levain (page 29)

Inclusions

50g dried morel mushrooms, chopped
200g hot water (170°F/77°C)

Dough

675g warm water (75 to 78°F/24 to 26°C) (approximately 87% hydration with the morel soaking liquid)
700g bread flour
200g stone-ground whole wheat flour
100g stone-ground whole-grain rye flour
25g diastic barley malt powder
25g pine or cedar bark flour (optional)
200g active levain
25g fine sea salt

Prepare the levain

1. Prepare the levain as directed on pages 29 to 30 in the Sourdough Starter Guide. Feed the active starter early in the morning (by 7 a.m.) the day you plan to mix the dough so that it is active and tripled in size after 4 to 6 hours. Alternatively, prepare the levain with a less active starter—approximately 10 percent inoculation (10g) calculated to the total weight of flours—the night before (by 10 p.m.) so it's ready in the morning, 8 to 10 hours later.

Rehydrate the mushrooms

2. One hour before mixing the dough, place the dried morels in a small bowl. Pour the hot water over the mushrooms to rehydrate them. Set aside to cool.

Autolyse and mix

3. This dough is easily mixed by hand in a large bowl or with a stand mixer fitted with the dough hook on low speed. Pour the warm water into the bowl. Add the bread flour, whole wheat flour, rye flour, malt powder, and pine flour (if using) and mix together until a shaggy dough forms with no dry patches, 2 to 3 minutes. Cover the dough with a kitchen towel or loose-fitting lid and let rest

continued . . .

in a warm (72 to 75°F/22 to 24°C), draft-free place for 1 hour (autolyse).

4. After the resting period, add the active levain to the dough and mix for 1 to 2 minutes. Cover the bowl and let sit for 10 minutes.

5. Add the salt and knead the dough using the Rubaud method as directed on page 33 (see photos on page 32) until it is smoother in appearance, feels more active, and has a little more elasticity, 5 to 6 minutes. (If using a stand mixer, knead the dough on medium speed.)

6. Add the rehydrated mushrooms and their soaking liquid to the dough and continue to mix for 1 more minute until well combined. The dough should pull away from the sides of the bowl. Let the dough rest for a couple of minutes.

Bulk ferment

7. Place the dough in a lightly oiled bowl or container that is four times the size of the dough and cover with a loose-fitting lid or kitchen towel. Place the dough in a warm (72 to 75°F/22 to 24°C), draft-free place. A constant temperature will ensure a consistent fermentation. Set a timer for 30 minutes.

8. When the timer goes off, perform the first set of stretch-and-folds as directed on pages 33 to 34. Again, set the timer for 30 minutes. Repeat the set of stretch-and-folds another two or three times over a 2-hour period, depending on how the dough feels (for a total of 3 hours of timed stretch-and-folds). Once the dough feels tighter and is doming, perform a couple of sets of coil folds as directed on page 34. Cover the dough and allow it to rest for 30 to 60 minutes, until you can see some fermentation bubbles and the dough has increased in volume by approximately 40 percent.

Pre-shape and bench rest

9. Gently remove the dough from the container and allow it to relax on an unfloured work surface for a minute. Using a bench knife, cut the dough into 2 equal pieces (1kg each). Working with 1 piece at a time, gently pre-shape the dough into a round ball. Cover the dough with a thin kitchen towel to prevent the top drying out. Allow the dough to bench rest until it has spread about an inch (2.5cm) in diameter and looks more relaxed, at least 30 minutes and up to 1 hour. (Follow the directions on pages 34 to 36; see photos on page 36.)

Final shape and overnight cold proof

10. Prepare 2 proofing baskets (for boules or bâtards) as directed on pages 36 to 37.

11. Shape the loaves into boules or bâtards as directed on pages 37 to 43. Allow the loaves to rest in a warm (72 to 75°F/22 to 24°C), draft-free place until increased in volume by approximately 20 percent, 30 to 60 minutes. This time will vary depending on how active the dough is.

12. Cover the loaves with a loose-fitting lid or plate and place them in the fridge to cold proof overnight, 16 to 18 hours.

Bake

13. The following day, score and bake the loaves as directed on pages 47 to 51.

14. See Storing Bread (page 51).

100% Rye Sourdough

Makes two 1kg tin loaves

Rye is one of my favourite grains. The natural sweet, earthy, and malty flavour it brings to any sourdough is always a great addition. Rye is also an effective cover crop that helps improve soil structure, reduces nitrogen loss from leaching, builds organic matter, and protects against water and wind erosion.

Other bread recipes might only call for 10 to 20 percent rye flour, because more than this can make country-style loaves too heavy and ferment too quickly. This 100 percent rye recipe has been developed at our bakery over time and is one of our more sour breads, with a high ratio of levain. It is a quick loaf to make but requires patience, as you must wait between 12 and 24 hours before slicing it, as the rye bread needs to fully set and develop in flavour and texture. For your patience, you will be rewarded with a delicious sourdough that has incredible flavour and is one of my favourites as toast, especially topped with avocado or wild mushrooms.

Seeds such as caraway are commonly added to rye loaves, as well as other flavourings such as molasses or cocoa, but rye's inherent maltiness is so pleasant on its own that I like to let the grain speak for itself.

note: *If you do not have a rye sourdough starter, before making this bread, take a small amount of your every-day wheat starter and feed it with a few refreshments of equal amounts water and rye flour (100 percent hydration) and a quarter of the amount of starter (25 percent inoculation). It will only take a couple of days before you have the rye starter needed. Continue feeding it in the same way to maintain this starter, storing it in the fridge if it is only needed once a week.*

Rye Levain

125g active rye starter

225g warm water (75 to 78°F/24 to 26°C) (100% hydration)

225g stone-ground whole-grain rye flour

Dough

750g warm water (75 to 78°F/24 to 26°C) (88% hydration)

550g active rye levain (see page 30)

850g stone-ground whole-grain rye flour, more for dusting

21g fine sea salt

Prepare the rye levain

1. Prepare the rye levain for this recipe following the method in the levain recipe as directed on page 29 in the Sourdough Starter by at 8 a.m. so you will be ready to mix the dough by 12 p.m. Using your hand, mix together the active rye starter, water, and rye flour in a medium bowl until a smooth paste forms. Use a spatula to scrape all the levain into a transparent 1L (4-cup) container or glass jar, then cover with a loose-fitting lid slightly askew. Draw a line or place a rubber band around the container to mark the top of the levain. This will indicate when the levain has doubled or tripled in size. Let sit in a warm (72 to 75°F/22 to 24°C), draft-free place until it has at least doubled or tripled in size, 3 to 4 hours. The levain should smell malty with a pleasant fruity tone.

Mix the dough

2. Pour the warm water into the bowl of a stand mixer fitted with the paddle. Add the active rye levain, rye flour, and salt and mix on medium-low speed to form a thick, homogeneous paste, 10 minutes.

3. Place the dough in a lightly oiled bowl or container that is four times the size of the dough and cover with a kitchen towel or loose-fitting lid. Place the dough in a warm (72 to 75°F/22 to 24°C), draft-free place. A constant temperature will ensure a consistent fermentation. Set a timer for 90 minutes. Check to see if the dough has started to ferment and increased in volume by approximately 30 percent. It may need an additional 30 to 60 minutes depending on the room temperature and activity of the levain. No stretch-and-folds are necessary, as there is minimal gluten development.

Shape and proof

4. Lightly spray two 1kg loaf tins with a neutral oil such as vegetable or sunflower oil and line the bottom and sides with parchment paper.

5. Lightly spray a large bowl with neutral oil and place it on a digital scale. Using wet hands (the dough is sticky), weigh 1075g of the dough. Wet your hands again and form the dough into an oval shape that will fit into the lined tin. Gently drop the dough into the tin. Repeat for the second loaf. Using wet hands or a dough scraper, flatten the top of the dough. From a height, generously dust the tops of the loaves with rye flour.

6. Allow the loaves to proof in a warm (72 to 75°F/ 22 to 24°C), draft-free place for 1½ to 2 hours.

7. After about 45 minutes, once the dough has started to proof and increase in height, place a large baking sheet on the middle rack of the oven. Remove the top rack to allow plenty of space for the breads to expand. Preheat the oven to 375°F (190°C).

Bake

8. Once the loaves have increased in volume by 30 to 40 percent, are domed on the top, and have cracked the flour, gently place them on the preheated baking sheet. Drop 2 or 3 ice cubes on the baking sheet and immediately close the door. Bake the bread for 45 to 50 minutes. If you are not using a convection oven, check the loaves halfway through, as they might need rotating. The loaves are done when a probe thermometer inserted into the centre reads above 200°F (93°C). Allow the loaves to cool in their tins for 15 to 20 minutes, then turn out onto a cooling rack to cool completely, 3 to 4 hours.

9. Transfer the cooled loaves to a container, bread bin, or linen bag and allow them to rest at room temperature for at least 12 and up to 24 hours before slicing. The rye bread will keep at room temperature, wrapped in a linen bag, for up to 5 days or can be frozen. See Storing Bread (page 51).

100% Rye Sourdough with Toasted Seeds and Flakes

Makes two 1kg tin loaves

Rye bread is integral to traditional Scandinavian cuisine, but ingredients such as sunflower seeds have been introduced to their breads only in the last 150 years, making seeded rye loaves quite modern indeed! This lovely variation of the 100% Rye Sourdough recipe can be easily adapted with other seeds or flakes. To make this loaf easy and fast to put together, I chose to increase the hydration of the dough rather than opt for a seed soaker. Toasting seeds in the oven brings out their natural oils and nuttiness before they're incorporated into the dough. Rolling the shaped loaf in raw seeds allows the raw seeds on the outside to toast during the bake, to match the flavour profile of the already-toasted seeds inside and so the overall result is consistent in flavour and texture.

note: *If you do not have a rye sourdough starter, before making this bread, take a small amount of your every-day wheat starter and a feed it with a few refreshments of equal amounts water and rye flour (100 percent hydration) and a quarter of the amount of starter (25 percent inoculation). It will only take a couple of days before you have the rye starter needed. Continue feeding it in the same way to maintain this starter, storing it in the fridge if only needed once a week.*

Rye Levain

150g active rye starter (see Note; 75% inoculation; see page 27)

200g warm water (75 to 78°F/24 to 26°C) (100% hydration)

200g stone-ground whole-grain rye flour

Inclusions

50g sesame seeds

50g pumpkin seeds

50g sunflower seeds

50g poppy seeds

50g flaxseeds

50g rye, spelt, or oat flakes (choose one or a mix)

Dough

750g warm water (75 to 78°F/24 to 26°C) (100% hydration)

550g active rye levain

750g stone-ground whole-grain rye flour

20g fine sea salt

Seed Mix, for rolling

50g sesame seeds

50g pumpkin seeds

50g sunflower seeds

50g poppy seeds

50g flaxseeds

50g rye, spelt, or oat flakes (choose one or a mix)

Prepare the rye levain

1. Prepare the rye levain for this recipe following the method in the levain recipe as directed on page 29 in the Sourdough Starter Guide at 8 a.m. so you will be ready to mix the dough by 12 p.m. Using your hand, mix together

continued . . .

the active rye starter, water, and rye flour in a medium bowl until a smooth paste forms. Use a spatula to scrape all the levain into a transparent 1L (4-cup) container or glass jar, then cover it with a loose-fitting lid slightly askew. Draw a line or place a rubber band around the container to mark the top of the levain. This will indicate when the levain has doubled or tripled in size. Let it sit in a warm (72 to 75°F/22 to 24°C), draft-free place until it has at least doubled or tripled in size, 3 to 4 hours. The levain should smell malty with a pleasant fruity tone.

Toast the Inclusions

2. One hour before making the dough, preheat the oven to 350°F (175°C).

3. Mix together the sesame seeds, pumpkin seeds, sunflower seeds, and poppy seeds on a small baking sheet. Bake until they are light golden brown, 5 minutes, stirring halfway through for an even colour. Set aside to cool.

Mix the dough

4. Pour the warm water into the bowl of a stand mixer fitted with the paddle. Add the active rye levain, toasted seeds, flaxseeds, grain flakes, rye flour, and salt and mix on medium speed to form a thick, homogeneous paste, 10 minutes.

5. Transfer the dough to a lightly oiled container or bowl that is four times the size of the dough and cover with a loose-fitting lid or kitchen towel. Place the dough in a warm (72 to 75°F/22 to 24°C), draft-free place. A constant temperature will ensure a consistent fermentation. Set a timer for 90 minutes. Check to see if the dough has started to ferment and increased in volume by approximately 30 percent. It may need an additional 30 to 60 minutes depending on the room temperature and activity of the levain. No stretch-and-folds are necessary, as there is minimal gluten development.

Shape and proof

6. Lightly spray two 1kg loaf tins with a neutral oil such as vegetable or sunflower oil and line the bottom and sides with parchment paper.

7. For the seed mix, in a large bowl or on a small baking sheet, combine the sesame seeds, pumpkin seeds, sunflower seeds, poppy seeds, flaxseeds, and grain flakes.

8. Lightly spray a large bowl with the neutral oil and place it on a digital scale. Using wet hands (the dough is sticky), weigh 1.2kg of the dough. Wet your hands again and form the dough into an oval shape that will fit into the lined tin. Gently drop the dough into the seed mix and roll it to completely cover the dough in seeds. Place the seeded dough in the prepared tin. Repeat for the second loaf.

9. Allow the loaves to proof in a warm (72 to 75°F/ 22 to 24°C), draft-free place for 1½ to 2 hours.

10. After about 45 minutes, once the dough has started to proof and increase in height, place a large baking sheet on the middle rack of the oven. Remove the top rack to allow plenty of space for the breads to expand. Preheat the oven to 375°F (190°C).

Bake

11. Once the loaves have increased in volume by 30 to 40 percent, are domed on the top, and have cracked the flour, gently place them on the preheated baking sheet. Drop 2 or 3 ice cubes on the baking sheet and immediately close the door. Because the loaves are baked in tins, you can put the ice cubes on the same baking sheet. Bake the bread for 45 to 50 minutes. If you are not using a convection oven, check the loaves halfway through, as they might need rotating. The loaves are done when a probe thermometer inserted into the centre reads above 200°F (93°C). Allow the loaves to cool in their tins for 15 to 20 minutes, then turn out onto a cooling rack to cool completely, 3 to 4 hours.

12. Transfer the cooled loaves to a container, bread bin, or linen bag and allow them to rest at room temperature for at least 12 and up to 24 hours before slicing. This seeded rye bread will keep at room temperature, wrapped in a linen bag, for up to 5 days or can be frozen. See Storing Bread (page 51).

Small Breads

Baguettes

Makes 2.1kg of dough; 4 full-size baguettes or 8 demi baguettes

Baguettes are best eaten on the day they are baked but make amazing toast or garlic bread over the next day or two. A linen bag is said to be the best way to store bread, allowing it to breathe and preventing it from drying out.

Start this dough in the morning or afternoon, as it will need to ferment in the fridge overnight before shaping, final proof, and baking.

Levain

1 batch Levain (page 29)

Dough

800g warm water (75 to 78°F/24 to 26°C)

1kg bread flour

125g stone-ground whole-grain spelt flour

150g active levain (6 to 8 hours after feeding

25g fine sea salt

25g coarse cornmeal, for dusting

Prepare the levain

1. Prepare the levain as directed on pages 29 to 30 in the Sourdough Starter Guide. Feed the active starter early in the morning (by 7 a.m.) the day you plan to mix the dough so that it is active and tripled in size after 4 to 6 hours. Alternatively, prepare the levain with a less active starter—approximately 10 percent inoculation (10g) calculated to the total weight of flours—the night before (by 10 p.m.) so it's ready in the morning, 8 to 10 hours later.

Autolyse and mix

2. This dough is easily mixed by hand in a large bowl or with a stand mixer fitted with the dough hook on medium-low speed. (Both methods work great for this recipe, as the dough doesn't need a lot of kneading.) Pour the warm water into the bowl. Add the bread flour and spelt flour and knead until a shaggy dough forms with no dry patches, 2 to 3 minutes. Cover the dough with a kitchen towel or loose-fitting lid and let rest for 1 hour (autolyse). It will not look any different after this time.

3. Add the active levain and salt and knead the dough by hand for another 5 minutes until a smooth dough forms. (If using a stand mixer, knead the dough on medium speed.)

Bulk ferment and overnight cold proof

4. Place the dough in a lightly oiled bowl or container that is four times the size of the dough and cover with a loose-fitting lid. Place the dough in a warm (72 to 75°F/ 22 to 24°C), draft-free place. A constant temperature will ensure a consistent fermentation. Set a timer for 30 minutes.

5. When the timer goes off, perform the first set of stretch-and-folds as directed on pages 33 to 34. Again, set the timer for 30 minutes. Repeat another set of stretch-and-folds (for a total of two stretch-and-folds). Allow the dough to rest for 2 hours, until you can see some fermentation bubbles and the dough is approximately doubled in the size. If the room is a little cooler, this may take up to 3 hours.

6. Place the covered dough in the fridge to cold proof overnight, 16 to 18 hours.

Pre-shape

7. The following day, gently remove the dough from the container and place it on a lightly floured work surface. Using a bench knife, divide the dough into equal pieces (4 baguettes of 525g each or 8 demi baguettes of 210g each). Gently pre-shape the dough as directed on pages 34 to 35 into ovals, 6 × 3 inches (15 × 8cm) for baguettes, or 3 × 1½ inches (8 × 4cm) for demi baguettes. Lightly cover the dough with a thin kitchen towel to prevent the top drying out. Allow the dough to bench rest until it has relaxed and spread about ½ inch (1cm) in diameter, 30 to 60 minutes.

continued . . .

Final shape and proof

8. A lightly floured baker's linen couche holds a baguette's shape during the proofing process and prevents the dough drying out. (Alternatively, you can shape the baguettes on parchment paper.)

9. Working with 1 piece at a time, transfer the dough to a lightly floured work surface. Start flattening the dough with your hand, so it expands a little into a rectangle or larger oval, 10 × 4 inches (25 × 10cm) for baguettes, or 5 × 2 inches (12 × 5cm) for demi baguettes. Using a bench knife, turn the dough over so the top surface becomes the bottom on the bench. With a long side facing you, using your thumbs and index fingers, fold the bottom of the dough up a third, then fold the top down to the middle, slightly overlapping the bottom edge and forming the dough into a smaller rectangle. Starting from the top edge of the dough, roll the dough towards you into a sausage shape. Compress the seam with the heel of your hand, firmly pressing the dough onto the work surface to seal it. Gently roll the baguette back and forth until it naturally starts to elongate and, moving your hands to the ends, roll to create two pointy ends (or you can choose to leave them squared).

10. If using a linen couche, place it on a large baking sheet for support. Lightly dust the couche all over with flour and cornmeal. Place the baguette seam side up at one end of the couche, then pull the material towards the baguette to support it, leaving ample space for it to grow during final proofing. (If using parchment paper, place the baguettes seam side down on the parchment and pull the parchment up to support it. You'll slide the parchment paper and baguettes onto the preheated baking stone, steel, or baking sheet.) Repeat with the other baguettes.

11. Dust the seam-side-up baguettes with a little cornmeal and loosely cover with the folded-up ends of the couche or with a kitchen towel. Allow to proof in a warm (72 to 75°F/22 to 24°C), draft-free place for 1 to 2 hours. Gently press the top of the dough with your finger: if the dough springs back slowly and your finger leaves a slight indent, the baguette is ready to be baked. If the dough bounces back immediately, let the dough proof a little longer.

Score and bake

12. While the loaves final proof, place a baking stone, steel, or large baking sheet on the middle rack of the oven. To create a deep golden crust, place another baking sheet on the lower rack for ice. Preheat the oven to 465°F (240°C).

13. If using a couche, you'll need a lightly floured baguette board or peel to move the baguettes without damaging the shape of the dough. Place the board next to each baguette and use the couche to roll the baguette onto it. The seam of the baguette should be facing up. Roll the baguettes onto a sheet of parchment paper so they are seam side down, leaving 2 inches (5cm) between demi baguettes, 3 inches (8cm) between baguettes.

14. Using a lame angled at 45 degrees, and with a confident and swift motion, lightly score the baguette down the centre, on a slight diagonal, overlapping the previous score by one-quarter. Three to five scores is usually enough, depending on the size of the baguette.

15. Remove the preheated baking surface from the oven and place it on the stovetop. As quickly and safely as possible, use the baguette board or peel to slide the baguettes with their parchment paper onto the hot baking surface. Place it back into the oven and add 2 cups of ice cubes to the baking sheet on the lower rack. Immediately close the oven door and set a timer for 15 minutes. When the timer goes off, rotate the baking surface to help with an even bake and release some of the steam from the oven. Again, set the timer for 15 minutes and bake the baguettes until they have a golden-brown crust. Depending on the oven and how dark you want the crust to be, they may need 5 minutes less or more to bake. Demi baguettes will take about 5 minutes less of total baking time than baguettes. Once baked, transfer the baguettes to a cooling rack to cool for 30 minutes before serving.

16. The baguettes are best eaten on the day of baking but can be stored in a linen bag or airtight container and toasted under a very hot broiler or reheated in the oven the following day. Once fully cooled, the baguettes can be wrapped in plastic wrap and stored in the freezer for up to 1 month. Defrost at room temperature for 2 hours. Reheat in a 400°F (200°C) oven for 5 to 7 minutes.

Sesame Burger Buns

Makes 14 buns

Many burger buns are made with a traditional dairy-and-egg brioche dough and coated in egg wash. This recipe makes an outstanding vegan burger bun with the perfect hint of sweetness and a light, fluffy internal texture with a flavourful chewy yet crunchy crust, highlighting that there is absolutely no need to use animal products to make delicious food!

If you are avoiding sesame because of an allergy, substitute poppy seeds for an equally good result.

Levain

1½ batches Levain (page 29)

Dough

200g warm water (78°F/26°C)

400g warm unsweetened oat milk (78°F/26°C)

300g active levain (75% hydration) (6 to 8 hours after feeding), or 25g fresh baker's yeast

100g extra-virgin coconut oil, melted

100g garlic oil or extra-virgin olive oil

75g pure maple syrup

900g bread flour

100g whole wheat flour

25g onion flakes or powder

25g garlic powder

25g fine sea salt

200g sesame seeds, for coating

Prepare the levain

1. Prepare the levain as directed on pages 29 to 30 in the Sourdough Starter Guide. Feed the active starter early in the morning (by 7 a.m.) the day you plan to mix the dough so that it is active and tripled in size after 4 to 6 hours. Alternatively, prepare the levain with a less active starter—approximately 10 percent inoculation (10g) calculated to the total weight of flours—the night before (by 10 p.m.) so it's ready in the morning, 8 to 10 hours later.

Autolyse and mix

2. Pour the warm water and oat milk into the bowl of a stand mixer fitted with the dough hook. Add the active levain, coconut oil, garlic oil, maple syrup, bread flour, whole wheat flour, onion flakes, and garlic powder and mix on medium-low speed until a shaggy dough forms with no dry patches, 2 to 3 minutes. Cover the dough with a kitchen towel or loose-fitting lid and let rest in a warm (72 to 75°F/22 to 24°C), draft-free place for 30 minutes (autolyse).

3. After the resting period, add the salt to the dough and mix on low speed for 10 minutes.

Bulk ferment and overnight cold proof

4. Lightly oil a bowl or container that is two or three times the size of the dough. Remove the dough from the mixer bowl and form it into a ball in your hands. Place the dough smooth side up in the oiled bowl and cover with a loose-fitting lid. Place the dough in a warm (72 to 75°F/22 to 24°C), draft-free place. Set a timer for 2 hours. (If you are using fresh baker's yeast, the dough will bulk ferment a lot quicker, so set the timer for 1 hour and perform just one set of folds, then proceed to the overnight cold proof.)

5. When the timer goes off, perform a coil fold as directed on page 34 if making sourdough buns and not

continued . . .

yeasted ones. Cover the dough and again set the timer for 2 hours. Repeat the coil fold. Once again, set the timer for 2 hours, then perform a final coil fold (about 6 hours in total). The dough should have doubled in size.

6. Cover with a loose-fitting lid and place in the fridge to cold proof overnight, 16 to 18 hours.

Shape and proof

7. The following day, line a large baking sheet or cutting board with parchment paper. Remove the dough from the fridge and transfer it to a lightly floured work surface. Using a bench knife, divide the dough into 14 equal portions (130g each). Roll the dough portions on a lightly floured surface into firm balls and then flatten them to 1 inch (2.5 cm) thickness.

8. Half-fill a small bowl with warm water. Place the sesame seeds in a second small bowl. Working with 1 portion of dough at a time, dip the bun top into the water, then into the sesame seeds to evenly coat

the top. Arrange the burger buns on the lined baking sheet, with at least 3 inches (8cm) between them. Loosely cover the buns with plastic wrap and let them rise in a warm (72 to 75°F/22 to 24°C), draft-free place until they have doubled in size, 1 to 2 hours.

Bake

9. Place a baking stone or large baking sheet on the middle rack of the oven. Preheat the oven to 475°F (240°C).

10. Slide the parchment with the buns onto the preheated baking surface. Lower the oven temperature to 400°F (200°C) and bake the buns until they are golden brown on top, 20 to 25 minutes. Transfer the buns to a cooling rack and let cool for 15 to 20 minutes before slicing.

11. These buns are best served sliced in half and toasted. Store the buns in an airtight container at room temperature for up to 3 days or in an airtight freezer bag in the freezer for up to 1 month.

Pocket Buns (Rustic Seeded Buns)

Makes 16 buns

Vanessa Kimbell of the Sourdough School in England made me aware of a very interesting fact: when marching, Roman soldiers would carry buns in their pockets for sustenance. The oval shape of our rustic seeded buns also resembles a pocket square; that is why they are so named.

These little buns were developed from our baguette recipe using the primitive form of wheat called emmer, which is a hulled wheat crop cultivated from the dawn of agriculture around ten thousand years ago in the Mediterranean. Emmer adds a delicious earthiness and softness to the crumb and amazing caramelization to the crust

Levain

1 batch Levain (page 29)

Dough

900g warm water (75 to 78°F/24 to 26°C)
(75% hydration)

800g bread flour

400g stone-ground whole-grain emmer, einkorn, or spelt flour

175g active levain (6 to 8 hours after feeding)

30g fine sea salt

500g seeds (I recommend sesame, poppy, nigella, cracked pumpkin, or a blend)

Prepare the levain

1. Prepare the levain as directed on pages 29 to 30 in the Sourdough Starter Guide. Feed the active starter early in the morning (by 7 a.m.) the day you plan to mix the dough so that it is active and tripled in size after 4 to 6 hours. Alternatively, prepare the levain with a less active starter—approximately 10 percent inoculation (10g) calculated to the total weight of flours—the night before (by 10 p.m.) so it's ready in the morning, 8 to 10 hours later.

Autolyse and mix

2. This dough is easily mixed by hand in a large bowl or with a stand mixer fitted with the dough hook on medium speed. Pour the warm water into the bowl. Add the bread flour and the whole-grain flour and mix together until a shaggy dough forms with no dry patches, 2 to 3 minutes. Cover the bowl with a kitchen towel or loose-fitting lid and let the dough rest in a warm (72 to 75°F/22 to 24°C), draft-free place for 1 hour (autolyse).

3. After the resting period, add the active levain and salt to the dough and knead using the Rubaud method as directed on page 33 (see photos on page 32) until the dough is smooth and has good strength and elasticity, 3 to 4 minutes. (If using a stand mixer, knead the dough on medium speed.)

Bulk ferment and overnight cold proof

4. Transfer the dough to a lightly oiled bowl or container that is four to five times larger than the dough and cover with a loose-fitting lid. Place the dough in a warm (72 to 75°F/22 to 24°C), draft-free place. A constant temperature will ensure a consistent fermentation. Set a timer for 30 minutes.

5. When the timer goes off, perform the first set of stretch-and-folds as directed on pages 33 to 34. Again, set the timer for 30 minutes. Repeat the set of stretch-and-folds (for a total of two stretch-and-folds). Allow the

continued . . .

dough to rest for 2 hours, until you can see some fermentation bubbles and the dough is approximately doubled in size. If the room is a little cooler, this may take up to 3 hours.

6. Place the covered dough in the fridge to cold proof overnight, 16 to 18 hours.

Shape and final proof

7. The following day, line a large baking sheet or cutting board with parchment paper. Remove the dough from the fridge and transfer it to an unfloured work surface. Using a bench knife, divide the dough into 4 equal pieces (575g each) using the method shown on page 36. Shape each portion into an oval and transfer to the lined baking sheet. Loosely cover the dough with a thin kitchen towel and let rest for 1 to 2 hours in a warm (72 to 75°F/22 to 24°C), draft-free place until they spread about ½ inch (1cm).

8. Fill a spray bottle with water. Spread the seeds on a small baking sheet. Lightly spray the dough with water. Working with 1 oval of dough at a time, use a bench knife to pick up the dough and place it smooth side down (top of the bun) into the seeds. Roll the dough back and forth to cover with seeds. Gently lift, turn over, and again roll the dough to cover the seam side in seeds. Return the seeded dough seam side down to the parchment paper. Allow to proof, uncovered, in a warm (72 to 75°F/22 to 24°C), draft-free place for 1 to 2 hours. Gently press the top of the dough with your finger: if the dough springs back slowly and your finger leaves a slight indent, the

buns are ready to be baked. If the dough bounces back immediately, let the dough rest a little longer.

Bake

9. Place a large baking stone or steel, or 2 stacked baking sheets on the rack of the oven. For additional steam, which creates a shiny and crunchy crust, place another baking sheet on the lower rack for ice. Preheat the oven to 465°F (240°C).

10. When the buns are proofed, on the cutting board or baking sheet the buns have been proofing on, use a bench knife to cut each piece of dough swiftly and cleanly into 4 equal-size triangular buns, 16 in total. The buns need at least 2 inches (5cm) between them so the heat can circulate for an even bake, so you may need to transfer half the buns to another parchment-lined baking sheet or cutting board, 8 buns on each sheet. (If using 2 baking sheets, bake in batches; no need to cover the buns waiting to go into the oven.)

11. Carefully slide the parchment with the buns onto the preheated baking surface. Add a handful of ice cubes to the baking sheet on the lower rack and immediately close the oven door. Bake the buns until they are golden brown all over, 20 to 30 minutes. Transfer the buns to a cooling rack and let cool for at least 30 minutes before serving.

12. These buns are best eaten warm from the oven with dinner, as a sandwich, or while marching with your Roman mates. Store the buns in an airtight container in a cool, dry place for up to 3 days.

Sourdough Pizza Dough

Makes 2 large or 3 medium pizza crusts

People absolutely love pizza, and getting children to top their own is a great way to make cooking for the family a fun activity. We have had some great pizza parties at our bakery, where we invite staff to bring a few friends and get everybody involved in shaping, topping, and loading the pizzas into our big oven with the bread peel.

note: *Before adding the toppings, I like to wet the crust with a little water and sprinkle on sesame seeds for extra flavour and texture. For a delicious charred flavour, just before loading the pizza into the preheated oven, set the oven to broil, then place the pizza in the oven. After 2 minutes, turn the oven temperature back to 500°F (260°C) and continue baking the pizza for 10 to 14 minutes, rotating it halfway through.*

Levain

1 batch Levain (page 29)

Dough

370g warm water (75 to 78°F/24 to 26°C)

485g 00 flour or bread flour

60g fine whole wheat flour

100g active levain (6 to 8 hours after feeding)

14g fine sea salt

Semolina flour, fine-grind cornmeal, or 00 flour, for dusting the work surface and pizza peel

Prepare the levain

1. Prepare the levain as directed on pages 29 to 30 in the Sourdough Starter Guide. Feed the active starter early in the morning (by 7 a.m.) the day you plan to mix the dough so that it is active and tripled in size after 4 to 6 hours. Alternatively, prepare the levain with a less active starter—approximately 10 percent inoculation (10g) calculated to the total weight of flours—the night before (by 10 p.m.) so it's ready in the morning, 8 to 10 hours later.

Autolyse and mix

2. Mix the dough in the morning or afternoon, as it will need to ferment in the fridge overnight before pre-shaping and final shaping the pizza. This dough is easily mixed by hand in a large bowl or with a stand mixer fitted with the dough hook on low speed. (Both methods work great for this recipe.) Pour the warm water into the bowl. Add the 00 flour and the whole wheat flour and mix together until a shaggy dough forms with no dry patches, 2 to 3 minutes. Cover the bowl with a kitchen towel or loose-fitting lid and let rest in a warm (72 to 75°F/ 22 to 24°C), draft-free place for 1 hour (autolyse).

3. After the resting period, add the active levain and salt to the dough and knead for 5 minutes, until a smooth dough forms. (If using a stand mixer, knead the dough on medium-low speed.) Cover the dough with a kitchen towel or loose-fitting lid and let it rest for 10 minutes. Then knead the dough for another 5 minutes to further develop the gluten and strengthen the dough. (If using a stand mixer, knead on medium speed.) You should start to notice a smoother appearance with more extendibility and activity.

Bulk ferment and overnight cold proof

4. Using extra-virgin olive oil, lightly oil a bowl or container that is four times the size of the dough.

continued . . .

Place the dough in the container and cover with a loose-fitting lid or kitchen towel. Place the dough in a warm (72 to 75°F/22 to 24°C), draft-free place. A constant temperature will ensure a consistent fermentation. Set a timer for 30 minutes.

5. When the timer goes off, perform the first set of stretch-and-folds as directed on pages 33 to 34. Again, set the timer for 30 minutes. Repeat the stretch-and-folds for a total of three times over a 90-minute period. Allow the dough to rest for 1 hour, until it is slightly domed. If the dough is still looking a little flat, perform another set of stretch-and-folds. Set the timer for 2 hours and allow the dough to ferment at room temperature, covered with a loose-fitting lid, until it is active and has increased in volume by 40 to 50 percent, with maybe a few fermentation bubbles.

6. Cover the dough with a loose-fitting lid or plate and place in the fridge to cold proof overnight, 16 to 18 hours.

Pre-shape, final shape, and bake

7. The following day, remove the dough from the fridge and transfer it to an unfloured work surface. Using a bench knife, divide the dough into two (500g each) or three (330g each) pieces. Working with 1 piece at a time, gently pre-shape the dough into a round ball. Loosely cover the dough with a kitchen towel to prevent the top drying out. Allow the dough to bench rest at room temperature (72°F/22°C) until it has spread by ½ to 1 inch (1 to 2.5cm), 30 to 60 minutes.

8. Meanwhile, place a pizza stone, baking steel, or large baking sheet on the middle rack of the oven and preheat the oven to 500°F (260°C) or as high as it will go.

9. Dust the work surface with semolina flour. Working with 1 piece of dough at a time, dust the ball with a little flour. Using the palm of your hand, press down on the dough to flatten it a little. Loosen the dough from the work surface and move it around to make sure it has enough flour underneath. Start stretching the dough by pressing your fingers into it about an inch from the outside to form the outer crust. Move your fingers around the pizza, stretching the dough in an outwards motion at the same time. Do not stretch it to full size yet.

10. Let the dough rest on a piece of parchment paper or a floured board for 15 minutes. Meanwhile, either prepare some toppings or start shaping the next pizza base.

11. After resting, return to shaping the dough. Carefully and confidently pick up the dough with both hands, an inch from its edge, rotating in one direction like you are steering the wheel of a car. Allow gravity to assist with gently stretching the pizza base to make it bigger and thinner. Then cup your hands over each other like you have a mug of cocoa and lay the dough over your hands. Gently pull your hands up and outwards, so the dough stretches like a parachute opening until you get to the desired size and thickness, being mindful not to rip the dough. Once the dough is approximately 12 inches (30cm) in diameter for a large pizza or 8 inches (20cm) for a medium pizza, place it back on the parchment paper or on a pizza peel lightly dusted with semolina flour.

12. Garnish the pizza with your desired toppings.

13. Slide the pizza from the peel or off the parchment paper onto the preheated baking surface and bake for 12 to 16 minutes, rotating the pizza halfway through if needed for even baking. Remove the pizza from the oven and slide it onto a cutting board to cool for 5 minutes before slicing it. Repeat with the remaining pizzas.

Seeded Bagels

Makes 8 bagels

The main reason for making these bagels is a love for Sunday brunching! Sunday has always been my favourite day to have off, as everything moves a little slower: the mood, people, music, and food. You can make these a few days ahead and enjoy them lightly toasted with a thick spread of cashew- or tofu-based cream cheese, carrot lox, capers, dill, and lemon.

Carrot Lox (page 344) is a plant-based alternative to smoked salmon. It's very easy to make and can be made up to five days ahead, making that Sunday brunch even easier.

Levain

1 batch Levain (page 29)

Dough

330g warm water (75 to 78°F/24 to 26°C)

60g active levain (80% to 90% hydration)
(6 to 8 hours after feeding)

50g barley malt syrup, divided

500g bread flour

75g fine whole wheat flour

5g diastatic barley malt powder

20g raw cane sugar or pure maple syrup

12g fine sea salt

Seed Mix

250g white sesame seeds

100g black sesame seeds

100g poppy seeds

50g nigella seeds

25g garlic powder or flakes

Prepare the levain

1. Prepare the levain as directed on pages 29 to 30 in the Sourdough Starter Guide. Feed the active starter early in the morning (by 7 a.m.) the day you plan to mix the dough so that it is active and tripled in size after 4 to 6 hours. Alternatively, prepare the levain with a less active starter—approximately 10 percent inoculation (10g) calculated to the total weight of flours—the night before (by 10 p.m.) so it's ready in the morning, 8 to 10 hours later.

Autolyse and mix

2. Pour the warm water into the bowl of a stand mixer fitted with the dough hook. Add the active levain, 20g of the malt syrup, bread flour, whole wheat flour, malt powder, and sugar. Mix on medium-low speed until a shaggy dough forms with no dry patches, 2 to 3 minutes. Cover the dough with a kitchen towel or loose-fitting lid and let rest in a warm (72 to 75°F/22 to 24°C), draft-free place for 30 minutes (autolyse).

3. After the resting period, add the salt to the dough and mix on low speed for 10 minutes.

Bulk ferment and overnight cold proof

4. Lightly oil a bowl or container that is two or three times the size of the dough. Remove the dough from the mixer bowl and form it into a ball in your hands. Drop the dough smooth side up into the oiled bowl and cover with a loose-fitting lid. Place the dough in a warm (72 to 75°F/22 to 24°C), draft-free place. A constant temperature will ensure a consistent fermentation. Set a timer for 1 hour.

5. When the timer goes off, perform a coil fold as directed on page 34. Cover the dough and set the timer for 3 hours. After the dough has bulk fermented for 4 hours, it should have doubled in size. It might need 1 more hour.

6. Place the covered dough in the fridge to cold proof overnight, 12 to 14 hours.

Shape and proof

7. The following day, remove the dough from the fridge and transfer it to an unfloured work surface. Using a bench knife, divide the dough into 8 equal portions (120g each). Roll the dough into firm balls and then flatten them slightly. Working with 1 piece of dough

continued . . .

at a time, push your thumb through the ball of dough to create a ring. Gently stretch the ring evenly on all sides while rotating the dough to create a bagel shape. The hole should be approximately 2 inches (5cm) wide so it doesn't close up during proofing or baking.

8. Lay the bagels on a lightly floured kitchen towel or parchment paper. Loosely cover with plastic wrap and let the bagels rest in a warm (72 to 75°F/22 to 24°C), draft-free place until doubled in size, 1 to 2 hours.

Prepare the seed mix, blanch, and bake

9. About 45 minutes before the bagels have finished proofing, cut a sheet of parchment paper to fit your baking stone or the base of a cast-iron bread pan; set aside. Place the baking surface on the bottom rack of the oven. Preheat the oven to 475°F (240°C).

10. In a large saucepan, combine 3L (12 cups) water and the remaining 30g malt syrup and bring to a boil.

11. While the water is coming up to a boil, prepare the seed mix. On a small baking sheet, combine the white sesame seeds, black sesame seeds, poppy seeds, nigella seeds, and garlic powder and mix well with your hands.

12. Once the water is boiling, working in batches of 2 to 4 bagels, blanch them in the boiling water for 30 to 40 seconds per side. Using a wire-mesh spider or slotted spoon, immediately transfer the bagels to the seed mix while they are still wet. Cover all sides of the bagels with seeds. Transfer the seeded bagels to the reserved parchment paper.

13. Once all the bagels have been blanched and coated in seeds, slide the parchment with the bagels onto the preheated baking surface. Reduce the oven temperature to 425°F (220°C) and bake the bagels until they are golden brown, 18 to 20 minutes. Transfer the bagels to a cooling rack and cool for 10 minutes before serving.

14. The bagels are best served sliced in half and toasted. Store the bagels in an airtight container at room temperature for up to 3 days or in an airtight freezer bag in the freezer for up to 1 month.

Pita Bread

Makes 8 pitas

Pita has deep roots in the Middle East, where it has been made for thousands of years. The word *pita* simply translates as "flatbread." It's a perfect little pocket bread that's eager to be filled with crunchy falafel, creamy tzatziki, crispy salad, some pickled chilies, and radish. The charred flavour from the thin exterior and the beautiful soft warm centre is pure heaven. Watching these thin breads puff as they hit the hot stone never gets boring.

Levain

 1½ batches Levain (page 29)

Dough

 240g warm water (78°F/26°C)

 225g active levain (6 to 8 hours after feeding)

 310g bread flour, divided

 8g fine sea salt

 25g extra-virgin olive oil

 15g raw cane sugar

 75g fine whole wheat flour

Prepare the levain

1. Prepare the levain as directed on pages 29 to 30 in the Sourdough Starter Guide. Feed the active starter early in the morning (by 7 a.m.) the day you plan to mix the dough so that it is active and tripled in size after 4 to 6 hours. Alternatively, prepare the levain with a less active starter—approximately 10 percent inoculation (10g) calculated to the total weight of flours—the night before (by 10 p.m.) so it's ready in the morning, 8 to 10 hours later.

Autolyse and mix

2. Pour the warm water into the bowl of a stand mixer fitted with the paddle. Add the active levain and 210g of the bread flour and mix on medium-low speed until a smooth batter forms. Cover the bowl with a kitchen towel or loose-fitting lid and let rest in a warm (72 to 75°F/ 22 to 24°C), draft-free place for 30 minutes (autolyse).

3. After the resting period, add the salt, olive oil, sugar, the remaining 100g bread flour, and the whole wheat flour. Mix with the dough hook on medium speed until a smooth dough forms, 5 minutes.

Bulk ferment

4. Lightly oil a bowl or container that is two or three times the size of your dough. Remove the dough from the mixer bowl and form it into a ball in your hands. Drop the dough smooth side up into the oiled bowl and cover with a loose-fitting lid. Set a timer for 30 minutes.

5. When the timer goes off, perform a set of three or four gentle stretch-and-folds as directed on pages 33 to 34. Return the dough to the bowl and cover. Again, set the timer for 30 minutes. Perform a set of three or four gentle stretch-and-folds and place the dough back in the bowl. Set a timer for 3 hours and let the dough rest in a warm (72 to 75°F/22 to 24°C), draft-free place until it has doubled in size. It might need up to another hour to rise, depending on the environment.

6. Place the covered dough in the fridge to cold proof overnight, 12 to 14 hours.

Shape and bake

7. The following day, cut a sheet of parchment paper to fit your baking stone or the base of a cast-iron baking pan; set aside. Place the baking surface on the middle rack of the oven and preheat to 475°F (240°C).

8. Remove the dough from the fridge and transfer it to an unfloured work surface. Using a bench knife, divide the dough into 8 equal portions (110g each). Roll the dough portions into firm balls and then flatten them slightly. Let the dough rest uncovered for 10 minutes.

continued . . .

9. Very lightly flour a work surface. Working with 1 piece of dough at a time, use a lightly floured rolling pin to roll out the dough into a 4 to 5-inch (10 to 12cm) circle or oval shape about ⅛ inch (3mm) thick. Place the pita on the parchment paper. Roll out the remaining pitas and place them on the parchment.

10. Transfer 4 pitas to the preheated baking surface using a peel and bake until puffed up and the bottoms are golden brown, 3 to 5 minutes (do not flip them). Wrap the baked pitas in a kitchen towel so they don't dry out while the second batch bakes. Repeat to bake the remaining pitas. The pitas are best eaten the day they are baked.

Naan Bread

Makes 8 naan

This thick, pillowy flatbread is a hallmark of Indian cuisine. It is traditionally baked stuck to the walls of a high-temperature wood- or charcoal-fired oven called a tandoor. Naan is chewy and buttery—a perfect marriage with a curry. This recipe yields the traditional Indian classic elevated with a garlic paste and butter.

Levain

1 batch Levain (page 29)

Dough

100g soy milk

100g coconut yogurt

150g active levain (see page 29) or sourdough discard

250g bread flour

50g stone-ground whole-grain spelt flour

5g baking powder

5g fine sea salt

5g garlic paste (about one clove crushed)

18g (4 teaspoons) coconut oil, for frying

75g vegan butter, melted

Garnish (optional)

1 bunch fresh cilantro, chopped

25g nigella seeds

Prepare the levain

1. Prepare the levain as directed on pages 29 to 30 in the Sourdough Starter Guide. Feed the active starter early in the morning (by 7 a.m.) the day you plan to mix the dough so that it is active and tripled in size after 4 to 6 hours. Alternatively, prepare the levain with a less active starter—approximately 10 percent inoculation (10g) calculated to the total weight of flours—the night before (by 10 p.m.) so it's ready in the morning, 8 to 10 hours later.

Mix

2. Warm the soy milk in a small saucepan over low heat to approximately 86°F (30°C).

3. Combine the warm soy milk, coconut yogurt, and active levain in a large bowl and stir together with a rubber spatula until smooth. Add the bread flour, spelt flour, baking powder, salt, and garlic paste. Using one hand to hold the bowl and the other to mix, knead until a shaggy dough forms with no dry patches, 1 minute. Cover the bowl with a kitchen towel or loose-fitting lid and let rest in a warm (72 to 75°F/22 to 24°C), draft-free place for 3 to 4 hours. The dough is ready if, when you gently press it with your finger, it springs back slowly and your finger leaves a slight indent.

Shape and bake

4. Transfer the dough to a lightly floured work surface. Gently knead the dough until it is smooth, 1 minute. Using a bench knife, cut the dough into 8 equal pieces (approximately 80g each). Shape the dough into balls and place them on a lightly floured work surface or a cutting board lined with parchment paper. Cover the dough with a kitchen towel or loose-fitting lid and let it proof in a warm (72 to 75°F/22 to 24°C), draft-free place for 30 minutes.

5. Have a sheet of parchment paper ready for the naan. Lightly flour the work surface. Working with 1 piece of dough at a time, roll out the ball into a teardrop shape about ¼ inch (5mm) thick. Place the dough on the parchment paper to prevent sticking while you continue to roll out the remaining dough.

6. Heat a large lidded cast-iron skillet over medium-high heat for 1 to 2 minutes. Add 1 teaspoon of the coconut oil to the hot skillet to melt.

7. Brush the tops of a couple of the naan with water and place them wet side down in the hot pan, then cover with the lid. Cook until bubbles start to appear on the surface of the dough and the naans puff up, 1 to 2 minutes. Brush the top with some melted butter, then use tongs to flip the naan. Cook until golden brown on the bottom, another 1 to 2 minutes. Transfer to a large plate. Carefully clean the pan with a damp cloth and repeat to cook the remaining naan.

8. Before serving, brush the naans with any remaining butter and heat under the broiler. Garnish with the chopped cilantro and nigella seeds, if using.

9. These naans are best eaten on the day they are baked but can be stored in an airtight container in the fridge for up to 2 days.

English Muffins

Makes 12 to 14 muffins

This classic breakfast option is enjoyed not only in England but in many countries around the world. Centuries ago, "muffin men" would go door to door selling these small flatbreads at a time when it was uncommon to have an oven in your house.

These English muffins are high in sourdough levain, which gives them an incredible sour flavour and a lightness that is perfect for toasting and topping with savoury or sweet options. My favourite accompaniment is a mix of crushed avocado, brown rice miso, tahini, lemon juice, black pepper, and loads of home-grown sprouts or grilled smoky tempeh, vine-ripe tomatoes, and baby gem lettuce. I highly recommend using a fork rather than a knife to split your English muffins. This will help retain the beautiful soft open crumb structure inside.

Levain

2 batches Levain (page 29)

Dough

450g unsweetened oat milk, at room temperature

340g active levain (40% hydration)
(6 to 8 hours after feeding)

50g soft vegan butter

600g bread flour

240g stone-ground whole wheat flour

30g pure maple syrup

17g fine sea salt

Cornmeal or semolina flour, for dusting the linen couche

Prepare the levain

1. Prepare the levain as directed on pages 29 to 30 in the Sourdough Starter Guide. Feed the active starter early in the morning (by 7 a.m.) the day you plan to mix the dough so that it is active and tripled in size after 4 to 6 hours. Alternatively, prepare the levain with a less active starter—approximately 10 percent inoculation (10g) calculated to the total weight of flours—the night before (by 10 p.m.) so it's ready in the morning, 8 to 10 hours later.

Mix

2. Pour the warm oat milk into the bowl of a stand mixer fitted with the dough hook. Add the active levain, butter, bread flour, whole wheat flour, maple syrup, and salt. Knead on low speed until smooth and pliable, 10 minutes.

Bulk ferment

3. Lightly oil a bowl or container that is four times the size of the dough. Remove the dough from the mixer bowl and form it into a ball in your hands. Drop the dough smooth side up into the bowl and cover with a loose-fitting lid. Place the dough in a warm (72 to 75°F/22 to 24°C), draft-free place until it has increased in volume by approximately 50 percent, 5 to 6 hours.

4. Place the covered dough in the fridge to cold proof overnight, 12 to 14 hours.

Shape and proof

5. The following day, line a large baking sheet with a linen couche or parchment paper. Scatter cornmeal or semolina flour over the surface. Set aside.

6. Remove the dough from the fridge and transfer it to a lightly floured work surface. Lightly flour the top of the dough and gently roll it out to 1 inch (2.5cm) thickness. Using a 3 to 4-inch (8 to 10cm) round cookie cutter, cut out discs of dough as close as possible to each other to

continued . . .

minimize trimmings. Arrange the rounds on the lined baking sheet, leaving a couple of inches between each one. Gather the trim, push it all together, roll out to 1 inch (2.5cm), and cut out extra rounds. Loosely cover the discs with a kitchen towel and let them proof in a warm (72 to 75°F/22 to 24°C), draft-free place for 2 to 3 hours. They should increase in volume by approximately 50 percent and slightly dome.

Dry-fry

7. Five minutes before the muffins have finished proofing, preheat a deep 10 to 12-inch (25 to 30cm) cast-iron or non-stick skillet over low heat.

8. Very carefully place 3 or 4 muffins into the hot pan (no oil needs to be added). Place a lid or upside-down metal bowl over the pan to help create steam and some additional heat around the muffins. Set a timer for 10 minutes. When the timer goes off, carefully remove the lid, being mindful of any steam so as not to scald yourself. Using a spatula, carefully flip the muffins and gently press the top with the spatula to ensure a flat surface on both sides. Again, set the timer for 10 minutes, cover, and cook on low heat. The muffins are done when a probe thermometer inserted into the centre reads 200°F (93°C) and they are golden brown on both sides. Transfer the muffins to a cooling rack to cool completely.

9. Wipe the pan with a damp cloth and repeat to cook the remaining muffins.

10. Poke a fork into the side of a cooled muffin and remove. Work your way around the outside, poking in and out until the muffin splits open. Toast the muffins until they are golden brown and enjoy them with toppings of your choice.

11. Store the English muffins in an airtight container at room temperature for up to 3 days or in an airtight freezer bag in the freezer for up to 1 month.

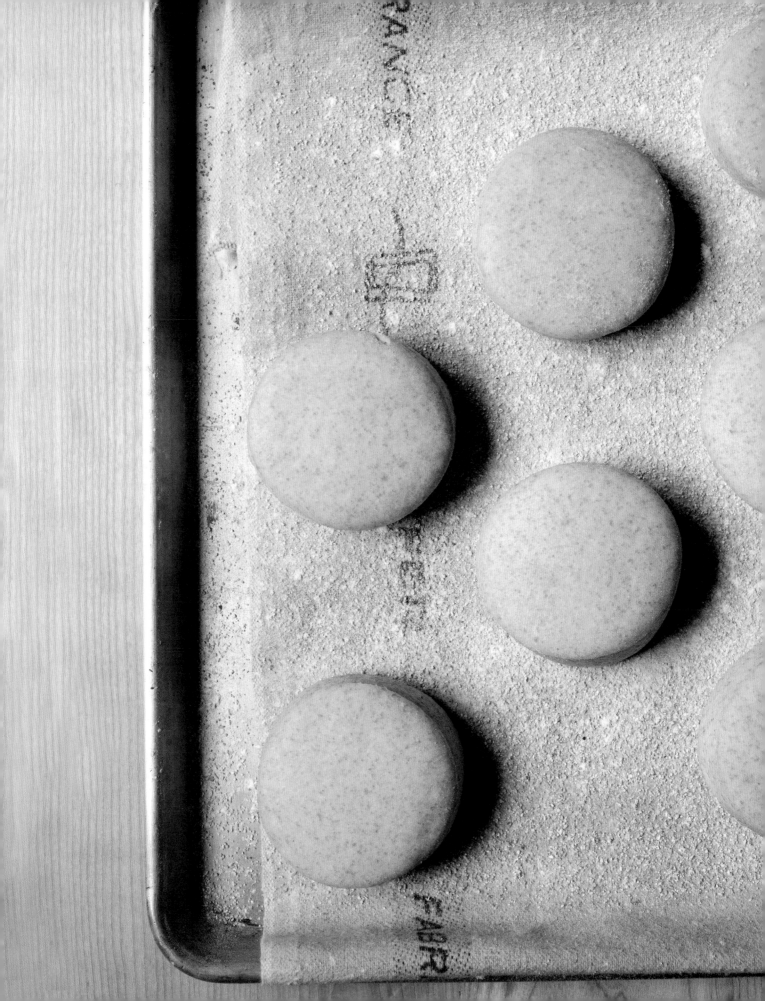

Porcini Mushroom and Thyme Grissini

Makes 20 to 22 long grissini

Grissini are beautiful crisp breadsticks with origins in Turin, Italy. They're perfect for dipping in dips and soft cheeses. I love making these, as they are fun to stretch, crunchy, and packed with flavour. They also look awesome on your dinner table—standing tall and proud in a vase or jar, they'll get your guests' attention straight away. I love the aromatic, earthy flavour of porcini mushrooms (also known as penny buns or cèpes). The porcini powder and the fresh thyme elevate this humble sourdough breadstick to the next level.

Levain

1 batch Levain (page 29)

Dough

200g warm water (75 to 78°F/24 to 26°C)

120g active levain (6 to 8 hours after feeding)

50g extra-virgin olive oil, plus 10g for brushing
   the dough

360g all-purpose flour

40g fine stone-ground whole wheat flour or
   spelt flour

8g fine sea salt

5g fine raw cane sugar

5g fresh thyme leaves

15g porcini powder

Prepare the levain

1. Prepare the levain as directed on pages 29 to 30 in the Sourdough Starter Guide. Feed the active starter early in the morning (by 7 a.m.) the day you plan to mix the dough so that it is active and tripled in size after 4 to 6 hours. Alternatively, prepare the levain with a less active starter—approximately 10 percent inoculation (10g) calculated to the total weight of flours—the night before (by 10 p.m.) so it's ready in the morning, 8 to 10 hours later.

Mix and proof

2. Pour the warm water into the bowl of a stand mixer fitted with the dough hook. Add the active levain, 50g of the olive oil, all-purpose flour, whole wheat flour, salt, sugar, thyme, and porcini powder. Knead the dough on low speed for 2 minutes. Stop the mixer and scrape down the sides and bottom of the bowl with a dough scraper to make sure there are no dry patches. Knead on medium speed for 6 minutes, until the dough is smooth and pulls away from the sides of the bowl. Let the dough rest in the bowl for 5 minutes.

3. Line a large baking sheet with parchment paper. Remove the dough from the mixer bowl and place it on a lightly floured work surface. Carefully form the dough into a long rectangle or oval approximately 3 inches (8cm) wide by 12 to 14 inches (30 to 35cm) long. Drizzle over the remaining 10g olive oil and gently massage the top of the dough with your hand. Loosely cover the dough with plastic wrap and allow it to proof in a warm (72 to 75°F/22 to 24°C), draft-free place for 3 hours, until some fermentation bubbles appear and the dough has doubled in size. It may need up to another hour.

Shape and bake

4. Arrange the oven racks in the upper and lower thirds of the oven and preheat to 375°F (190°C). Line 2 large baking sheets with parchment paper.

5. With a long side of the dough facing you on the baking sheet that the dough proofed on, using a bench knife or kitchen knife, cut the dough into 20 to 22 strips, each ½ inch (1cm) wide, pushing the dough away from the previous strip as you cut so they don't stick together.

6. Working with 1 strip at a time, carefully pick up the strip at the ends and pull it in opposite directions to stretch to a thin, even string approximately 12 inches (30cm) long and ¼ inch (5mm) wide. Carefully transfer each dough string to the lined baking sheets (10 to 12 strings per sheet), leaving a little space between them.

7. Bake the grissini until golden brown and crispy, 22 to 26 minutes. The porcini powder will make the dough light brown, so make sure the grissini bake for at least 22 minutes, otherwise they won't be crunchy and won't last as long. Transfer the grissini to a cooling rack and let them cool for at least 15 minutes before serving.

8. Store the grissini in a paper bag at room temperature to keep them dry for up to 3 days.

Focaccia

Makes one 13 × 9 × 2-inch (33 × 23 × 5cm) focaccia, serves 8 to 10

This classic lovely, light, flavoursome, fun sourdough bread is great for sharing over dinner or a picnic with friends and family. The dough is fermented for 24 hours in total to achieve the texture and flavour that I feel this amazing Italian staple should have. Yes, this sourdough takes time, but the actual active baking time is minimal, and trust me, it is worth it.

Levain

1 batch Levain (page 29)

Dough

450g warm water (75 to 78°F/24 to 26°C)
   (83% hydration including the bassinage;
   see below)

115g active levain (6 to 8 hours after feeding)

25g extra-virgin olive oil

550g bread flour

50g whole wheat flour

12g fine sea salt

50g warm bassinage (75 to 78°F/24 to 26°C)
   (8% hydration)

Toppings

Leaves from 2 sprigs fresh rosemary, lightly chopped

Leaves from 10 sprigs fresh thyme, lightly chopped

25 to 50g extra-virgin olive oil

5 to 10g flaky sea salt

Prepare the levain

1. Prepare the levain as directed on pages 29 to 30 in the Sourdough Starter Guide. Feed the active starter early in the morning (by 7 a.m.) the day you plan to mix the dough so that it is active and tripled in size after 4 to 6 hours. Alternatively, prepare the levain with a less active starter—approximately 10 percent inoculation (10g) calculated to the total weight of flours—the night before (by 10 p.m.) so it's ready in the morning, 8 to 10 hours later.

Autolyse and mix

2. Pour the 450g warm water into a large bowl. Add the active levain, olive oil, bread flour, and whole wheat flour and mix together until a shaggy dough forms with no dry patches, 2 to 3 minutes. Cover the bowl with a kitchen towel or loose-fitting lid and let rest in a warm (72 to 75°F/22 to 24°C), draft-free place for 30 to 60 minutes (autolyse). The dough will not change in appearance, but a longer rest is better.

3. Evenly scatter the fine salt over the dough and pour over the 50g warm water (bassinage). Using slightly wet hands, knead the dough by squeezing and pinching it until the salt water is fully incorporated.

4. Knead the dough using the Rubaud method as directed on page 33 (see photos on page 32) until it is smooth and has good strength and elasticity, 3 to 4 minutes. Cover the bowl with a loose-fitting lid and set a timer for 30 minutes.

5. When the timer goes off, perform the first set of stretch-and-folds as directed on pages 33 to 34. Again, set the timer for 30 minutes. Repeat the set of stretch-and-folds another two or three times over a 2-hour period, depending on how the dough feels (for a total of 3 hours of timed stretch-and-folds). Once the dough feels tighter, is doming, and has good strength, cover it with a kitchen towel or loose-fitting lid and allow it to proof for 1 to 2 hours at room temperature.

continued . . .

6. Brush a 13 × 9 × 2-inch (33 × 23 × 5cm) baking sheet or baking pan with a little olive oil and line with parchment paper. Brush a little extra oil over the parchment.

7. Using wet hands and a wet dough scraper, gently loosen the dough from the bowl. Transfer the dough smooth side up into the prepared pan. With wet hands, gently encourage the dough to flatten a little. Cover with a loose-fitting lid or kitchen towel and let proof in a warm (72 to 75°F/22 to 24°C), draft-free place for 20 minutes.

8. Once the dough has relaxed, with wet hands, gently press it to manipulate it a little more to the sides of the pan. Cover the pan with plastic wrap or a lid and place it in the fridge to cold proof overnight, 16 to 18 hours.

Final proof and dimple

9. The following day, remove the focaccia from the fridge and allow it to slowly warm up to room temperature, 3 to 4 hours depending how cold your fridge is and how active the dough was the day before. (I have left the dough at room temperature for up to 6 hours and had amazing results, so be patient.) The dough will increase at least a further 50 percent in volume.

10. Once the dough is ready, lightly drizzle with the 25 to 50g olive oil and gently smear it all over the surface of the dough using your hands. Hold your fingers like claws and push your fingers into the dough, right to the base. Start at one end of the pan and work your way along in rows.

The dough will bubble and some areas might deflate, but this is normal. Sprinkle the rosemary and thyme over the dough. Set aside, uncovered, for 30 minutes to relax and proof a little more. The resulting uneven crumb and bubbles give the bread its signature style.

Bake

11. Meanwhile, place an oven rack in the middle position and place a baking sheet on a lower rack. Preheat the oven to 400°F (200°C).

12. When ready to bake, sprinkle the flaky sea salt over the focaccia dough and transfer to the oven. Add a little hot water or a few ice cubes to the hot baking sheet underneath the focaccia and immediately close the door. The steam will help the crust to caramelize. Bake the focaccia for 10 minutes, then reduce the oven temperature to 350°F (175°C) and continue baking for another 15 to 20 minutes, until the bread is a beautiful dark golden brown.

13. Remove the focaccia from the oven and allow it to cool in the pan for 5 minutes. Carefully remove the bread from the pan and transfer it to a cooling rack. Allow the focaccia to rest for 30 minutes. Enjoy the bread warm.

14. Store the focaccia in an airtight container in the fridge for up to 3 days or in an airtight freezer bag in the freezer for up to 1 month. Warm on a griddle or in the oven after the first day for extra texture and softness.

Sweet Sourdough

Dark Chocolate, Cherry, Cocoa, and Red Wine Sourdough

Makes two 1kg boules

This decadent bread is rich in dark chocolate and packed with red wine–soaked cherries. It is complex, with a balance of sweet and savoury notes. This is a sourdough to share with friends and family or gift for a special celebration. It is indulgent and incredible freshly baked from the oven or toasted with a smothering of vegan butter the day after.

Bassinage (see page 33) refers to adding part of the water to the dough after initial kneading has caused some gluten development. This makes for a more hydrated dough and an attractive open crumb. I find with breads like this that contain inclusions like fruit, chocolate, and/or nuts that bringing the loaves out of the fridge a little while before baking prevents a shock to the dough, resulting in more oven spring and that much sought-after open crumb.

Levain

1 batch Levain (page 29)

Dough

650g warm water (75 to 78°F/24 to 26°C)

75g stone-ground whole-grain rye flour

275g fine stone-ground whole wheat flour

400g bread flour

25g extra-virgin coconut oil

25g dark cocoa powder

20g fine raw cane sugar

150g active levain (6 to 8 hours after feeding

18g fine sea salt

50g warm bassinage (75 to 78°F/24 to 26°C)

200g dairy-free dark chocolate (chips or chopped)

Macerated Cherries

200g dried sour cherries

150g organic vegan red wine

50g boiling water

Prepare the levain

1. Prepare the levain as directed on pages 29 to 30 in the Sourdough Starter Guide. Feed the active starter early in the morning (by 7 a.m.) the day you plan to mix the dough so that it is active and tripled in size after 4 to 6 hours. Alternatively, prepare the levain with a less active starter—approximately 10 percent inoculation (10g) calculated to the total weight of flours—the night before (by 10 p.m.) so it's ready in the morning, 8 to 10 hours later.

Macerate the cherries

2. When the levain has at least doubled in size, about 1 hour, place the cherries in a medium bowl with the red wine and boiling water. The hot water will rehydrate and plump up the dried fruit and the wine will add flavour. Allow the cherries to macerate, stirring every 20 minutes until cool, 1 hour. (This step can be done the evening before; store the cooled cherries in their liquid in an airtight container in a cool, dry place.)

Autolyse and mix

3. This dough is easily mixed by hand in a large bowl or in a stand mixer fitted with the dough hook on medium speed. Pour the 650g warm water into the bowl. Add the rye flour, whole wheat flour, and bread flour and mix until a shaggy dough forms with no dry patches or lumps, 2 to 3 minutes. Cover the dough with a kitchen towel or loose-fitting lid and let rest in a warm (72 to 75°F/ 22 to 24°C), draft-free place for 30 minutes (autolyse).

4. Melt the coconut oil in a small saucepan over low heat until it is a warm liquid but not too hot, whisk in the cocoa powder and sugar to form a smooth paste. Set aside to cool.

continued . . .

5. Add the active levain and salt to the dough and mix for 2 to 3 minutes. During the first minute of mixing, add the 50g warm water (bassinage) a little at a time, until it is all incorporated. Add the cooled coconut and cocoa paste and knead the dough using the Rubaud method as directed on page 33 (see photos on page 32) for another 4 minutes, until the dough looks and feels smoother and has more activity and elasticity. (If using a stand mixer, knead the dough on medium speed.) Cover the dough with a loose-fitting lid and let sit for 10 minutes.

6. Knead the dough a final time at a faster speed to stretch it a little more, 5 to 7 minutes, until the dough is smoother in appearance. The dough should pull away from the sides of the bowl. (If using a stand mixer, knead on medium-high speed.)

Bulk ferment

7. Lightly oil a bowl or container that is four times the size of the dough. Remove the dough from the mixer bowl and form it into a ball in your hands. Drop the dough smooth side up into the bowl and cover with a kitchen towel or loose-fitting lid. Set a timer for 10 minutes.

8. Strain the cherries through a sieve, reserving the liquid for another use (perhaps reducing it to a syrup and serving with ice cream). When the timer goes off, scatter the cherries and chocolate over the top of the dough—the inclusions don't need to be fully mixed in just yet, as during the bulk proof stage and folding they will be evenly dispersed. Set the timer for 20 minutes.

9. When the timer goes off, perform the first set of stretch-and-folds as directed on pages 33 to 34, gently incorporating the inclusions into the dough. Cover the dough with a kitchen towel or loose-fitting lid and again set the timer for 30 minutes. Repeat the set of stretch-and-folds another three times over a 90-minute period.

10. Allow the dough to continue bulk fermentation until it is domed and has increased in volume by approximately 50 percent, 1 to 2 hours depending on the room's temperature.

Pre-shape, final shape, and overnight cold proof

11. Gently remove the dough from the container and place it on an unfloured work surface. Using a bench knife, cut the dough into 2 equal pieces (1kg each). Working with 1 piece at a time, gently pre-shape the dough into a round ball. Loosely cover the dough with a kitchen towel and allow it to rest for 30 minutes. (Follow the directions on pages 34 to 36; see photos on page 36.)

12. Prepare 2 round proofing baskets as directed on pages 36 to 37.

13. Lightly dust the tops of the loaves with flour. Using a bench knife, pick up the dough and turn it onto its floured side. Gently shape the dough into a boule as directed on pages 37 to 39. Repeat for the second loaf. Cover the loaves with a kitchen towel and let proof in a warm (72 to 75°F/22 to 24°C), draft-free place until the loaves have increased in volume by approximately 20 percent, 30 to 60 minutes.

14. Cover the loaves with a loose-fitting lid or plate and place in the fridge to cold proof overnight, 12 to 18 hours.

Bake

15. The following day, cut a sheet of parchment paper to fit your baking stone, a large baking sheet, or the base of a cast-iron bread pan; set aside. Place the baking surface on the middle rack of the oven. (If using a stone or baking sheet, place another baking sheet on the bottom rack for ice; the steam will enhance oven spring and caramelization of the crust.) Preheat the oven to 425°F (220°C).

16. About 15 minutes before baking, remove the boules from the fridge and place them on the work surface to warm up a little.

17. If using a cast-iron bread pan, you will have to bake one loaf at a time and leave the other in the fridge until the first loaf is half-baked. If using a baking stone or baking sheet, you should be able to bake both loaves at the same time. Turn the loaves out seam side down onto the reserved parchment paper. Using a lame or very sharp knife, score the top of each loaf as directed on page 47. Carefully transfer the boules (with the parchment) to the oven seam side down and add a few ice cubes to the bottom baking sheet. Place 1 ice cube in the cast-iron pan to create additional steam.

18. Bake for 20 minutes. Remove the bread pan lid or rotate the loaves front to back on the baking sheet or baking stone. Reduce the oven temperature to 400°F (200°C) and continue baking for 20 to 25 minutes, until the crust is nicely browned. It is a little trickier to know when this loaf is perfectly baked because of the darkness of the cocoa powder, so use your senses— smelling the bread, tapping the base to check if the loaf sounds hollow, and the overall appearance should tell you when it is done.

19. Transfer the loaves to a cooling rack and allow to cool for at least 1 hour before slicing. This will be a real test, as the chocolate fragrance will fill the air, but be strong—it will be worth the wait!

20. Store the sourdough in a linen bag or wooden or metal container at room temperature for up to 5 days.

Orange, Cardamom, and Olive Oil Brioche with Toasted Hazelnuts

Makes four 7⅞ × 3⅙ × 3⅙-inch (20 × 8 × 8cm) tin loaves

Brioche originates in France and is centuries old. It is thought that when peasants had no bread before the French Revolution, Marie Antionette said, "Qu'ils mangent de la brioche," which has been mistranslated as "Let them eat cake." Although brioche requires both bread and pastry skills (due to its being generally heavily loaded with eggs, butter, and cream), there are so many ways to enrich dough by using only plant-based products such as coconut milk and oil or some tasty vegan butters. We say, "Let vegans eat brioche!"

T85 flour is a blend of hard red winter and hard red spring wheats. It is neither strictly white nor strictly whole-grain flour. I use medium Matfer Bourgeat Exoglass Loaf Moulds for this recipe.

This loaf is light and buttery and makes for an indulgent brunch, perhaps topped with chocolate hazelnut spread, or even as French toast if it is stale. It also makes a lovely gift to share with friends or family.

Levain

2 batches Levain (page 29)

Brioche Dough

1 medium orange (150g)

300g aquafaba (liquid from two 14 oz/400mL cans of chickpeas; see page 333)

300g extra-virgin olive oil

240g unsweetened soy milk

100g raw cane sugar

25g ground cardamom

350g active levain (6 to 8 hours after feeding)

500g T85 flour or fine stone-ground whole wheat flour

500g bread flour

20g fine sea salt

"Egg" Wash

40g unsweetened soy milk

5g pure maple syrup

5g organic canola oil

For decorating

100g Elderflower Syrup (page 235)

150g chopped toasted hazelnuts

Prepare the levain

1. Prepare the levain as directed on pages 29 to 30 in the Sourdough Starter Guide. Feed the active starter early in the morning (by 7 a.m.) the day you plan to mix the dough so that it is active and tripled in size after 4 to 6 hours. Alternatively, prepare the levain with a less active starter—approximately 10 percent inoculation (10g) calculated to the total weight of flours—the night before (by 10 p.m.) so it's ready in the morning, 8 to 10 hours later.

Autolyse, mix, bulk ferment, and overnight cold proof

2. Trim the ends off the orange, cut it into quarters, and remove any seeds. Place the orange in a food processor and pulse for 30 to 60 seconds, until puréed with small pieces of zest. Measure out 200g (7 oz) of the purée and set aside.

3. Pour the aquafaba and olive oil into the bowl of a stand mixer fitted with the dough hook.

4. Slightly warm the soy milk in a small saucepan over low heat to 68 to 72°F (20 to 22°C). Add the milk to the aquafaba mixture.

5. Add the sugar, cardamom, blended orange, active levain, T85 flour, and bread flour. Mix on low speed until a shaggy dough forms with no dry patches, 3 to 4 minutes. Stop the mixer and scrape down the sides as needed.

continued . . .

6. Cover the bowl with a kitchen towel or loose-fitting lid and let rest in a warm (72 to 75°F/22 to 24°C), draft-free place for 30 minutes (autolyse).

7. After the resting period, add the salt and knead the dough on medium speed until it is smooth and shiny, 8 to 10 minutes. After mixing, allow the dough to rest for 2 to 3 minutes. Perform the windowpane test to check if the dough is sufficiently mixed and developed: Pull away a small piece of dough and stretch it between your fingers to create a "window." If you can see light without tearing the dough, enough gluten has developed and the dough is strong. If the dough rips quite easily, continue kneading for 3 to 5 minutes longer, allow the dough to relax for a minute, then repeat the windowpane test.

8. Place the dough in a lightly oiled bowl or container that is three to four times the size of the dough and cover with a loose-fitting lid. Place the dough in a warm (72 to 75°F/22 to 24°C), draft-free place until it has doubled in size, 2 to 3 hours.

9. Place the covered dough in the fridge to cold proof overnight, 12 to 16 hours.

Shape the loaves

10. The following day, lightly oil four (7⅞ × 3⅙ × 3⅙ inches/ 20 × 8 × 8cm) loaf tins and line the bottom and sides with parchment paper.

11. Gently remove the dough from the container and transfer to an unfloured work surface. Using a bench knife, cut the dough into 12 equal pieces (200g each). On a lightly floured work surface, shape each piece into a tight ball. Place 3 dough balls snugly together in each tin.

12. Loosely cover the tins with plastic wrap or a kitchen towel and let the dough proof in a warm (72 to 75°F/ 22 to 24°C), draft-free place until doubled in size, 3 to 4 hours.

"Egg" wash and bake

13. One hour before baking, arrange the oven racks in the upper and lower thirds of the oven and preheat to 350°F (175°C).

14. To make the "egg" wash, in a small bowl, whisk together the soy milk, maple syrup, and canola oil. Just before baking, brush the top of each loaf with the "egg" wash.

15. Bake the brioches for 20 minutes. Lower the oven temperature to 325°F (160°C) and continue baking until golden brown, 20 minutes. If you are not using a convection oven, you might need to rotate the brioches top to bottom and front to back halfway through.

16. Remove the loaves from the oven and let them cool in their tins on a cooling rack for 10 to 15 minutes. Remove the brioches from the tins and return them to the cooling rack.

Decorate the loaves

17. Meanwhile, simmer the elderflower syrup in a small saucepan over medium heat until reduced to a thick syrup consistency, 3 minutes. Brush the syrup generously all over the top of the turned-out brioches while still warm. Sprinkle the chopped hazelnuts on top. Let the loaves cool completely.

18. Store the loaves in an airtight container in the fridge for up to 3 days or wrap in plastic wrap and freeze for up to 1 month. Thaw for a few hours before toasting.

Toasted Walnut and Golden and Black Raisin Sourdough

Makes two 9 × 5 × 4-inch (23 × 12 × 10cm) Pullman loaves

This sourdough loaf can be enjoyed as part of a sweet or a savoury meal. The recipe is in the sweet sourdough chapter, but all its sweetness comes naturally from the macerated raisins. Toasting the walnuts adds a lovely depth of flavour, texture, and colour. This bread is best enjoyed with a simple vegan butter or nut butter and is also a delectable addition to a vegan cheese board.

A Pullman pan has a lid to create the perfect quadrilateral loaf and minimize crust development. The name came about after the bread's adoption by the Pullman Railway Company because the square-sided loaves took up less space than domed loaves in the small train kitchens.

Levain

1 batch Levain (page 29)

Dough

300g walnut halves

150g golden raisins

150g black raisins

600g warm water (75 to 78°F/24 to 26°C) (85% hydration)

420g bread flour

210g stone-ground whole wheat flour

70g stone-ground whole-grain rye flour

30g non-diastatic barley malt powder or barley malt syrup

175g active levain (100% hydration)

15g fine sea salt

Prepare the levain

1. Prepare the levain as directed on pages 29 to 30 in the Sourdough Starter Guide. Feed the active starter early in the morning (by 7 a.m.) the day you plan to mix the dough so that it is active and tripled in size after 4 to 6 hours. Alternatively, prepare the levain with a less active starter—approximately 10 percent inoculation (10g) calculated to the total weight of flours—the night before (by 10 p.m.) so it's ready in the morning, 8 to 10 hours later.

Toast the nuts and hydrate the raisins

2. Two hours before mixing the dough, preheat the oven to 340°F (170°C). Scatter the walnuts on a small baking sheet and lightly toast them in the oven until golden brown, 5 minutes. Set aside to cool.

3. Place the golden raisins and black raisins in a medium bowl, cover with boiling water, and let expand and rehydrate, 30 to 60 minutes. Once the raisins are plump, drain them back to the bowl and set aside to cool.

Autolyse and mix

4. This dough is easily mixed by hand in a large bowl or with a stand mixer fitted with the dough hook on medium speed. Pour the warm water into the bowl. Add the bread flour, whole wheat flour, rye flour, and malt powder and mix together until a shaggy dough forms with no dry patches, 2 to 3 minutes. Cover the bowl with a kitchen towel or loose-fitting lid and let rest in a warm (72 to 75°F/22 to 24°C), draft-free place for 1 hour (autolyse). The dough will not change in appearance.

5. After the resting period, add the active levain to the dough and mix for 1 to 2 minutes. Cover the dough and let sit for 10 minutes.

6. Add the salt and knead the dough using the Rubaud method as directed on page 33 (see photos on page 32)

continued . . .

until the dough is smoother in appearance, feels more active, and has a little more elasticity, 6 to 8 minutes. (If using a stand mixer, knead the dough on medium-high speed.) The dough should pull away from the sides of the bowl. Allow the dough to rest in the bowl for 2 minutes.

7. Using your hands, break up the walnuts a little, then scatter the nuts and raisins over the top of the dough. Gently fold the dough over and around to mix in the fruit and nuts a little. Don't worry about fully incorporating them just yet, as the stretch-and-folds will help.

Bulk ferment

8. Place the dough in a lightly oiled bowl or container that is four times the size of the dough and cover with a loose-fitting lid or damp kitchen towel. Place the dough in a warm (72 to 75°F/22 to 24°C), draft-free place. A constant temperature will ensure a consistent fermentation. Set a timer for 30 minutes.

9. When the timer goes off, perform the first set of stretch-and-folds as directed on pages 33 to 34. Again, set the timer for 30 minutes. Repeat the set of stretch-and-folds another two or three times over a 2-hour period, depending on how the dough feels (for a total of 3 hours of timed stretch-and-folds). Once the dough feels tighter and is doming, perform a couple of sets of coil folds as directed on page 34. Cover the dough and allow it to rest for 30 to 60 minutes, until you can see some fermentation bubbles and the dough has increased in volume by approximately 40 percent.

Pre-shape, final shape, and overnight cold proof

10. Gently remove the dough from the container and place it on an unfloured work surface. Using a bench knife, cut the dough into 2 equal pieces (approximately 1050g each). Working with 1 piece at a time, gently pre-shape the dough into a round ball. Loosely cover the dough with a kitchen towel and let the dough rest for 30 to 40 minutes. (Follow the directions on pages 34 to 36; see photos on page 36.)

11. Lightly oil two 9 × 5 × 4-inch (23 × 12 × 10cm) Pullman loaf tins—don't forget the inside of the lid—and line the bottom with parchment paper. This will help to prevent the bottom of the bread from overcolouring from the natural sugars.

12. Shape each loaf into a simple rectangle as shown on page 44. Very lightly flour the dough and carefully place it seam side down in the lined tins. Cover with the lids and allow the loaves to proof at room temperature until they have started to increase in volume and dome a little, anywhere between 1 and 2 hours depending on the warmth of your kitchen.

13. Gently re-cover the tins with their lids and place the loaves in the fridge to cold proof overnight, 12 to 18 hours.

Bake

14. The following day, check the loaves to see how much they have risen. I like to make sure they have risen to the top of the tins. Let the loaves come to room temperature, at least 1 to 2 hours. This is necessary because of the high quantity of inclusions (fruit and nuts).

15. When the loaves are almost at room temperature, preheat the oven to 375°F (190°C).

16. Bake the loaves with the lids on for 30 minutes. Lower the oven temperature to 350°F (175°C) and continue baking the bread for another 20 minutes, until it is dark golden brown. Remove the tins from the oven, take the lids off (to maintain a crispy crust), and place the tins on a cooling rack for 5 minutes. Turn the loaves out of the tins and allow the bread to cool for at least 1 hour before slicing.

17. See Storing Bread (page 51).

Sourdough Stroopwafels

Makes 12 or 13 waffles

The stroopwafel is a Dutch classic that is cooked in its own special hot iron waffle press. They are a kind of sandwich cookie—two thin waffle rounds sandwiching a cinnamon caramel filling. A nice way to enjoy this delicious treat is to place them over a hot drink, such as coffee or tea, to warm the cookie and soften the caramel. Stroopwafels were first made in the Netherlands during the late eighteenth century by bakers repurposing crumbs and scraps. By 1870 they had garnered a lot of attention, with over a hundred bakeries making the treat, and then other cities started making them too.

Levain

1 batch Levain (page 29)

Waffles

20g ground flaxseed

155g unsweetened oat milk

200g vegan butter, melted until just liquid

100g active levain (6 to 8 hours after feeding)

500g all-purpose flour

150g raw cane sugar or coconut sugar

3g fine sea salt

Caramel Filling

400g pure maple syrup

200g coconut sugar

40g vegan butter

3g ground cinnamon

Prepare the levain

1. Prepare the levain as directed on pages 29 to 30 in the Sourdough Starter Guide. Feed the active starter early in the morning (by 7 a.m.) the day you plan to mix the dough so that it is active and tripled in size after 4 to 6 hours. Alternatively, prepare the levain with a less active starter—approximately 10 percent inoculation (10g) calculated to the total weight of flours—the night before (by 10 p.m.) so it's ready in the morning, 8 to 10 hours later.

Make the waffle dough, proof, then cold proof overnight

2. To make your flax egg, whisk together the flaxseed and oat milk in a large bowl until a smooth paste forms. If there are any lumps, push a small rubber spatula against the side of the bowl to break them up. Let sit for 10 minutes to bloom and thicken.

3. Add the melted (but not hot) butter to the flax egg and whisk to combine. Add the active levain, flour, sugar, and salt. Mixing with one hand while the other hand holds the bowl, thoroughly incorporate all the ingredients until a smooth dough has formed. Knead the dough with your hand for 2 minutes, to develop the gluten a little.

4. Very lightly oil a separate large bowl or container that is two or three times the size of the dough. Remove the dough from the mixing bowl and form it into a ball with your hands, then place it smooth side up in the oiled bowl. Cover with a kitchen towel or loose-fitting lid. Place the dough in a warm (72 to 75°F/22 to 24°C), draft-free place until it has increased in volume by 30 to 50 percent, 2 to 4 hours.

5. Place the covered dough in the fridge to cold proof overnight, 12 to 14 hours.

continued . . .

Shape and cook

6. The next morning, line a large baking sheet with parchment paper or a silicone baking mat. Remove the waffle dough from the fridge and transfer it to an unfloured work surface. Divide the dough into 2-inch (5cm) pieces (85g each). You should have 12 or 13 balls. It is a good idea to test this size/weight first in your stroopwafel iron to see if it is suitable. Place the balls on the lined baking sheet. Cover them with a kitchen towel and let sit until they come up to room temperature, about 1 hour.

7. Preheat the stroopwafel iron. Once it is hot, place 1 or 2 balls of dough (depending whether yours is a single or double iron) and press them onto the hot irons. Close the iron to compress the dough. Cook the waffles until the steam has slowed and the waffles are golden brown, 40 to 50 seconds.

8. Remove the waffles from the iron and immediately trim the outside with a cookie cutter. Using a small serrated knife, cut the waffles in half like a pita bread. Set them aside and continue to cook the remaining waffles.

Make the caramel filling

9. Place the maple syrup, coconut sugar, butter, and cinnamon in a medium saucepan and gently warm over medium-low heat. Once melted, stir the mixture once gently to make sure there are no lumps, and then stop mixing and allow the sugars to start to caramelize. Keep the saucepan on the heat until a beautiful golden-brown liquid caramel has formed. Then remove the caramel from the heat.

Fill the waffles

10. Arrange the cooled stroopwafels in two rows, with both halves facing each other.

11. While the caramel is still warm, divide it among the 6 bottom halves and quickly spread it to the edges using a small spoon. Top with the other half and gently press the sandwich together. Be careful—once the waffles are cool, they are very brittle.

12. Enjoy the stroopwafels on the day they are made or store in an airtight container at room temperature for up to 3 days.

Dark Chocolate and Miso Babka

Makes one 9 × 5 × 3-inch (23 × 12 × 8cm) loaf, serves 7 to 8

The word *babka* is Yiddish for "little grandmother," thought to be attributed to the fluted pan it is traditionally baked in, whose shape is akin to the skirts of elderly women. Babka is a Jewish staple eaten on special occasions, a cross between bread and cake. It consists of a twisted or braided yeasted buttery brioche dough with various fillings folded in. A dark filling, like chocolate, creates the most beautiful marble effect when sliced. The miso in this recipe adds another depth to the flavour, with a little bit of salt and nutty umami undertones.

I don't warm the milk for this dough. The long mixing time generates enough heat with all the friction.

Levain

1 batch Levain (page 29)

Tangzhong (see Note, page 81)

80g unsweetened soy milk

20g bread flour

20g brown rice miso

Babka Dough

15g ground flaxseed

90g unsweetened soy milk

110g unsweetened oat milk

50g raw cane sugar

100g active levain (40% hydration)
   (6 to 8 hours after feeding)

300g bread flour

20g stone-ground whole-grain spelt flour

5g fine sea salt

75g cold vegan butter, cut into ½-inch (1cm) cubes

Dark Chocolate Ganache

100g dairy-free dark chocolate, chopped

50g vegan butter

50g vegan icing sugar, sifted

20g dark cocoa powder, sifted

100g unsweetened soy milk

Glaze

85g pure maple syrup

75g raw cane sugar

80g water

Prepare the levain

1. Prepare the levain as directed on pages 29 to 30 in the Sourdough Starter Guide. Feed the active starter early in the morning (by 7 a.m.) the day you plan to mix the dough so that it is active and tripled in size after 4 to 6 hours. Alternatively, prepare the levain with a less active starter—approximately 10% inoculation (10g) calculated to the total weight of flours—the night before (by 10 p.m.) so it's ready in the morning, 8 to 10 hours later.

Make the tangzhong

2. Whisk together the soy milk and bread flour in a small saucepan. Place the pan over medium-low heat and cook, whisking constantly, until the paste is smooth and thickened, 2 to 3 minutes, then whisk in the miso until smooth. Cover and set it aside to cool to room temperature.

Mix, bulk ferment, and cold proof

3. To make your flax egg, whisk together the flaxseed and soy milk in a small bowl until a smooth paste forms. If there are any lumps, push a small rubber spatula against the side of the bowl to break them up. Let sit for 10 minutes to bloom and thicken.

4. In the bowl of a stand mixer fitted with the dough hook, combine the oat milk, sugar, active levain, flax egg,

continued . . .

bread flour, spelt flour, and tangzhong. Mix on low speed until a shaggy dough forms with no dry patches, 2 to 3 minutes. Cover with a kitchen towel or loose-fitting lid and let rest for 10 minutes.

5. Add the salt and mix the dough on medium speed for 3 minutes. With the mixer running, gradually add the cold butter in 3 additions (25g each), waiting until the butter is fully incorporated before making the next addition. If the butter is added too quickly, the dough will split. You may need to stop the mixer and use a rubber spatula to push the butter from the sides of the bowl back into the dough. Keep adding the butter until it's all incorporated; this will take 5 to 10 minutes. After all the butter is incorporated, continue to mix the dough for another 8 to 10 minutes to allow the dough to fully develop and strengthen until it is smooth and pulls away from the sides of the bowl. Try to keep the dough temperature under 85°F (30°C).

6. Lightly oil a bowl or container that is three to four times the size of the dough. Remove the dough from the mixer bowl and form it into a ball in your hands. Place the dough smooth side up in the bowl and cover with a kitchen towel or loose-fitting lid. Allow the dough to sit in a warm (72 to 75°F/22 to 24°C), draft-free place until doubled in size, 2 to 4 hours.

7. Cover the dough with a loose-fitting lid or plate and place in the fridge to cold proof overnight, 12 to 14 hours.

Make the dark chocolate ganache

8. The following morning, place the chocolate and butter in a medium heatproof bowl. Place the bowl over a saucepan of barely simmering water (the bowl should not touch the water). Stir occasionally until the chocolate and butter are melted and smooth, 5 to 6 minutes. Remove the bowl from the pan and immediately use a rubber spatula to mix in the icing sugar and cocoa powder until the mixture is smooth. Add the soy milk and mix until smooth and shiny. Set aside, stirring every 5 to 10 minutes until the ganache has cooled and thickened. This should take 30 to 60 minutes.

Roll the dough and proof

9. Remove the dough from the fridge. The colder the dough, the easier it will be to roll and handle. On a lightly floured work surface, immediately roll out the chilled dough into a rectangle 12 × 8 inches (30 × 20cm) and ¼ inch (5mm) thick, with a long side facing you. Work quickly and efficiently—this dough is very soft, so the more you roll and touch it, the more difficult it will be to handle.

10. Using an offset spatula, spread the dark chocolate ganache over the dough in an even layer all the way to the edges. I like to start at one end and work my way along to keep the ganache in a nice even layer. Starting at the long edge closest to you, roll up the dough, creating a tight roulade and pinch the seam to seal. Transfer the dough seam side down to a baking sheet or cutting board and place in the fridge for 30 minutes to allow for easier shaping and neatness.

11. Lightly spray a 9 × 5 × 3-inch (23 × 12 × 8cm) loaf pan with oil and line the bottom and sides with parchment paper.

12. Remove the dough from the fridge and transfer it to a lightly floured work surface. Using a large chef's knife, cut the log down the centre lengthwise. Arrange the halves side by side with a short side closest to you and the chocolate layers facing up. Cross one half over the other to make an X, then repeat this at the bottom of the roulade and at the top, making 3 twists in total. Make sure the chocolate side is exposed. Lightly compress the twisted dough so it will fit into the loaf tin by pushing the ends towards the middle. Keeping the cut layers facing up, place the babka in the tin.

13. Loosely cover the babka with a large sandwich bag or loose-fitting plastic wrap. Allow the babka to sit in a warm (72 to 75°F/22 to 24°C), draft-free place until it has doubled in size, 2 to 4 hours.

Bake

14. Place an oven rack in the middle position and remove the upper rack to allow lots of space for the babka to rise. Place a large baking sheet on the rack. Preheat the oven to 350°F (175°C).

15. Once the babka is domed and doubled in size, gently place the loaf on the preheated baking sheet along with 2 or 3 ice cubes. The ice will create some steam within the oven and prevent the babka from colouring too quickly. Bake for 35 to 40 minutes, until the babka is a beautiful golden brown. A probe thermometer should read above 200°F (93°C).

16. Transfer the babka to a cooling rack and let it cool in the tin for 10 minutes. This will help the babka hold its shape. Gently remove the babka from the tin and return it to the cooling rack.

Meanwhile, make the glaze and brush the loaf

17. Combine the maple syrup, sugar, and water in a small saucepan and bring to a boil over medium heat. Cook, without stirring, until the glaze has thickened and is tacky between the fingertips, 2 to 3 minutes. Do not over-reduce or the sugars will crystallize. Brush the babka with a double coating of glaze. The second coating gives the bread a beautiful shine.

18. The babka is best eaten on the day it is baked but can be stored in an airtight container in the fridge for up to 3 days. Slice and toast under the broiler until golden brown.

Roasted Apple and Vanilla Custard-Filled Buns with an Oat and Almond Crumble

Makes 10 buns

This warming brioche-style bun is filled with custard and seasonal roasted fruit and finished with a toasted nutty crumble. This recipe is very versatile and you can use whatever local fruit is available to you depending on the time of year. I've made this recipe with pears, blueberries, peaches, and plums and switched out spices to complement the fruit.

Levain

1 batch Levain (page 29)

Bun Dough

30g ground flaxseed

400g unsweetened oat milk

100g extra-virgin coconut oil, melted

35g pure maple syrup

150g active levain (6 to 8 hours after feeding)

400g bread flour

140g stone-ground whole wheat flour

25g ground cinnamon

5g ground nutmeg

12g fine sea salt

10g fresh baker's yeast (optional)

Apple Topping

1kg/2.2 lb unpeeled Braeburn, McIntosh, Fuji, or Gala apples (5 to 6 medium apples)

28g extra-virgin coconut oil, melted

25g coconut sugar

Vanilla Custard

30g cornstarch

400g unsweetened oat milk

50g raw cane sugar

20g pure vanilla extract

1g ground turmeric

A pinch fine sea salt

Oat and Almond Crumble

50g cold vegan butter

50g coconut sugar or raw cane sugar

50g oat flakes

50g whole wheat flour

50g sliced natural almonds

Maple Glaze

120g pure maple syrup

150g raw cane sugar

150g water

Prepare the levain

1. Prepare the levain as directed on pages 29 to 30 in the Sourdough Starter Guide. Feed the active starter early in the morning (by 7 a.m.) the day you plan to mix the dough so that it is active and tripled in size after 4 to 6 hours. Alternatively, prepare the levain with a less active starter—approximately 10 percent inoculation (10g) calculated to the total weight of flours—the night before (by 10 p.m.) so it's ready in the morning, 8 to 10 hours later.

Mix

2. To make your flax egg, whisk together the flaxseed and oat milk in a medium bowl until a smooth paste forms. If there are any lumps, push a small rubber

continued . . .

spatula against the side of the bowl to break them up. Let sit for 10 minutes to bloom and thicken.

3. In the bowl of a stand mixer, combine the flax egg, melted coconut oil, and maple syrup. Whisk by hand to combine.

4. Add the active levain, bread flour, whole wheat flour, cinnamon, nutmeg, salt, and baker's yeast, if using. Attach the dough hook and mix on medium-low speed for 5 minutes. Allow the dough to rest for 5 minutes.

5. Continue kneading on medium-high speed until the dough looks smooth and pulls away from the sides of the bowl, 5 to 7 minutes. Use a probe thermometer to ensure the dough does not go above 82°F (28°C), which would overcook the yeasts and affect the rise.

Bulk ferment and overnight cold proof

6. Place the dough in a lightly oiled bowl or container that is four times the size of the dough and cover with a loose-fitting lid or kitchen towel. Place the dough in a warm (72 to 75°F/22 to 24°C), draft-free place. A constant temperature will ensure a consistent fermentation. Set a timer for 30 minutes.

7. When the timer goes off, perform the first set of stretch-and-folds as directed on pages 33 to 34. Again, set the timer for 30 minutes. (If you are using fresh baker's yeast, the dough will bulk ferment a lot quicker, so you will only need to perform one set of stretch-and-folds and then, after an hour's proof, proceed to the overnight cold proof.) Repeat the set of stretch-and-folds another three times over a 2-hour period, depending on how the dough feels (for a total of four timed stretch-and-folds over 3 hours). Cover the dough with a kitchen towel or loose-fitting lid and allow to rest for 45 minutes.

8. After the resting period, gently perform a coil fold as directed on page 34. Cover the dough and allow it to rest for 1 to 2 hours, until you can see some fermentation bubbles and the dough has increased in volume by approximately 40 percent.

9. Cover the dough with a loose-fitting lid or plate and place in the fridge to cold proof overnight, 12 to 14 hours. This will allow the dough to fully ferment and develop

some great flavours and textures. Chilling the dough also makes it a lot easier to shape.

Prepare the apple topping

10. The next morning, preheat the oven to 380°F (195°C). Line a large baking sheet with parchment paper or a silicone baking mat.

11. Wash the apples (no need to peel them). Stand them upright on a cutting board and, using a chef's knife, cut both sides off as close to the core as possible. Cut the remaining two sides off. Discard the cores. Cut each half into three equal-size wedges. Place the apples in a medium bowl and lightly toss with the melted coconut oil and the coconut sugar. Spread the apple wedges on the lined baking sheet and roast them until softened and lightly browned, 20 to 25 minutes. Set aside to cool.

Make the vanilla custard

12. Place the cornstarch in a medium bowl. In a small saucepan, whisk together the oat milk, sugar, vanilla, turmeric, and salt. Pour a quarter of the oat milk mixture over the cornstarch and whisk until a smooth paste forms. Add the remaining oat milk mixture to the paste and continue to whisk until fully incorporated. Pour the mixture into the saucepan and bring to a simmer over medium-low heat, whisking constantly to prevent sticking. Once the custard is gently simmering, reduce the heat to low and cook, stirring occasionally with a rubber spatula, until thickened and there is no floury aftertaste, 10 minutes. Set aside to cool.

Shape and proof

13. Line 2 large baking sheets with parchment paper or silicone baking mats.

14. Remove the dough from the fridge and transfer it to a lightly floured work surface. Using a bench knife, divide the dough into 10 equal pieces (125g each). Shape each piece into a ball.

15. Working with 1 ball at a time, flatten it into a disc. Working from 12 o'clock, pull the dough into the centre. Keep going all the way round the disc. This shaping technique is used to strengthen the dough before its final shape. Turn the ball over and slightly cup your hands and form the dough into a ball shape (see pages 106 to 107 for shaping photos).

16. Using the palm of your hand, flatten the ball. Using your fingertips, start to push down ½ inch (1cm) from the outside to form a crust, like a small pizza, 3 to 4 inches (8 to 10cm) in diameter. Repeat to shape the remaining balls. Transfer the shaped dough to the lined baking sheets, leaving 3 inches (8cm) between them. (I would recommend 5 buns per large baking sheet.) Loosely cover the dough with plastic wrap and place in a warm (72 to 75°F/22 to 24°C), draft-free place to proof for 30 minutes.

Meanwhile, prepare the oat and almond crumble

17. Combine the butter, coconut sugar, oat flakes, whole wheat flour, and almonds in a medium bowl. Using your fingertips, rub the ingredients together until fully mixed and a crumbly texture. Set aside.

18. Fill a spray bottle with water. After the 30-minute first proof, divide the vanilla custard equally among the dough discs, spreading it inside the raised edge. Be quite generous, as the apples will add weight. Arrange the roasted apple wedges on top of the custard. Proof, uncovered, in a warm (72 to 75°F/22 to 24°C), draft-free place until the buns have doubled in size, 60 to 90 minutes. Halfway through the proofing time, mist the exposed dough with a little water to prevent the dough from drying.

19. Meanwhile, arrange the oven racks in the upper and lower thirds of the oven and preheat to 375°F (190°C).

Bake

20. Sprinkle the oat and almond crumble over the apples (but not over the crust). Bake until the crust is golden brown, 16 to 20 minutes. If you are not using a convection oven, you might need to rotate the buns halfway through. Carefully transfer the buns to a cooling rack set over a baking sheet to catch any glaze. Let cool completely.

Make the maple glaze and brush the buns

21. In a small saucepan, combine the maple syrup, sugar, and water. Bring to a simmer and cook until reduced and slightly tacky between your fingertips, 5 to 6 minutes. Do not over-reduce or the sugars will crystallize. Brush the crust a few times with the glaze to create a beautiful shine.

22. These brioche buns are best eaten on the day of baking but can be stored in an airtight container in the fridge for up to 3 days, then reheated in the oven at 350°F (175°C) for 10 minutes.

Sourdough Cinnamon Buns

Makes about 15 buns

Cinnamon buns, rolls, swirls, or sticky buns? People from all corners of the globe have their own name and interpretation for this incredibly popular treat said to have originated in Sweden. In North America, it is customary to top cinnamon buns with icing like our Cream Cheeze Frosting (page 183).

At the bakery we use real, or "true," organic cinnamon sourced from Sri Lanka rather than Saigon cinnamon, or cassia. The taste and aroma are far superior. Also, the richness of organic extra-virgin coconut oil compared to refined coconut oil is what makes these cinnamon buns incredibly delicious and what the bakery is best known for as far as treats are concerned. Not only this, but we mill our own red spring wheat flour, adding more depth of flavour to the buns.

Levain

40g or 50g active starter

200g warm water (75 to 78°F/24 to 26°C)

150g bread flour or all-purpose flour, more for dusting

50g stone-ground whole wheat flour

Bun Dough

60g ground flaxseed

800g unsweetened oat milk, divided

170g extra-virgin coconut oil, melted

70g pure maple syrup

280g active levain

20g fresh baker's yeast (optional)

845g bread flour

280g stone-ground whole wheat flour

30g ground organic Sri Lankan cinnamon

10g ground cardamom

25g fine sea salt

Filling

225g extra-virgin coconut oil

225g raw cane sugar

50g ground organic Sri Lankan cinnamon

15g ground cardamom (optional)

Glaze

170g pure maple syrup

150g raw cane sugar

177g water

Prepare the levain

1. Prepare the levain for this recipe following the method for the levain recipe as directed on pages 29 to 30 in the Sourdough Starter Guide. Feed the active starter early in the morning (by 7 a.m.) the day you plan to mix the dough so that it is active and tripled in size after 4 to 6 hours. Alternatively, prepare the levain with a less active starter—approximately 10 percent inoculation (10g) calculated to the total weight of flours—the night before (by 10 p.m.) so it's ready in the morning, 8 to 10 hours later. There will be some discard, which you can use in zero-waste recipes.

Mix

2. To make your flax egg, whisk together the flaxseed and 200g of the oat milk in a medium bowl until a smooth paste forms. If there are any lumps, push a small rubber spatula against the side of the bowl to break them up. Let sit for 10 minutes to bloom and thicken.

3. In the bowl of a stand mixer, combine the remaining 600g oat milk, the flax egg, melted coconut oil, and maple syrup. Whisk by hand to combine.

4. Add the active levain, baker's yeast (if using), bread flour, whole wheat flour, cinnamon, cardamom, and salt. Attach the dough hook and mix on medium-low speed for 5 minutes. Let the dough rest for 5 minutes.

continued . . .

5. Knead the dough a final time on medium-high speed until it looks smooth and pulls away from the sides of the bowl, 5 to 7 minutes.

Bulk ferment and overnight cold proof

6. Place the dough in a lightly oiled bowl or container that is four times the size of the dough and cover with a loose-fitting lid or kitchen towel. Place the dough in a warm (72 to 75°F/22 to 24°C), draft-free place. A constant temperature will ensure a consistent fermentation. Set a timer for 30 minutes.

7. When the timer goes off, perform the first set of stretch-and-folds as directed on pages 33 to 34. Again, set the timer for 30 minutes. (If you are using fresh baker's yeast, the dough will bulk ferment a lot quicker, so you will only need to perform one set of stretch-and-folds and then, after an hour's proof, proceed to the overnight cold proof.) Repeat the set of stretch-and-folds another three times over a 2-hour period, depending on how the dough feels (for a total of four timed stretch-and-folds over 3 hours). Allow the dough to rest for 45 minutes.

8. After the resting period, gently perform a coil fold as directed on page 34. Cover the dough and allow it to rest for 1 to 2 hours, until you can see some fermentation bubbles and the dough has increased in volume by approximately 40 percent.

9. Cover the dough with a loose-fitting lid or plate and place in the fridge to cold proof overnight, 12 to 14 hours. This will allow the dough to fully ferment and develop some great flavours and textures. Chilling the dough also makes it a lot easier to shape.

Make the filling

10. The next morning, in the bowl of a stand mixer fitted with the paddle, combine the coconut oil, sugar, cinnamon, and cardamom, if using. Mix on low speed while you roll out the dough. This allows time for the fats, sugar, and spices to fully emulsify and makes the filling a lot easier to spread evenly.

Roll and proof

11. Lightly oil 3 extra-large muffin tins (13 × 8½ inches/ 33 × 22cm; wells 3½ inches/9cm in diameter) or 1 large deep baking pan (13 × 9 inches/33 × 23 cm) with a little coconut oil or vegetable oil.

12. Remove the dough from the fridge and transfer it to a lightly floured work surface. Roll the dough into a rectangle approximately 10 × 40 inches (25cm × 1m) and about ¼ inch (5mm) thick, with a long side facing you.

13. Using an offset spatula or spoon, evenly spread the filling to cover the dough. Starting at the long side closest to you, roll the dough up into a tight roulade. Work along like you are playing scales on the piano, moving from one side of the dough to the other. Once the dough is rolled, pat it into shape to make it neat and cylindrical.

14. With the seam side down, cut the dough with a sharp knife into about 15 pieces (approximately 170 to 180g each), wiping the blade after each cut to ensure clean-cut edges. Place the buns cut side up in the prepared tins and loosely cover with a kitchen towel or plastic bag. Let the buns sit in a warm (72 to 75°F/ 22 to 24°C), draft-free place for 1 to 2 hours, until they have doubled in size and the dough looks puffy.

Bake

15. Meanwhile, preheat the oven to 385°F (195°C) for 45 minutes.

16. Bake the buns until golden brown, 16 to 18 minutes. Allow the buns to cool in the tins for 5 minutes so they hold their shape. Remove the buns from the tins and transfer to a cooling rack set over a baking sheet to catch any glaze.

Make the glaze and brush the buns

17. In a small saucepan, combine the maple syrup, sugar, and water over medium heat. Bring to a simmer without stirring and reduce until it is tacky between the fingertips, 5 to 6 minutes. Do not over-reduce or the sugars will crystallize. Brush the cinnamon buns with a double coating of glaze. The second coating gives the buns a beautiful shine.

18. Store the cinnamon buns in an airtight container at room temperature for up to 2 days. They are best cut in half and toasted under the broiler until golden brown. This is better than heating them in the oven, where the glaze can burn and the buns can dry out.

Wild Blackberry and Walnut Sticky Buns

Makes 12 sticky buns

Sticky buns are traditionally made with baker's yeast, but we love true sourdough and try to make everything without adding yeast, so it is optional in this recipe.

The main difference between this recipe and our Sourdough Cinnamon Buns (page 157) is how we bake the sticky buns all together upside down in a pan filled with caramel and walnuts, rather than individually in muffin tins then finished with a glaze.

Blackberries grow abundantly at lower elevations, and this recipe is a delicious way to enjoy them. Pick your own blackberries if possible. Foraging is one of our most precious pastimes, but many people are nervous about harvesting plants and mushrooms, and rightly so. Blackberries are probably the easiest thing to recognize; we have great memories of getting scratched by thorns and having juicy red faces picking blackberries as kids. You can substitute seasonal berries of your choice.

Levain

40g or 50g active starter

200g warm water (75 to 78°F/24 to 26°C)

150g bread flour or all-purpose flour

50g whole wheat flour

Brioche Dough

75g ground flaxseed

800g canned full-fat coconut milk, divided

70g pure maple syrup

450g active levain (40% hydration)
   (or 30g fresh baker's yeast)

26g pure vanilla extract

15g ground cinnamon

5g ground nutmeg

285g fine whole wheat flour

845g bread flour

28g fine sea salt

170g cold vegan butter

Blackberry Chia Jam

400g wild blackberries

40g raw cane sugar

20g white chia seeds

Caramel

400g toasted walnut halves

100g vegan butter

100g coconut sugar

150g pure maple syrup

15g pure vanilla extract

"Egg" Wash

40g unsweetened soy milk

5g pure maple syrup

5g canola oil

Prepare the levain

1. Prepare the levain for this recipe following the method in the levain recipe as directed on pages 29 to 30 in the Sourdough Starter Guide. Feed the active starter early in the morning (by 7 a.m.) the day you plan to mix the dough so that it is active and tripled in size after 4 to 6 hours. Alternatively, prepare the levain with a less active starter—approximately 10 percent inoculation (10g) calculated to the total weight of flours—the night before (by 10 p.m.) so it's ready in the morning, 8 to 10 hours later.

Autolyse and mix

2. To make your flax egg, whisk together the flaxseed and 250g of the coconut milk in a medium bowl until a smooth paste forms. If there are any lumps, push a small rubber spatula against the side of the bowl to break them up. Let sit for 10 minutes to bloom and thicken.

3. Pour the remaining 550g coconut milk into the bowl of a stand mixer fitted with the dough hook. Add the maple

continued . . .

syrup, flax egg, active levain, vanilla, cinnamon, nutmeg, whole wheat flour, and bread flour and mix on medium speed until a shaggy dough forms with no dry patches, 3 minutes. Cover the bowl with a kitchen towel or loose-fitting lid and let it rest in a warm (72 to 75°F/ 22 to 24°C), draft-free place for 30 minutes (autolyse).

4. After the resting period, add the salt to the dough and mix on medium speed for 3 minutes. Continue mixing on medium speed while slowly adding the cold butter, 1 teaspoon at a time, mixing well after each addition, for 5 minutes. Stop the mixer every minute or so and scrape down the sides of the bowl. Continue mixing until all the butter is incorporated and the dough looks smooth and pulls away from the sides of the bowl, 5 more minutes. Allow the dough to rest for 1 minute.

Bulk ferment and overnight cold proof

5. Place the dough in a lightly oiled bowl or container that is four times the size of the dough and cover with a loose-fitting lid or kitchen towel. Place the dough in a warm (72 to 75°F/22 to 24°C), draft-free place. A constant temperature will ensure a consistent fermentation. Set a timer for 30 minutes.

6. When the timer goes off, perform the first set of stretch-and-folds as directed on pages 33 to 34. Again, set the timer for 30 minutes. (If you are using fresh baker's yeast, the dough will bulk ferment a lot quicker, so you will only need to perform one set of stretch-and-folds and then, after an hour's proof, proceed to the overnight cold proof.) Repeat the set of stretch-and-folds another three times over a 2-hour period, depending on how the dough feels (for a total of four timed stretch-and-folds over 3 hours). Cover with a kitchen towel or loose-fitting lid and allow the dough to rest for 45 minutes.

7. After the resting period, gently perform a coil fold as directed on page 34. Cover the dough and allow it to rest for 1 to 2 hours, until you can see some fermentation bubbles and the dough has increased in volume by approximately 40 percent.

8. Cover the dough with a loose-fitting lid or plate and place in the fridge to cold proof overnight,

12 to 14 hours. This will allow the dough to fully ferment and develop some great flavours and textures. Chilling the dough also makes it a lot easier to shape.

Make the blackberry chia jam

9. The following morning, combine the blackberries and sugar in a medium saucepan and gently simmer over low heat for 5 minutes. Stir in the chia seeds and continue to simmer and stir until the jam is thickened and a good spreadable consistency, 10 to 15 minutes. Transfer the jam to a medium bowl and let cool. Cover and keep it in the fridge until needed.

Meanwhile, toast the walnuts and make the caramel

10. Preheat the oven to 350°F (175°C). Scatter the walnuts on a small baking sheet and toast in the oven until they are golden brown, 5 minutes. Set aside.

11. Lightly oil a 13 × 9 × 2-inch (33 × 23 × 5cm) baking pan and line the bottom and sides with parchment paper.

12. Combine the butter, sugar, and maple syrup in a small saucepan and simmer, stirring, over medium heat until melted and smooth, 1 minute. Remove from the heat and stir in the vanilla, then pour it into the lined baking pan, covering the bottom entirely. Scatter the toasted walnuts evenly over the caramel and set aside.

Roll and proof

13. Remove the dough from the fridge and carefully transfer it to a floured work surface. Roll out the dough into a rectangle approximately 18 × 6 inches (45 × 15cm) and ¼ inch (5mm) deep, with a long side facing you.

14. Evenly spread the blackberry chia jam over the dough, leaving a ½-inch (1cm) border on all sides. Starting at the long side closest to you, roll the dough up into a tight roulade.

15. Using a sharp knife, cut the roll into 12 equal pieces. Place each piece cut side up in the pan on top of the walnuts, evenly spaced. Cover the pan with plastic wrap and allow to proof in a warm (72 to 75°F/22 to 24°C), draft-free area until the buns have doubled in size, 2 to 3 hours.

"Egg" wash and bake

16. An hour before baking, preheat the oven to 350°F (175°C).

17. To make the "egg" wash, in a small bowl, whisk together the soy milk, maple syrup, and canola oil. Just before baking, brush the proofed dough with the "egg" wash.

18. Bake the buns until they are golden brown and the internal temperature is above 200°F (93°C), 30 minutes.

19. Transfer the buns to a cooling rack and let them cool in the pan for 5 minutes. Do not let the buns sit too long or the caramel will cool too much and stick to the pan. Place a cutting board or serving dish on top of the pan and with a fast and confident motion, flip upside down so the walnuts are now on display. Allow the buns to cool for another 20 minutes before serving. Gently pull the buns apart to serve.

20. These buns are best eaten on the day they are baked but can be stored in an airtight container in the fridge for up to 3 days. Reheat them in the oven at 350°F (175°C) for 10 minutes.

Panettone Buns

Makes 18 buns

These buns are inspired by the flavours of the classic Italian sweet bread that takes days to make, although this version takes just two days to put together. I wanted to make this recipe as simple as possible by adding the vegan butter at the beginning rather than incorporating it once the dough had been developed. I had great results, with a super-soft and delicate crumb structure packed with almonds, citrus, and raisins. A tiny amount of saffron or turmeric gives the bread a lovely golden colour usually achieved by adding a lot of eggs, though you won't be able to taste the spice. This dough also works well as larger buns, but those take a little longer at the final proof stage. You can use store-bought candied peel or make your own following the instructions in the Note. If making your own, plan to make it at least a day in advance.

note: *To make your own candied peel, using a vegetable peeler, peel 2 lemons and 2 oranges into long strips. Cut the peels into ¼-inch (5mm) wide strips. Place the citrus peel in a small saucepan, cover with cold water, bring to a boil, and simmer for 5 minutes. Drain the water and repeat the process three more times. Then cover the citrus peel with 470g water and 200g raw cane sugar and bring to a simmer. Slowly cook for 1 hour, until the peel is very soft and translucent. Drain the peel and scatter it evenly on a baking sheet or plate to air-dry at room temperature overnight or up to 48 hours. Store in an airtight container in the fridge for up to 1 week or in the freezer for up to 1 month. Chop the peel into raisin-size pieces when needed.*

Levain

1 batch Levain (page 29)

Bun Dough

100g black raisins

100g sultana raisins

1 teaspoon saffron threads (or 1g/a pinch of ground turmeric)

40g ground flaxseed

400g unsweetened oat milk, divided

200g active levain (6 to 8 hours after feeding) (or 30g fresh baker's yeast)

125g cold vegan butter

50g pure maple syrup

25g pure vanilla extract

140g fine whole wheat flour

420g bread flour

11g fine sea salt

100g finely chopped candied peel (see Note to make your own)

40g fresh lemon juice and 10g zest

40g fresh orange juice and 10g zest

100g sliced natural almonds

25g dark rum

25g unsweetened soy milk, for brushing

Maple Glaze

50g water

25g fresh orange juice

50g coconut sugar

50g pure maple syrup

Garnishes

50g sliced, crushed natural almonds

25g pearl sugar

continued . . .

Prepare the levain

1. Prepare the levain as directed on pages 29 to 30 in the Sourdough Starter Guide. Feed the active starter early in the morning (by 7 a.m.) the day you plan to mix the dough so that it is active and tripled in size after 4 to 6 hours. Alternatively, prepare the levain with a less active starter—approximately 10 percent inoculation (10g) calculated to the total weight of flours—the night before (by 10 p.m.) so it's ready in the morning, 8 to 10 hours later.

Mix

2. Place the black raisins and sultana raisins in a medium bowl. Cover with boiling water, stir, and allow the raisins to expand and rehydrate, 1 hour. Drain the raisins, return them to the bowl, and set aside.

3. In a small bowl, soak the saffron in 10g boiling water for at least 10 minutes.

4. To make your flax egg, whisk together the flaxseed and 200g of the oat milk in a medium bowl until a smooth paste forms. If there are any lumps, push a small rubber spatula against the side of the bowl to break them up. Let sit for 10 minutes to bloom and thicken.

5. In the bowl of a stand mixer fitted with the dough hook, combine the flax egg, the remaining 200g oat milk, active levain, butter, maple syrup, vanilla, whole wheat flour, bread flour, and salt. Knead on medium speed for 5 minutes. Allow the dough to rest, uncovered, for 5 minutes. Continue kneading the dough on medium-high speed until it looks smooth and pulls away from the sides of the bowl, 8 to 10 minutes. Allow the dough to rest, uncovered, for 5 minutes.

6. Scatter the candied peel over the top of the dough, followed by the saffron (and soaking liquid), lemon zest and juice, orange zest and juice, drained raisins, almonds, and rum. Knead on medium speed or by hand for 1 minute to incorporate the ingredients into the dough.

Bulk ferment and overnight cold proof

7. Place the dough in a lightly oiled bowl or container that is four times the size of the dough and cover with a loose-fitting lid or kitchen towel. Place the dough in a warm (72 to 75°F/22 to 24°C), draft-free place. A constant temperature will ensure a consistent fermentation. Set a timer for 30 minutes.

8. When the timer goes off, perform the first set of stretch-and-folds as directed on pages 33 to 34. Again, set the timer for 30 minutes. (If you are using fresh baker's yeast, the dough will bulk ferment a lot quicker, so you will only need to perform one set of stretch-and-folds and then, after an hour's proof, proceed to the overnight cold proof.) Repeat the set of stretch-and-folds another three times over a 2-hour period, depending on how the dough feels (for a total of four timed stretch-and-folds over 3 hours). Allow the dough to rest for 45 minutes.

9. After the resting period, gently perform a coil fold as directed on page 34. Cover the dough and allow it to rest for 1 to 2 hours, until you can see some fermentation bubbles and the dough has increased in volume by approximately 50 percent.

10. Cover the dough with a loose-fitting lid or plate and place in the fridge to cold proof overnight, 12 to 18 hours. This will allow the dough to fully ferment and develop some great flavours and textures. Chilling the dough also makes it a lot easier to shape.

Shape and bake

11. The following day, lightly oil 3 large 6-cup popover tins or 3 large 6-cup straight-sided muffin tins with a little coconut oil or vegetable oil.

12. Remove the dough from the fridge and transfer it to a lightly floured work surface. Using a bench knife, divide it into 18 equal portions (100g each) and roll each into a rough ball shape. Working with 1 dough ball at a time, flatten it into a disc on a floured surface. Working from 12 o'clock, pull the dough into the centre. Keep going all the way round the disc. This shaping technique is used to strengthen the dough before its final shape. Turn the ball over and slightly cup your hands and form the dough into a ball shape (see pages 106 to 107 for shaping photos) and gently place them seam side down in the prepared tins. Cover with plastic wrap or a kitchen towel and allow the buns to proof in a warm

(72 to 75°F/22 to 24°C), draft-free place for 2 to 3 hours, until at least doubled in size.

13. Once the buns are domed, position the racks in the two upper thirds of the oven and preheat to 370°F (185°C). Spread the almonds on a small baking sheet and toast in the oven until light golden brown, 3 to 4 minutes. Set aside to cool.

14. Using a soft pastry brush, lightly brush the buns with the soy milk. Gently place them in the oven and bake until they are golden brown, 15 to 17 minutes. If you are not using a convection oven, you might need to rotate the tins top to bottom and back to front halfway through. Remove from the oven and allow the buns to cool in the tins for a few minutes. Carefully remove the buns from the tins and transfer to a cooling rack.

Make the maple glaze and garnish the buns

15. In a small saucepan, combine the water, 25g orange juice, coconut sugar, and maple syrup. Bring to a simmer and cook until reduced to a thick syrup consistency and the mixture is tacky between your fingertips, 5 to 6 minutes. Do not over-reduce or the sugars will crystallize and the glaze will be matte rather than shiny. Brush the tops of the buns with two or three layers of glaze and immediately top them with the pearl sugar and toasted almonds.

16. Store the buns in an airtight container at room temperature for up to 3 days or wrapped in plastic wrap and freeze for up to 1 month. Thaw the frozen buns at room temperature for a few hours before slicing the panettone in half and toasting under the broiler.

Chai-Spiced Pumpkin Sourdough Doughnuts Filled with Cranberry and Raspberry Jam

Makes 12 large (100g), 14 medium (85g), or 16 small (75g) doughnuts

People go crazy for doughnuts! They're one of those foods that bring back the joy of childhood and never go out of fashion. When we were growing up in England, we loved to get jam-filled doughnuts encrusted with thick white crunchy sugar, often referred to as Berliners.

We created these sourdough doughnuts for a Thanksgiving potluck, accompanied by some homemade vegan whisky cream liqueur. They were a hit! The jam is more on the tart side, which helps bring out the fruits' natural flavours. Pumpkin is naturally high in starch, so it acts as an egg replacement by emulsifying the dough. You can easily replace it with other squash or even sweet potato.

If you do not like spice, you can use *just* cane sugar for coating the doughnuts, but I highly recommend the chai spice mix as it adds so much flavour. (The doughnuts in the photograph are medium-sized.)

Levain

1 batch Levain (page 29)

Dough

250g canned full-fat coconut milk

80g extra-virgin coconut oil, melted until just liquid

75g coconut sugar or raw cane sugar

150g roasted pumpkin or squash

150g active levain (6 to 8 hours after feeding)

450g bread flour, more for dusting

50g fine stone-ground whole wheat flour

10g fine sea salt

Cranberry and Raspberry Jam

600g fresh or frozen cranberries

400g fresh or frozen raspberries

300g raw cane sugar

Zest and juice of 1 lemon

100g water

Chai-Spiced Sugar

3g anise seeds

3g cardamom seeds

3 whole cloves

15g ground cinnamon

10g ground ginger

10g garam masala

5g ground nutmeg

5g ground allspice

3g black pepper

2g cayenne pepper

250 to 500g raw cane sugar

4 to 6 quarts (4 to 6L) organic canola oil, for frying

Prepare the levain

1. Prepare the levain as directed on pages 29 to 30 in the Sourdough Starter Guide. Feed the active starter early in the morning (by 7 a.m.) the day you plan to mix the dough so that it is active and tripled in size after 4 to 6 hours. Alternatively, prepare the levain with a less active starter—approximately 10 percent inoculation (10g) calculated to the total weight of flours—the night before (by 10 p.m.) so it's ready in the morning, 8 to 10 hours later.

continued . . .

Mix and overnight cold proof

2. In the bowl of a stand mixer fitted with the dough hook, combine the coconut milk and coconut oil. Add the coconut sugar, roasted pumpkin, active levain, bread flour, and whole wheat flour. Mix on low speed until a shaggy dough forms with no dry patches, 5 minutes. Cover the dough with a kitchen towel or loose-fitting lid and allow it to rest for 10 minutes.

3. Add the salt and knead the dough on medium speed until smooth and elastic, 5 to 10 minutes. Perform the windowpane test to check if the dough is sufficiently mixed and developed: Pull away a small piece of dough and stretch it between your fingers to create a "window." If you can see light without tearing the dough, enough gluten has developed and the dough is strong. If the dough rips quite easily, continue kneading for 2 to 3 minutes longer, allow the dough to relax for a minute, then repeat the windowpane test.

4. Lightly oil a large bowl or container that is three or four times the size of the dough. Remove the dough from the mixer and form a ball or droplet shape in your hands. Place the dough smooth side up in the bowl and cover with a kitchen towel or loose-fitting lid. Allow the dough to sit in a warm (72 to 75°F/22 to 24°C), draft-free place until doubled in size, 2 to 4 hours.

5. Cover the dough with a loose-fitting lid or plate and place in the fridge to cold proof overnight, 12 to 14 hours.

Shape and proof

6. The next morning, remove the dough from the fridge. Leave the dough in the container and allow it to warm up for approximately 1 hour. This makes shaping the dough easier. Line a large baking sheet with parchment paper or a silicone baking mat.

7. Lightly flour a work surface with some bread flour. Using a bench knife or chef's knife, divide the dough into equal-size balls (100g each for large doughnuts; 85g each for medium doughnuts; 75g each for small doughnuts).

8. Working with 1 dough ball at a time, flatten it into a disc. Working from 12 o'clock, pull the dough into the centre. Keep going all the way round the disc. This shaping technique is used to strengthen the dough before its final shape. Turn the ball over and slightly cup your hands and form the dough into a ball shape (see pages 106 to 107 for shaping photos). Place the dough-nut on the lined baking sheet. Continue to shape the rest of the dough balls, leaving 2 inches (5cm) between them on the baking sheet.

9. Loosely cover the doughnuts with plastic wrap or a kitchen towel. Place the doughnuts in a warm (72 to 75°F/22 to 24°C), draft-free place until doubled in size, 2 to 3 hours. Every 20 to 30 minutes check that the cover is not sticking to the doughnuts, loosening it if necessary to allow some space and prevent damage.

Make the cranberry and raspberry jam

10. Combine the cranberries, raspberries, sugar, lemon zest and juice, and water in a medium saucepan. Cook over medium-low heat, stirring occasionally, until the fruit is reduced to a jam consistency, 15 to 20 minutes. Remove from the heat and allow the jam to cool for 5 minutes. Leave the jam as is if you prefer a textured jam or, for a smooth texture, strain the jam through a fine-mesh sieve. It's delicious either way! Transfer the jam to a piping bag fitted with a No. 6 plain tip. Set aside.

Make the chai-spiced sugar

11. In a spice grinder or mortar, blend or grind the anise seeds, cardamom seeds, and cloves into a fine powder. Add the cinnamon, ginger, garam masala, nutmeg, allspice, black pepper, and cayenne pepper and continue to blend or grind until everything is fully mixed. Transfer the spice mixture to a medium bowl. Add sugar to taste. How much sugar you add depends on how spiced you want your doughnuts to be.

Deep-fry and coat the doughnuts

12. Thirty minutes before you want to deep-fry the doughnuts, half-fill a deep-fryer or large saucepan with the canola oil and heat over medium-low heat until it reaches 345 to 350°F (174 to 175°C) on a digital probe thermometer. Set a cooling rack over a baking sheet to catch excess oil after frying.

13. Gently pick up 1 doughnut at a time with your hands and carefully place it in the hot oil. Fry the doughnuts in batches of 3 to 5 at a time. This will give the doughnuts lots of space to cook evenly and make sure the oil temperature doesn't drop (making the doughnuts greasy). Fry for 3 minutes, until they are a nice golden-brown colour on the bottom. Turn the doughnuts using a slotted spoon or wire-mesh spider and fry for another 3 minutes.

14. Using a slotted spoon or spider, remove one of the doughnuts from the hot oil and check that the internal temperature is 200°F (93°C), showing they are cooked through. Transfer the doughnuts to the cooling rack to drain excess oil.

15. Working with 1 doughnut at a time, immediately roll the doughnuts in the chai-spiced sugar to coat all over.

Return the doughnuts to the rack. Repeat to deep-fry and coat the remaining doughnuts.

Fill the doughnuts

16. Using a skewer or small knife, make a hole in the bottom or side of each doughnut and fill with the cranberry and raspberry jam. It will take a little practice to gauge how much jam to pipe into the doughnut. As you hold the doughnut with one hand and pipe with the other, you should feel it get heavier. You could also place the doughnut on a scale and precisely fill each with a set amount, approximately 35g.

17. These doughnuts are best enjoyed on the day they are made but can be stored in an airtight container at room temperature for up to 3 days.

Cakes, Muffins, and Scones

Banana, Fig, and Brazil Nut Cake

Makes one 9 × 5 × 3-inch (23 × 12 × 8cm) cake, serves 7 to 8

Bread or cake? Whatever you call it, there's no denying it's delicious! Keeping to our values of eating ethically and sustainably—even though bananas are not seasonal in Canada—I was inspired to make the best banana cake I could using second-grade organic and fair-trade very ripe bananas, thus minimizing food waste. In the winter, we must source ingredients from farther afield, so this is a winter feature at our bakery. You can use any bananas that are not green: ripe or overripe.

The coconut sugar adds a delicious caramel flavour, and the dried figs bring a chewy texture. I decided to use Brazil nuts as I'd never had them in a cake before and knew they would add another great dimension, with a crunchy bite. The lemon juice will prevent the bananas from going brown and help bring out more flavours. This cake is finished with slices of caramelized banana.

Cake

30g (¼ cup) ground flaxseed

95g (⅓ cup) unsweetened oat milk

135g (⅔ cup) cold vegan butter

135g (¾ cup + 2 teaspoons) coconut sugar or raw cane sugar, more for sprinkling

155g (1¼ cups) all-purpose flour

10g (2 teaspoons) baking powder

10g (1 teaspoon) baking soda

15g (2 tablespoons) cornstarch

3g (1 teaspoon) ground cinnamon

3g (½ teaspoon) fine sea salt

250g/½ lb very ripe bananas (2 to 3 medium) + 1 banana (to top the batter)

Juice of ½ lemon

5g (1 teaspoon) pure vanilla extract

225g (1 cup) dried figs, stems trimmed, figs cut in half

100g (¾ cup) natural Brazil nuts, coarsely chopped

Caramelized Banana (optional)

1 banana

Coconut sugar or raw cane sugar, for sprinkling

1 batch Cream Cheeze Frosting (page 183)

Make the cake

1. Preheat the oven to 325°F (160°C). Lightly coat a 9 × 5 × 3-inch (23 × 12 × 8cm) loaf pan with canola oil spray, then line the bottom and sides with parchment paper.

2. To make your flax egg, whisk together the flaxseed and oat milk in a small bowl until a smooth paste forms. If there are any lumps, push a small rubber spatula against the side of the bowl to break them up. Let sit for 10 minutes to bloom and thicken.

3. In the bowl of a stand mixer fitted with the paddle, cream the butter and coconut sugar on medium speed until smooth, light, and fluffy, 2 to 3 minutes.

4. In a medium bowl, sift together the flour, baking powder, baking soda, cornstarch, cinnamon, and salt. Whisk together and set aside.

5. In a small bowl and using a fork, lightly mash the bananas with the lemon juice until it forms a lumpy purée with some small pieces of banana for texture.

6. Add the mashed banana, vanilla, and flax egg to the mixer bowl. Mix on medium-low speed until incorporated, 1 to 2 minutes.

7. With the mixer on low speed, add the flour mixture in 3 additions, mixing after each addition until just combined and stopping to scrape down the sides of the bowl before the next addition. (Mixing on a low speed prevents gluten development.) Remove the bowl from the mixer.

8. Add the figs and Brazil nuts and mix gently with a rubber spatula or wooden spoon until they are just incorporated. Pour the batter into the prepared loaf pan and gently level the top with a spoon.

continued . . .

9. Slice the whole banana in half lengthwise. Lay the halves cut side up on top of the batter. Sprinkle the coconut sugar just on the banana halves so it caramelizes during baking. Bake until the cakes are golden brown and a skewer inserted in the centre of the cake comes out clean, 50 to 60 minutes. Allow the cake to cool in the pan for 15 to 20 minutes. Turn it out onto a cooling rack, turn right side up, and let cool for 1 hour. If making this cake in advance, store it in an airtight container in the fridge for up to 3 days. Bring the cake to room temperature and decorate with caramelized banana (if using) before serving.

Meanwhile, prepare the caramelized banana (if using)

10. Slice the banana crosswise on a slight angle into seven or eight 1-inch (2.5cm) pieces. Lay the slices on a small baking sheet and sprinkle them with coconut sugar or cane sugar. Using a kitchen torch, carefully caramelize the banana slices until golden brown. This will give them a crème brûlée texture. Allow the caramelized bananas to cool. (The caramelized banana will last for a few hours before losing its texture; only torch enough bananas for the day eaten.)

Ice the cake and finish

11. Fill a piping bag fitted with a No.6 plain tip with the cream cheeze frosting. Slice the cooled cake crosswise into 7 or 8 slices, keeping the slices together in the shape of the loaf. Pipe a little cream cheeze frosting on top of each slice. Top each slice with a piece of caramelized banana. I like to alternate which side has the cream cheeze and caramelized banana on each cake slice.

12. Store the cake, undecorated, in an airtight container at room temperature for up to 3 days or tightly wrapped in plastic wrap and freeze for up to 1 month.

Caramelized Plum and Lemongrass Upside-Down Cake

Makes one 9-inch (23cm) round cake, serves 10 to 12

An upside-down cake is baked with the toppings at the bottom. When you turn out the cake, the caramelized bottom becomes the top. The pineapple version was incredibly popular during the 1950s and '60s, so this is a bit of a retro recipe! Since pineapples are not native to Canada, we opt for plum and lemongrass, which are both grown by our local grower Seed to Culture on their magical farm in Lillooet.

This cake is one of my favourites, best served warm with a big scoop of coconut yogurt. A cast-iron skillet is ideal for an upside-down cake because the heavy metal prevents the base from burning. This cake may seem a little darker than you are used to, but don't worry because that adds extra flavour—of course, as long as it's not burnt! If you find your oven runs a bit hotter, I suggest baking at 340°F (170°C) or loosely cover the cake with foil for the last 15 minutes.

Lemongrass Powder

1 stalk of lemongrass (or 7g/2 teaspoons loose lemongrass tea)

Caramel Plum Layer

450g (2 cups) cold vegan butter

50g (⅓ cup) coconut sugar

50g (⅓ cup) raw cane sugar

2g (1 teaspoon) ground ginger

15g (1 tablespoon) unsweetened oat milk

450g/1 lb organic plums (10 to 12 plums), cut into ⅛ to ¼-inch (3 to 5mm) slices

Sponge

30g (¼ cup) ground flaxseed

155g (⅔ cup) unsweetened oat milk

240g (1 cup) unsweetened soy milk

30g (¼ cup) apple cider vinegar

175g (¾ cup) cold vegan butter

300g (1½ cups) raw cane sugar

28g (2 tablespoons) pure vanilla extract

300g (2 cups + 6 tablespoons) all-purpose flour

15g (1 tablespoon) baking powder

4g (¾ teaspoon) fine sea salt

Coconut Yogurt (page 327; optional), for serving

Make the lemongrass powder

1. Set a dehydrator to 150°F (65°C). Trim the root end from the lemongrass stalk and chop the stalk (as green as possible on the end, as this will add a more rounded flavour) into very small pieces. Spread the lemongrass pieces on the dehydrator tray. Dehydrate for 8 to 12 hours, until the lemongrass is completely dry. (Alternatively, spread the lemongrass on a baking sheet and dehydrate in the oven on the lowest setting possible until completely dry, 2 to 4 hours.)

2. In a high-speed blender, blend the dehydrated lemongrass into a fine powder. Transfer 7g (2 teaspoons) to a small bowl and set aside. The remaining lemongrass can be stored in an airtight container in the freezer for up to 1 year.

Make the caramel plum layer

3. Lightly coat a 9-inch (23cm) springform pan with canola oil spray, then line the bottom and sides with parchment paper.

continued . . .

4. In a medium saucepan, combine the butter, coconut sugar, and cane sugar and simmer, stirring, over medium heat to form an emulsified liquid, 1 minute. Remove from the heat. Using a spatula, stir in the ginger and oat milk until emulsified and smooth. Pour the caramel into the prepared springform pan and, working quickly before the caramel sets, tip the pan from side to side so the caramel covers the entire base. You can use the back of a spoon to help you out.

5. Starting in the centre of the pan, arrange the plum slices over the caramel in a tight spiral pattern, working outwards to cover the entire base. The neater and more uniform this layer is, the more structure the cake will have when turned out upside down. Set aside.

Make the sponge and bake

6. Preheat the oven to 350°F (175°C).

7. To make your flax egg, whisk together the flaxseed and oat milk in a small bowl until a smooth paste forms. If there are any lumps, push a small rubber spatula against the side of the bowl to break them up. Let sit for 10 minutes to bloom and thicken.

8. Combine the soy milk and apple cider vinegar in a small bowl. Let sit for 10 minutes to sour.

9. Meanwhile, in the bowl of a stand mixer fitted with the paddle, beat the butter and cane sugar until creamy, starting on low speed and increasing to medium, 2 to 3 minutes. Scrape down the sides and bottom of the bowl halfway through to ensure there are no lumps or dry patches.

10. Add the soured milk mixture, flax egg, and vanilla and beat for 1 minute. At this stage, the batter will probably look split, but once the dry ingredients are added, it will form a smooth batter.

11. In a medium bowl, sift together the flour, baking powder, lemongrass powder, and salt. With the mixer on medium-low speed, add the dry ingredients in 2 additions, gently mixing after each addition until a smooth batter forms, 1 minute.

12. Pour the batter over the plums and smooth the top with a small offset or rubber spatula. Bake until the cake is dark golden brown and a skewer inserted into the centre of the cake comes out clean, 55 to 60 minutes. You will have to bake this cake longer than you might think due to the moisture of the plums. Let the cake cool in the pan on a cooling rack for 10 minutes. If the cake is left in the pan too long, the caramel on the bottom will set and the cake will become stuck.

13. Place a serving plate upside down over the pan and release the sides of the pan. With the plate and pan firmly pressed together, and with a quick movement, invert the cake onto the plate. Allow to cool completely.

14. Store the cake in an airtight container in the fridge for up to 3 days. Before serving, I recommend warming the cake in the oven at 375°F (190°C) for 6 to 8 minutes to really bring out the amazing fruit and lemongrass flavours. Serve with a dollop of coconut yogurt, if using.

Espresso Coffee Cake

Makes one 9-inch (23cm) round 2-layer cake, serves 10 to 12

In the UK, coffee cake is literally a cake with coffee in it. When I was thinking of my favourite cakes to include in this cookbook, I found out that in North America coffee cake is a cake that you can eat with a cup of coffee—rather like how English tea cake does not actually contain tea but does pair well with tea.

Coffee was first cultivated in or around Ethiopia and gained popularity on the Arabian Peninsula in the sixteenth century, spreading into Europe a century or two later. The Dutch and Germans are credited with bringing the concept of drinking coffee with various cakes (such as streusel-topped cakes and Bundt cakes) to North America, a time-honoured favourite ever since. Some coffee cake recipes from the late 1800s onwards contain coffee, but not many are vegan like this one!

Coffee Frosting

125g (½ cup) cold vegan butter

250g (1½ cups + 3 tablespoons) vegan icing sugar

250g (1 cup) vegan cream cheese

30mL (2 tablespoons) dark rum or coffee liqueur

30mL (2 tablespoons) brewed espresso, cooled

5.5g (1¼ teaspoons) pure vanilla extract

Sponge

30g (3 tablespoons + ¾ teaspoon) ground flaxseed

360g (1½ cups) unsweetened soy milk

250g (1 cup + 3 tablespoons) organic canola oil

250g (1 cup) coconut sugar

2 shots brewed espresso (or 60mL/¼ cup strong coffee), cooled

28g (2 tablespoons) pure vanilla extract

5.5g (1½ teaspoons) apple cider vinegar

300g (2⅔ cups) all-purpose flour

75g (⅔ cup) stone-ground whole-grain spelt flour

10g (2 teaspoons) ground cinnamon

10g (2 teaspoons) ground espresso beans

10g (2¼ teaspoons) baking powder

10g (2 teaspoons) baking soda

4g (¾ teaspoon) fine sea salt

For decorating (optional)

Cocoa powder

Shaved dairy-free dark chocolate

Toasted whole or sliced natural almonds

Make the coffee frosting

1. In the bowl of a stand mixer fitted with the paddle, cream the butter on medium-high speed until soft, 1 to 2 minutes. Add the icing sugar and beat on medium-high speed until smooth.

2. Add the cream cheese and beat on medium-high speed until smooth and creamy, 1 to 2 minutes. Add the rum, brewed espresso, and vanilla and mix until smooth. Scrape the frosting into an airtight container and place in the fridge to set up for a couple of hours. Clean the bowl so there is no residue of coffee frosting.

continued . . .

Make the sponge and bake

3. Preheat the oven to 350°F (175°C). Lightly coat two 9-inch (23cm) springform pans with canola oil spray, then line the bottoms with parchment paper.

4. To make your flax egg, whisk together the flaxseed and soy milk in the bowl of a stand mixer until a smooth paste forms. If there are any lumps, push a small rubber spatula against the side of the bowl to break them up. Let sit for 10 minutes to bloom and thicken.

5. Whisk in the canola oil, coconut sugar, flax egg, brewed espresso, vanilla, and apple cider vinegar.

6. In a large bowl, whisk together the all-purpose flour, spelt flour, cinnamon, espresso powder, baking powder, baking soda, and salt.

7. Add the dry ingredients to the wet ingredients. Using the paddle, beat on medium speed until a smooth batter forms, 1 to 2 minutes. Stop the mixer halfway through and use a rubber spatula to scrape down the sides and bottom of the bowl to ensure there are no lumps or dry patches.

8. Divide the batter evenly between the prepared pans, about 700g per pan. Bake until a skewer inserted in the centre of the cakes comes out clean, 25 to 30 minutes. Let the cakes cool in their pans on a cooling rack for 15 to 20 minutes. Remove the ring from the pan and let the cake layers cool completely before frosting, about 60 minutes.

Assemble the cake

9. Remove the coffee frosting from the fridge. Transfer 1 cake layer to a serving plate. Using a piping bag fitted with a plain tip or an offset spatula, pipe or spread a third of the chilled coffee frosting over the cake layer. Place the other cake layer on top and lightly press it down. Pipe or spread a third of the frosting around the sides and then the remaining frosting over the top. Pipe some decorative droplets. Decorate by sifting cocoa powder or sprinkling shaved chocolate or toasted nuts over the top, if using. Place the finished cake back in the fridge for at least 30 minutes to let the frosting set.

10. Store the cake in an airtight container in the fridge for up to 5 days.

Spiced Carrot and Walnut Cake

Makes one 9 × 5 × 3-inch (23 × 12 × 8cm) cake, serves 7 to 8

Carrot cake is so ancient that historians do not quite agree on exactly where it came from, but it has enjoyed immense popularity since the Second World War in Britain, a time when carrots were used to add sweetness to cakes when sugar was being rationed.

This cake is so good that our best friends in Scotland chose it to be their wedding cake. For a delicious celebration cake, it can easily be doubled and baked in two or three 9-inch (23cm) springform pans, then layered with Cream Cheeze Frosting. It is easier to make a big batch of frosting in a stand mixer, but if you only have a hand-held electric mixer, you can halve the recipe below. Leftover icing can be stored in an airtight container in the fridge for up to 2 weeks or in the freezer for up to 1 month. The frosting should be thawed in the fridge overnight before using.

note: *Toasting the walnuts first adds a deep flavour throughout the cake. We use beautiful local carrots from Helmer's Organic Farm in Pemberton, as their sweet and fruity flavour is incredible. I highly recommend making this cake when you can find local carrots, as it will take your cake to the next level.*

Have you noticed your walnuts turning a little black inside the baked cake? Try lightly coating them in a small amount of flour, then shaking in a strainer to remove the excess flour before mixing through the batter. The vinegar and baking soda can cause a reaction that discolours the nuts. The flour acts as a barrier to prevent blackening.

Cream Cheeze Frosting
(makes enough for 2 cakes)

- 75g (¼ cup) cold vegan butter
- 125g (¾ cups) vegan icing sugar
- 125g (½ cup) vegan cream cheese

Sponge

- 250g (2½ cups) chopped walnuts
- 35g (3½ tablespoons) ground flaxseed
- 310g (1¼ cups + 1 tablespoon) unsweetened oat milk
- 100g (¼ cup + 3 tablespoons) organic canola oil
- 135g (⅔ cup) fine raw cane sugar
- 10g (2 teaspoons) pure vanilla extract
- 10g (2 teaspoons) apple cider vinegar
- 165g (1⅓ cups) all-purpose flour
- 75g (½ cup) whole wheat flour
- 7g (1½ teaspoons) baking powder
- 7g (1 teaspoon) baking soda
- 3g (a pinch) fine sea salt
- 5g (1 teaspoon) ground cinnamon
- 5g (1 teaspoon) ground ginger
- 3g (a pinch) ground nutmeg
- 250g (2¾ cups) grated unpeeled carrots
  (grated on the large holes of a box grater)

Topping

- Zest of 1 lemon (using a microplane)

Make the cream cheeze frosting

1. In the bowl of a stand mixer fitted with the paddle, beat the butter on medium-high speed until soft, 1 to 2 minutes. Add the icing sugar and continue beating on medium-high speed until smooth, 2 to 3 minutes.

2. Add the cream cheese and beat on medium-high speed, gradually increasing the speed to high until smooth, 2 to 3 minutes. Scrape the frosting into an airtight container and chill in the fridge for 2 to 3 hours.

Make the sponge and bake

3. Preheat the oven to 350°F (175°C). Lightly coat a 9 × 5 × 3-inch (23 × 12 × 8cm) loaf pan with a neutral vegetable or sunflower oil spray and line the bottom and sides with parchment paper.

continued . . .

4. Spread the walnuts on a small baking sheet and lightly toast in the oven until golden brown, 5 to 6 minutes. Let cool.

5. To make your flax egg, whisk together the flaxseed and oat milk in the bowl of a stand mixer until a smooth paste forms. If there are any lumps, push a small rubber spatula against the side of the bowl to break them up. Let sit for 10 minutes to bloom and thicken.

6. To the flax egg, add the canola oil, cane sugar, vanilla, and apple cider vinegar. Mix on medium speed with the paddle for 1 to 2 minutes to combine.

7. In a large bowl, whisk together the all-purpose flour, whole wheat flour, baking powder, baking soda, salt, cinnamon, ginger, and nutmeg.

8. Add the dry ingredients to the wet ingredients and mix on medium-low speed until just incorporated, 1 to 2 minutes.

9. Add the grated carrots and 150g (1½ cups) of the toasted walnuts (reserve the remaining walnuts for decorating). Lightly mix on low speed for 1 minute. Remove the bowl from the mixer. Using a rubber spatula, stir the batter from the bottom to check that everything is fully mixed together.

10. Scrape the batter into the prepared loaf pan and smooth the top with a rubber spatula. Bake until a skewer inserted into the centre of the cake comes out clean, 60 to 70 minutes. Let the cake cool in the pan for 15 to 20 minutes. Turn it out onto a cooling rack, turn right side up, and let cool completely, at least 60 minutes, before frosting.

Frost the cake

11. Spoon on the chilled frosting and use a small offset spatula to spread it over the top of the cake, gently swirling and decorating with as much of the frosting as you like. Sprinkle the lemon zest over the cake and finish with a generous scattering of the reserved toasted walnuts.

12. As this cake is oil-based, it's very moist and can be stored in an airtight container in the fridge for up to 5 days.

Jamaican Rum and Ginger Cake

Makes one 9 × 5 × 3-inch (23 × 12 × 8cm) cake, serves 7 to 8

Jamaica was one of the first British colonies, and ginger produced there was exported to Europe. Jamaican ginger cake, redolent of ginger, dark rich sugar, and rum, quickly became a popular dessert. This is a beautiful recipe that has gone through lots of testing not just to get the balance of flavours right, but also because I love eating it. It is not overly sweet, it is deliciously moist and sticky, and a great companion for a cup of coffee. With the ginger and spices, it does pack a punch too!

This cake is amazing as is, but other serving suggestions include topping with Cream Cheeze Frosting (page 183) or warm Vanilla Custard (page 153), or simply lightly toasting and spreading with vegan butter.

40g (⅓ cup) ground flaxseed

310g (1 cup + 1 tablespoon + ¾ teaspoon) unsweetened oat milk

150g (⅔ cup) Medjool or honey dates, pitted

150g (¾ cup) boiling water

25g (2 tablespoons) dark Jamaican rum

140g (½ cup) organic canola oil

40g (3 tablespoons) black treacle or blackstrap molasses

100g (½ cup) demerara sugar

100g (½ cup) all-purpose flour

100g (½ cup) whole wheat flour

10g (2¼ teaspoons) baking powder

10g (2 teaspoons) baking soda

25g (4½ tablespoons) ground ginger

10g (1 teaspoon) ground allspice

10g (1 teaspoon) ground cinnamon

10g (2 tablespoons) dark cocoa powder

5g (¾ teaspoon) fine sea salt

50g (¼ cup) chopped crystallized ginger

1. Preheat the oven to 325°F (160°C). Lightly grease a 9 × 5 × 3-inch (23 × 12 × 8cm) loaf pan with a neutral vegetable or sunflower oil spray, then line the bottom and sides with parchment paper.

2. To make your flax egg, whisk together the flaxseed and oat milk in a large bowl until a smooth paste forms. If there are any lumps, push a small rubber spatula against the side of the bowl to break them up. Let sit for 10 minutes to bloom and thicken.

3. Place the dates in a separate medium bowl. Pour the boiling water over the dates and stir to make sure they are all submerged. Allow the dates to rehydrate and soften, 5 to 10 minutes. Drain the dates in a fine-mesh sieve, then squeeze and crush them to remove any excess water and form a paste. If the date paste weighs more than 175g, continue to squeeze out more water, compressing them with a spoon against the sides of the sieve. Check to ensure there are no pits remaining. Transfer the paste to a small bowl and stir in the dark rum. Set the dates aside to macerate for at least 10 minutes.

4. To the flax egg combine the canola oil, treacle, demerara sugar, and date paste. Whisk together to form a creamy batter.

5. In a separate large bowl, combine the all-purpose flour, whole wheat flour, baking powder, baking soda, ground ginger, allspice, cinnamon, cocoa powder, and salt. Whisk together.

6. Add half of the dry ingredients to the wet ingredients and gently stir with a large spatula or wooden spoon until incorporated. Add the remaining dry ingredients and continue stirring until the batter is smooth with no dry lumps. Stir in the crystallized ginger until just mixed.

7. Pour the batter into the prepared loaf pan and smooth the top a little with a rubber spatula. Bake until the cake is a dark golden brown and a skewer inserted into the centre of the cake comes out clean, 60 minutes. Allow the cake to cool in the pan for 15 to 20 minutes. Turn it out onto a cooling rack, turn right side up, and let cool for at least 1 hour before slicing.

8. The cake can be stored in an airtight container in the fridge for up to 3 days.

Zucchini, Toasted Hazelnut, and Lime Cake

Makes one 9 × 5 × 3-inch (23 × 12 × 8cm) cake, serves 7 to 10

Zucchini is the Italian name used in many English-speaking countries. In the UK and of course France, however, the French word *courgette* is common. Despite their various names and near-global cultivation, all types of squash originate from the Americas.

160g (1 cup + 1 tablespoon) toasted skin-on natural hazelnuts

175g (1⅓ cups) grated zucchini (grated on the large holes of a box grater)

35g (3½ tablespoons) ground flaxseed

275g (1 cup + 1 tablespoon) unsweetened oat milk

165g (1⅓ cups) all-purpose flour

75g (½ cup) whole wheat flour

10g (1 teaspoon) baking soda

5g (1 teaspoon) baking powder

2.5g (½ teaspoon) fine sea salt

100g (¼ cup + 3 tablespoons) organic canola oil

135g (⅔ cup) raw cane sugar

10g (2 teaspoons) apple cider vinegar

10g (2 teaspoons) pure vanilla extract

Zest of 2 limes, divided

Juice of 1 lime

To finish

1 batch Cream Cheeze Frosting (page 183)

Fresh zucchini flowers (optional)

Make the cake

1. Preheat the oven to 350°F (175°C). Lightly coat a 9 × 5 × 3-inch (23 × 12 × 8cm) loaf pan with canola oil spray, then line the bottom and sides with parchment paper.

2. Spread the hazelnuts on a small baking sheet. Toast in the oven until fragrant and blistered, 5 to 7 minutes. Wrap the warm hazelnuts in a kitchen towel and rub them through the cloth to remove most of the skins. Once cooled, pulse the nuts in a food processor or roughly chop with a knife.

3. Place the grated zucchini on a kitchen towel and bring the edges together to form a ball. Squeeze out the excess liquid to prevent your batter being too wet and sinking after baking.

4. To make your flax egg, whisk together the flaxseed and oat milk in a medium bowl until a smooth paste forms. If there are any lumps, push a small rubber spatula against the side of the bowl to break them up. Let sit for 10 minutes to bloom and thicken.

5. In a large bowl, whisk together the all-purpose flour, whole wheat flour, baking soda, baking powder, and salt.

6. In a separate large bowl, whisk together the canola oil, sugar, apple cider vinegar, vanilla, the zest of 1 lime, and the lime juice. Whisk in the flax egg.

7. Using a rubber spatula or wooden spoon, gently incorporate half of the dry ingredients into the wet ingredients. Mix until smooth and no flour lumps remain. Repeat with the remaining dry ingredients. Add the grated zucchini and 130g (1 cup) of the toasted hazelnuts (reserve the remaining hazelnuts for decorating), and gently fold into the batter.

8. Scrape the batter into the prepared loaf pan, guiding the mixture with a rubber spatula and smoothing the top. Bake until the cake is cracked and a beautiful golden brown, and a skewer inserted into the centre of the cake comes out clean, 50 to 60 minutes. Let the cake cool in the pan for 20 minutes. Turn it out onto a cooling rack, turn right side up, and let cool completely for at least 1½ hours before decorating.

Frost and finish the cake

9. Using an offset spatula, evenly spread the cream cheeze frosting on top of the cake. Sprinkle the remaining lime zest over the frosting, then top with the remaining chopped hazelnuts and the zucchini flowers, if using.

10. Store the cake, without the zucchini flowers, in an airtight container in the refrigerator for up to 5 days.

Raspberry, Lemon, and Coconut Cake

Makes two 1 lb/450g cakes, or one 2 lb/900g cake, serves 14 to 16

This cake is a light and fruity favourite at our bakery, especially for Mother's Day, when you can garnish with edible flowers to give it a special springtime look. We usually bake this cake as a loaf in a medium Matfer Bourgeat Exoglass Pan (7⅞ × 3⅛ × 3⅛ inches/ 20 × 8 × 8cm), but you could use a larger loaf pan (9 × 5 × 3 inches/23 × 12 × 8cm) and bake it for 5 minutes longer than instructed. I have also made it in a Bundt pan and as a round birthday cake. It'll take 45 to 55 minutes to bake in a Bundt pan. Always check the centre of the cake with a skewer just to be sure.

This versatile cake is a crowd-pleaser for any occasion and it stays moist. Make sure to use frozen raspberries as fresh ones can result in a sunken cake. Freeze-dried raspberries also make a bright and decorative garnish and add more zest than dehydrated ones.

note: *As this cake is oil-based, it keeps extremely well, so it can be baked the day before, stored unglazed in an airtight container in the fridge, and decorated the following day.*

Sponge

350g (1½ cups) canned full-fat coconut milk

110g (½ cup) extra-virgin coconut oil

300g (2 cups) all-purpose flour

16g (1½ teaspoons) baking soda

9.5g (2 teaspoons) baking powder

250g (1 cup) raw cane sugar

50g (½ cup) unsweetened shredded coconut

3g (½ teaspoon) fine sea salt

3g (1 teaspoon) psyllium husk powder

10g (2 teaspoons) coconut extract or pure vanilla extract

15g (2½ tablespoons) lemon zest (about 4 lemons)

45g (3 tablespoons + ¾ teaspoon) lemon juice (about 2 lemons)

150g (1¼ cups) frozen raspberries (unthawed)

Toppings

80g (1½ cups) coconut ribbons

Zest of 1 lemon

200g (1⅔ cups) fresh, dehydrated, or freeze-dried raspberries (optional)

Glaze

40g (¼ cup) lemon juice

175g to 200g (about 2 cups) vegan icing sugar, sifted

Make the sponge and bake

1. Preheat the oven to 340°F (170°C). Lightly coat 2 small (1 lb/450g each) loaf pans (or one 2 lb/900g loaf pan) with a neutral vegetable or sunflower oil spray, then line the bottom and sides with parchment paper.

2. In a medium saucepan, heat the coconut milk and coconut oil over low heat until the oil is just melted. Avoid overheating the coconut oil or it will evaporate. Remove from the heat.

3. In a large bowl, sift the flour, baking soda, and baking powder. Add the cane sugar, shredded coconut, and salt. Whisk together.

4. In a medium bowl, whisk the psyllium husk powder with a small amount of the coconut milk mixture until a paste forms. Let sit for 5 minutes. Gradually whisk in the remaining coconut milk mixture until all the liquid is incorporated. Add the coconut extract, lemon zest, and lemon juice and whisk until combined, 1 minute.

5. In a small bowl, break up the frozen raspberries a little, then set aside.

6. Gently but quickly incorporate the wet ingredients into the dry ingredients using a rubber spatula or your hand. Less mixing is best—developing too much gluten will make the cake chewy and tough. Once the ingredients are just incorporated, add the frozen raspberries and give everything just a 10-second stir.

continued . . .

7. Evenly divide the batter between the prepared
1 lb/450g loaf pans (or fill one 2 lb/900g loaf pan),
smoothing the tops with a rubber spatula. Bake until
a skewer inserted in the centre of the cakes comes
out clean, 35 to 45 minutes. Allow the cakes to cool for
30 minutes in their pans. Reduce the oven temperature
to 325°F (160°C). Transfer the cakes to a cooling rack to
continue to cool for at least 1½ hours before decorating.

8. Meanwhile, spread the coconut ribbons on a small
baking sheet and bake until lightly toasted, 2 to 3 minutes.
Set the coconut aside on a plate to cool completely.

Make the glaze and decorate the cake

9. Pour the lemon juice into a medium bowl. Gradually
add the icing sugar, stirring constantly to form a thick
paste, adding the sugar until the desired thickness is
achieved.

10. Pour a line of glaze lengthwise down the centre of
the cakes and use a spoon or offset spatula to gently
push it towards the edges to form drips. Scatter the
lemon zest over the glaze, followed by the toasted
coconut ribbons and raspberries, if using.

11. Store the cakes in an airtight container in the
refrigerator for up to 5 days. Bring to room temperature
before serving.

Blueberry Muffins with a Hazelnut and Oat Crumble

Makes about 10 large muffins

Up in the BC mountains, wild blueberries grow abundantly and are a favourite food for bears. We source our organic berries from Hare's Farm in Pemberton. JD, the farmer, has the best blueberries in the world, and we get to use his second-grade underripe or overripe frozen berries throughout the winter when other local fruits are unavailable.

There is much debate on whether this is a muffin or a scone; it started as a scone recipe, but we found baking them in muffin tins ensures more consistency in size and shape. This recipe calls for large, deep muffin tins, but you could use standard muffin tins to yield 16 muffins.

Blueberry and Chia Jam

500g/1.1 lb (3 cups) fresh or frozen blueberries

250g (1 cup + 1 tablespoon) water

100g (¼ cup + 3 tablespoons) raw cane sugar

Juice of ½ lemon

25g (2 tablespoons + 1 teaspoon) white or black chia seeds

Hazelnut and Oat Crumble

50g (¼ cup) cold vegan butter

50g (¼ cup) coconut sugar or raw cane sugar

50g (½ cup) oat flakes

50g (¼ cup + 1 tablespoon) red spring wheat or whole wheat flour

50g (⅓ cup) chopped blanched natural hazelnuts

Muffin Batter

40g (¼ cup + 1 teaspoon) psyllium husk powder

400g (1½ cups + 1 tablespoon) unsweetened oat milk or soy milk

180g (¾ cup + 1 tablespoon) cold vegan butter

100g (½ cup) raw cane sugar

420g (2½ cups + 2 tablespoons) all-purpose flour

100g (½ cup + 2 tablespoons) stone-ground whole-grain spelt flour

80g (½ cup) coarse cornmeal

20g (1½ tablespoons) baking powder

3g (2 tablespoons) chopped fresh rosemary

10g (1¾ teaspoons) fine sea salt

300g (1½ cups) fresh blueberries

Garnish (optional)

A handful of fresh blueberries

Edible flowers, such as violas

Make the blueberry and chia jam

1. In a large saucepan, combine the blueberries, water, cane sugar, and lemon juice. Bring to a simmer over medium heat, stirring occasionally, and cook until the blueberries have softened and the liquid has reduced a little, 10 minutes.

2. Stir in the chia seeds and continue to simmer, stirring frequently, until a thick jam consistency is reached, 10 to 15 minutes. Transfer the jam to a bowl or container and let cool completely. The jam needs to be fully cooled before it is used; if you make it a day ahead, store in the fridge and use it straight from the fridge.

Make the hazelnut and oat crumble

3. Make this a day ahead to save time, if you wish. In a medium bowl, combine the butter, coconut sugar, oat

continued . . .

flakes, red spring wheat flour, and hazelnuts. Rub everything together with your fingertips until fully mixed and a crumbly texture. Set aside.

Make the muffin batter

4. Place an oven rack in the middle position if both muffin pans fit on one rack, or in the upper and lower thirds of the oven. Preheat the oven to 375°F (190°C). Lightly coat 10 cups of 2 large deep muffin tins with neutral vegetable or sunflower oil spray.

5. To make your egg replacer, place the psyllium husk powder in a medium bowl. Add a little oat milk and mix with a rubber spatula to form a thick paste. Add the remaining oat milk a little at a time, stirring constantly to prevent lumps, until the mixture is thick, smooth, and gummy.

6. In the bowl of a stand mixer fitted with the paddle, cream together the butter and sugar on medium speed until paler in colour, 2 to 3 minutes. Add the psyllium egg replacer and beat until emulsified, 1 to 2 minutes.

7. Sift the all-purpose flour into a large bowl. Add the spelt flour, cornmeal, baking powder, rosemary, and salt and whisk together.

8. With the mixer on low speed, add the flour mixture in 4 additions, beating after each addition until combined. Stop to scrape down the sides of the bowl as needed. (Mix on low speed so you don't develop too much gluten; overmixing will result in a chewy, rubbery muffin.)

Remove the bowl from the mixer, add the blueberries, and fold through with a rubber spatula.

Assemble and bake

9. Place the prepared muffin tin on a digital scale. Using a small spoon, portion between 150 and 160g of the batter into each large muffin cup (or 100g into each standard muffin cup). (Alternatively, divide the batter evenly among the muffin cups, filling about three-quarters full.)

10. Have a cup of warm water ready. Dip a small spoon into the water, then make a hole in the centre of each muffin about 1 inch (2.5cm) deep, wetting the spoon as needed. Fill the holes with the blueberry and chia jam. Fully cover the top of the muffins with the hazelnut and oat crumble.

11. Bake until the muffins are golden brown and a skewer inserted in the centre of a muffin comes out clean, 20 to 25 minutes. If you are not using a convection oven, you might need to rotate the pans top to bottom and front to back halfway through. Allow the muffins to cool completely in the tins for 45 to 60 minutes before removing, as they are very soft from the jam in the centre and can collapse when fresh out of the oven. Carefully remove the muffins from the tins. Just before serving, garnish with fresh blueberries and flowers, if using.

12. Store the muffins, without garnishes, in an airtight container at room temperature for up to 3 days.

Organic Pemberton Rhubarb Muffins

Makes about 10 large or 12 standard muffins

Although technically a vegetable, the tartness of rhubarb's crimson stalks makes for a delightful pie, crumble, or jam. The stalks are so pretty, especially sliced on a mandoline and then dehydrated, which gives them a translucent stained-glass-window effect. The jagged rhubarb chips snap and melt in your mouth like candy, while adding to the aesthetic grandeur of your bake! I like to garnish these with delicious sweet cicely, which is in season at the same time as rhubarb and adds a beautiful liquorice-mint flavour.

Rhubarb Chips (optional)

100g (¼ cup + 3 tablespoons) raw cane sugar

100g (¼ cup + 3 tablespoons) boiling water

2 stalks pink or red young rhubarb, cut crosswise into 3-inch (8cm) pieces

Rhubarb and Chia Jam (makes 800g/1.76 lb)

1kg/2.2 lb rhubarb, cut crosswise into ½-inch (1cm) pieces (6 cups)

250g (2 cups) water

200g (1 cup) raw cane sugar

Zest and juice of 1 lemon

50g (¼ cup + 1 tablespoon) white chia seeds

Muffin Batter

40g (¼ cup + 1 teaspoon) psyllium husk powder

400g (1½ cups + 1 tablespoon) unsweetened oat milk or soy milk

180g (¾ cup + 1 tablespoon) cold vegan butter

100g (½ cup) raw cane sugar

420g (2½ cups + 2 tablespoons) all-purpose flour

100g (½ cup + 2 tablespoons) stone-ground whole-grain spelt flour

20g (1½ tablespoons) baking powder

80g (½ cup) oat flakes, pulsed in a food processor until coarsely ground

3g (1 teaspoon) elderflower powder or chamomile powder

10g (1¾ teaspoons) fine sea salt

400g (1¼ cups) Rhubarb and Chia Jam (recipe at left), divided

1 batch Hazelnut and Oat Crumble (page 193; optional)

To finish

1 batch Cream Cheeze Frosting (page 183)

Fresh elderflower blossoms and herbs, for garnish (optional)

Make the rhubarb chips (if using; dehydrate the rhubarb up to 3 days before you plan to make the muffins)

1. Place the sugar in a medium bowl. Pour the boiling water over the sugar and stir until dissolved. Let cool completely.

2. Once the syrup is cooled, very thinly slice the rhubarb pieces lengthwise with a mandoline or vegetable peeler. Place the rhubarb in the syrup and gently stir until fully coated.

3. Set a dehydrator to 135°F (57°C). Spread the rhubarb on the dehydrator trays. Dehydrate overnight (8 to 12 hours) until the rhubarb is completely dry. (Alternatively, set the

continued . . .

oven to its lowest setting possible until completely dry, 2 to 4 hours.) Remove the rhubarb chips from the trays while they are still warm for easier removal. Let the rhubarb chips cool completely. Store in an airtight container at room temperature for up to 3 days.

Make the rhubarb and chia jam (make a few hours in advance or a day ahead)

4. In a large saucepan, combine the rhubarb, water, sugar, and lemon zest and juice. Bring to a simmer over medium heat, cover, and cook, stirring occasionally, for 15 minutes. Remove the lid and continue cooking over low heat until reduced by half and the rhubarb has softened.

5. Stir in the chia seeds and simmer, stirring constantly, until a thick jam consistency is reached, 10 to 15 minutes. Transfer the jam to a bowl or container and let cool completely. The jam needs to be fully cooled before it is used.

Make the muffin batter

6. Place an oven rack in the middle position of the oven if both muffin pans fit on one rack, or in the upper and lower thirds of the oven. Preheat the oven to 375°F (190°C). Lightly coat 10 cups of 2 large deep muffin tins with a neutral vegetable or sunflower oil spray.

7. To make your egg replacer, place the psyllium husk powder in a medium bowl. Add a little oat milk and mix with a rubber spatula to form a thick paste. Add the remaining oat milk a little at a time, stirring constantly to prevent lumps, until the mixture is thick, smooth, and gummy.

8. In the bowl of a stand mixer fitted with the paddle, cream together the butter and sugar on medium speed until paler in colour, 2 to 3 minutes. Add the psyllium egg replacer and beat until emulsified, 1 to 2 minutes.

9. Sift the all-purpose flour into a large bowl. Add the spelt flour, baking powder, ground oat flakes, elderflower powder, and salt and whisk together.

10. With the mixer on low speed, add the dry ingredients to the wet ingredient in 4 additions, beating after each addition until combined. Stop to scrape down the sides of the bowl as needed. (Mix on low speed so you don't develop too much gluten; overmixing will result in a chewy, rubbery muffin.) Remove the bowl from the mixer. Add 300g (1 cup) of the rhubarb and chia jam and fold through with a rubber spatula.

Assemble and bake

11. Place the prepared muffin tin on a digital scale. Using a small spoon, portion between 150 and 160g of the batter into each muffin cup. (Alternatively, divide the batter evenly among the muffin cups, filling about three-quarters full.)

12. Have a cup of warm water ready. Dip a small spoon into the water, then make a hole in the centre of each muffin about 1 inch (2.5cm) deep, wetting the spoon as needed. Fill the holes with the remaining 500g (2 cups) rhubarb and chia jam (50g/2½ tablespoons per muffin). Fully cover the top of the muffins with the hazelnut and oat crumble, if using.

13. Bake until the muffins are golden brown on top and a skewer inserted in the centre of a muffin comes out clean, 20 to 25 minutes. If you are not using a convection oven, you might need to rotate the pans top to bottom and front to back halfway through. Allow the muffins to cool completely in the tins for 45 to 60 minutes before removing, as they are very soft from the jam in the centre and can collapse when fresh out of the oven. Carefully remove the muffins from the tins and transfer to a cooling rack to cool completely.

Decorate

14. Once fully cooled, pipe or spoon some cream cheeze frosting on top of each muffin. Just before serving, garnish with the dehydrated rhubarb chips and fresh elderflower blossoms and herbs, if using.

15. The muffins can be stored, without rhubarb chips and blossoms, in an airtight container at room temperature for up to 3 days.

Hazelnut Madeleines

Makes 12 to 14 madeleines

A madeleine is a little shell-shaped sponge cake that is very popular in Europe. Similarly, a financier is a pocket-size almond sponge cake. Both cakes are packed with flavour and texture, but the main difference between them is that traditionally madeleines are made with whole eggs and baking powder, while financiers are made with egg whites and no added leavening. I've taken inspiration from both madeleines and financiers and created this simple and delicious recipe.

I use a Chicago Metallic 12-cup non-stick madeleine tin, but you could use a mini muffin tin. If you only have one madeleine mould or mini muffin tin, bake in two batches on the middle rack. Enjoy these very soft, delicate, and flavoursome cakes freshly baked and still a little warm.

160g (1¼ cups) skin-on natural hazelnuts
125g (½ cup) vegan butter (I recommend Miyoko's, as it will brown)
120g (1 cup) all-purpose flour, sifted
30g (¼ cup) stone-ground whole-grain spelt flour
15g (1 tablespoon) cornstarch
5g (1 teaspoon) baking powder
3g (½ teaspoon) fine sea salt
90g (⅔ cup) cold aquafaba (liquid from canned chickpeas)
110g (½ cup packed) brown sugar
28g (2 tablespoons) pure maple syrup
15g (1 tablespoon) pure vanilla extract

1. Arrange the oven racks in the upper and lower thirds of the oven and preheat to 350°F (180°C). (If using one madeleine tin and baking in two batches, place an oven rack in the middle position.) Lightly grease the madeleine moulds with coconut oil spray or vegan butter and dust them with all-purpose flour, tapping out excess.

2. Scatter the hazelnuts on a small baking sheet and lightly toast in the oven until turning golden, 5 minutes. Set aside to cool, and don't worry about removing the skins.

3. Melt the butter in a small saucepan over medium heat, stirring often, until lightly browned with a nutty aroma, 3 to 5 minutes. Set aside to cool.

4. Pulse the hazelnuts in a food processor to break them up a little, 30 seconds. Remove 50g (⅓ cup) of the nuts and set aside for the topping. Pulse the remaining hazelnuts until they are ground to a flour, about 1 minute. Add the all-purpose flour, spelt flour, cornstarch, baking powder, and salt and pulse for another 30 seconds to combine everything.

5. Pour the aquafaba into the bowl of a stand mixer fitted with the whisk. Lightly whip until soft peaks form, 2 to 3 minutes. Add the brown sugar, maple syrup, and vanilla and gently mix using a large rubber spatula.

6. Add the dry ingredients to the wet ingredients and gently fold with a spatula until a smooth batter forms. Pour the browned butter around the outer edge of the batter and fold it through with a spatula until just mixed.

7. Evenly divide the batter among the madeleine moulds with a spoon, about 25g per mould; it should rise two-thirds of the way up the sides of the moulds. Top the batter with a sprinkle of the reserved chopped hazelnuts. Bake the madeleines until golden brown, 10 to 12 minutes. (If baking on two racks, rotate the tins halfway through.) Let cool in the tins on a cooling rack for 10 minutes. Carefully remove the madeleines from the moulds and return them to the cooling rack to cool completely.

8. If baking a second batch, wipe out the madeleine tin with a dry cloth and coat with coconut oil or vegan butter and dust them with all-purpose flour, tapping out excess as you did in step 1. Bake the remaining madeleines in the same pan.

9. Store the madeleines in an airtight container at room temperature for up to 3 days.

Kimchi, Green Onion, and Cilantro Scones

Makes 8 to 10 scones

Kimchi is salted and fermented cabbage—a bit like a Korean spicy sauerkraut—that's used in many dishes or as a condiment. The fact that I love kimchi is probably no surprise, since I love every fermented food, but I especially enjoy spicy fermented cabbage! For this recipe, I made my own kimchi and fermented it for three months in our fridge, but this isn't necessary as there are plenty of amazing artisan producers around the world making incredible variations of it. If you are not a fan of spice or kimchi, I have made these scones with sauerkraut and dill instead, and they were just as delicious! I love to eat these scones still warm from the oven with a little vegan butter or lightly toasted the following day.

Scones

110g (½ cup) vegan butter

450g (3 cups) all-purpose flour

40g (2 tablespoons + 2¼ teaspoons) baking powder

5g (1 teaspoon) fine sea salt

1.5g (¼ teaspoon) cayenne pepper

25g (5 teaspoons) nutritional yeast

200g (1⅓ cups) kimchi, patted dry to remove excess liquid and roughly chopped

50g (¾ cup) thinly sliced green onions (all parts; about 5 onions)

20g (1 cup) finely chopped fresh cilantro stems and leaves

200g (¾ cup + 1 tablespoon) unsweetened soy milk

Glaze

20g (1 tablespoon + 1 teaspoon) unsweetened soy milk

2g (1 teaspoon) dry mustard

Make the scones

1. Cut the butter into ¼-inch (5mm) cubes and freeze until needed.

2. Preheat the oven to 350°F (175°C). Line a large baking sheet with parchment paper or a silicone baking mat.

3. Sift together the flour, baking powder, salt, and cayenne pepper into a large bowl. Add the nutritional yeast and whisk everything together.

4. Add the frozen butter. Using your fingertips, rub the butter into the flour until the mixture is like breadcrumbs. Add the kimchi, green onion, cilantro, and soy milk. Using one hand while the other hand holds the bowl still, gently incorporate everything together just until a soft dough forms and no dry patches remain. Do not overmix.

5. Lightly flour your work surface and the dough. Roll out the dough into a rectangle ¾ to 1 inch (2 to 2.5cm) thick. Using a large chef's knife, cut the dough crosswise into 4 rectangles, then cut each rectangle diagonally to make 8 equal-size triangles. Arrange them upside down on the lined baking sheet, leaving a little space between them to allow for growth and even baking. (The side that was on the work surface becomes the top, which helps with the rise and creates a nicer finished appearance.)

Glaze and bake

6. In a small bowl, stir together the soy milk and mustard. Using a pastry brush, lightly brush the tops of the scones with the glaze a couple of times.

7. Bake until golden brown on top, 15 to 17 minutes. Transfer the scones to a cooling rack to cool for at least 10 minutes before serving.

8. Store the scones in an airtight container in the fridge for up to 3 days.

Macadamia Feta and Herb Scones (Biscuits)

Makes 8 to 10 scones

You have got to love the English language for its various dialects and cultural differences! Here is a case in point: a British biscuit is what North Americans call a cookie, but biscuits in North America are more like British scones. Is there a difference between an American biscuit and a British scone? A southern biscuit has more butter and acidity from buttermilk, making them flakier and fluffier, while scones rely on richer ingredients, like cream and eggs, to get a sturdy yet crumbly texture. Given that I am vegan, so do not use any dairy or eggs, this recipe is a cross between a biscuit and a scone. Call it as you please!

I've used my Macadamia Feta (page 343) in this recipe to add a delicious creamy flavour and wonderful softness to the scones. The feta brings the slight acidity you would get from buttermilk and works with the soy milk as an egg replacer. I love to add a few different herbs for their flavour, aroma, and appearance. These scones are best served warm or lightly toasted with some extra feta, sliced pickled onions, herbs, and arugula, or simply with some vegan butter.

Scones

110g (½ cup) cold vegan butter

400g (2½ cups) all-purpose flour

40g (2 tablespoons + 2¼ teaspoons) baking powder

50g (⅓ cup) stone-ground whole-grain spelt flour

25g (½ cup) nutritional yeast

5g (1 teaspoon) fine sea salt

2.5g (½ teaspoon) cracked black pepper

250g (1 cup) unsweetened soy milk

200g (1¾ cups) Macadamia Feta (page 343),
    cut into ¼-inch (5mm) cubes

50g (⅔ cup) finely chopped fresh herbs
    (such as dill, parsley, and chives)

Glaze

20g (1 tablespoon + 2 teaspoons) unsweetened
    soy milk

5g (1 teaspoon) pure maple syrup

2.5g (½ teaspoon) olive oil

Make the scones

1. Cut the butter into ¼-inch (5mm) cubes and freeze until needed.

2. Preheat the oven to 350°F (175°C). Line a large baking sheet with parchment paper or a silicone baking mat.

3. Sift together the all-purpose flour and baking powder into a large bowl. Add the spelt flour, nutritional yeast, salt, and pepper and whisk everything together.

4. Add the frozen butter. Using your fingertips, rub the butter into the flour until the mixture looks like bread-crumbs. Add the soy milk, macadamia feta, and chopped herbs. Using one hand while the other hand holds the bowl still, gently incorporate everything together just until a soft dough forms and no dry patches remain. Do not overmix.

5. Lightly flour the work surface and the dough. Roll out the dough into a rectangle ¾ to 1 inch (2 to 2.5cm) thick. Using a large chef's knife, cut the dough crosswise into 4 rectangles, then cut each rectangle diagonally to make 8 equal-size triangles. Arrange them upside down on the lined baking sheet, leaving a little space between them to allow for growth and even baking. (The side that was on the work surface becomes the top, which helps with the rise and a nicer finished appearance.)

Glaze and bake

6. In a small bowl, stir together the soy milk, maple syrup, and olive oil. Using a pastry brush, lightly brush the tops of the scones a couple of times.

7. Bake until the tops are golden brown, 15 to 17 minutes. Transfer the scones to a cooling rack to cool for at least 10 minutes before serving.

8. Store in an airtight container in the fridge for up to 3 days. Lightly toast before serving.

Biscuits, Cookies, and Tarts

Anzac Cookies

Makes 14 cookies

ANZAC is the acronym for the Australia and New Zealand Army Corps. Each year Anzac Day, April 25, marks the anniversary of the first major military action fought by Australian and New Zealand forces during the First World War, in 1915. The original Anzac cookie was created by the soldiers' wives, with the idea being that the biscuits would stay fresh for weeks: they took so long to reach their husbands overseas. Because they were baked for longer, they were very crunchy, and apparently ground up by the soldiers and added to their porridge. I mean, why not have a cookie for breakfast?

When my wife, Natasha, and I lived and worked in Australia, we loved these cookies. Whistler generally has a large Australian community too, so these cookies are a home comfort to many of the seasonal workers in the resort town. Anzac cookies are one of my favourites as they tick all the boxes: not too sweet, crunchy, soft, chewy, and easy to make.

400g (2 cups packed) brown sugar

250g (1 cup + 2 tablespoons) vegan butter

100g (¼ cup) golden syrup

300g (2 cups) red spring wheat flour or
   whole wheat flour

225g (2½ cups) oat flakes

100g (1½ cups) unsweetened coconut flakes

5g (1 teaspoon) baking soda

40g (3 tablespoons) unsweetened oat milk

1. Line 3 large baking sheets with parchment paper or silicone baking mats.

2. In a medium saucepan, combine the brown sugar, butter, and golden syrup and gently melt over low heat. This will only take a couple of minutes. It does not need to be hot, just melted to a liquid.

3. In a large bowl, mix together the flour, oat flakes, coconut flakes, and baking soda. Add the melted butter mixture. Switch to your hands and mix just until a dough forms. Do not overmix.

4. Weigh the dough into 100g portions (or use a 3½ oz/ 100g ice cream scoop), then roll into balls between your palms. Place the balls on the lined baking sheet and slightly flatten each ball into a 2½-inch (6cm) circle, ¾ inch (2cm) thick, leaving about 2 inches (5cm) between them as they will spread during baking.

5. Transfer the sheets to the fridge and chill for at least 1 hour to allow the dough to rest and set into its new shape. (Chilling solidifies the fats in the dough, so as the cookies bake, the fat takes longer to melt.)

6. When ready to bake, arrange the oven racks in the upper and lower thirds of the oven and preheat to 325°F (160°C).

7. Remove 2 sheets of cookies from the fridge and immediately transfer to the oven. Bake until golden brown all over, 14 to 17 minutes. The baking time may vary depending on your oven; we bake for 17 minutes, which results in a beautiful crunchy exterior and soft middle, the perfect balance for this cookie. If you are not using a convection oven, you may need to rotate the cookies halfway through. Allow the cookies to cool on the baking sheets for at least 30 minutes. Meanwhile, reposition the top rack to the middle of the oven and bake the third sheet of cookies.

8. Store the cookies in an airtight container at room temperature for up to 5 days.

Dark Chocolate, Oat, and Sea Salt Cookies

Makes 12 cookies

These dark chocolate cookies have been on offer at the bakery since we opened our doors. This must tell you how good they are! Investing in high-quality ingredients, such as the chocolate, will elevate these cookies to a higher level. We use Callebaut 70.5% extra bitter chocolate chips, as I like the balance of the bitterness of the chocolate with the sweetness from the cane sugar. This company has improved their efforts in sourcing sustainable and ethical cocoa in recent years. We recommend using fair-trade chocolate so you can feel good when it tastes good.

The espresso is used to add more flavour, like a spice with its complex flavour profile. Nobody has ever commented on the subtle taste of the coffee in these extremely popular cookies. I also like to finish them with a sprinkle of sea salt flakes from Vancouver Island Salt Company. This helps bring out more flavours from the cinnamon and grains and adds a nice contrast.

15g (1 tablespoon + ¾ teaspoon) ground flaxseed

40g (3 tablespoons) unsweetened oat milk

300g (1¼ cups + 2 tablespoons) cold vegan butter

265g (1 cup) raw cane sugar

85g (1 cup) unsweetened shredded coconut

5g (1 teaspoon) pure vanilla extract

230g (1¾ cups) stone-ground whole wheat flour

215g (2½ cups) rolled quick-cooking oats

10g (2 tablespoons) ground espresso beans

15g (1½ teaspoons) baking soda

5g (1 teaspoon) baking powder

3g (1 teaspoon) ground cinnamon

1.5g (¼ teaspoon) fine sea salt

335g (2 cups + 2 tablespoons) 70% dairy-free dark chocolate chips

7g (1 teaspoon) flaky sea salt, for sprinkling

1. To make your flax egg, whisk together the flaxseed and oat milk in a medium bowl until a smooth paste forms. If there are any lumps, push a small rubber spatula against the side of the bowl to break them up. Let sit for 10 minutes to thicken and bloom.

2. In the bowl of a stand mixer fitted with the paddle, cream together the butter and sugar on medium speed until paler, 3 to 5 minutes.

3. Add the coconut, vanilla, and flax egg and beat on medium speed until slightly creamy, 2 minutes.

4. In a large bowl, whisk together the flour, oats, espresso, baking soda, baking powder, cinnamon, and fine salt.

5. Gradually add the flour mixture to the wet ingredients, gently mixing with your hand. Be careful not to overmix the dough or the cookies will be tough and chewy.

6. Add the chocolate chips and mix them with your hand until they are evenly distributed.

7. Cover the bowl and chill the cookie dough for 30 minutes. This will firm up the dough and make weighing and shaping easier and less messy.

8. Line 2 large baking sheets with parchment paper or silicone baking mats. Divide the dough into 12 equal portions (125g/4.4 oz each), and using your hands, roll the dough into balls. On a work surface, use your hands to shape the balls into 3 to 4-inch (8 to 10cm) discs, about ½ inch (1cm) thick. Arrange 6 cookies on each lined baking sheet, leaving ample space between them. Place the sheets in the fridge to chill the cookies for at least 1 hour or overnight before baking.

9. When ready to bake, arrange the oven racks in the upper and lower thirds of the oven and preheat to 350°F (175°C).

10. Bake the cookies until they are golden brown all over, 14 to 16 minutes. If you are not using a convection oven, you may need to rotate the cookies halfway through. Remove the cookies from the oven and immediately sprinkle the flaky sea salt over them so that it sticks to the melted chocolate. Allow the cookies to cool on the baking sheet for at least 30 minutes before transferring to cooling racks.

11. Store the cookies in an airtight container at room temperature for up to 2 days or in the fridge for up to 3 days.

Cocoa Nib, Orange, Chocolate, and Black Pepper Drop Cookies

Makes 16 to 18 cookies

These easy drop cookies can be pulled together in no time. The name "drop cookie" refers to the technique of dropping batter onto a baking sheet. Using a blended whole orange gives a brownie-like cake texture and prevents waste. Adding black pepper gives the chocolate a subtle spicy kick. Red chili flakes also work well.

Because of the cocoa powder, it's harder to judge when these cookies are done. To nail your timing, you could bake one or two cookies first.

2 medium oranges (300g/10.5 oz total)

300g (1⅓ cups) cold vegan butter

140g (⅔ cup) raw cane sugar

140g (⅔ cup) coconut sugar

155g (⅔ cup) unsweetened oat milk

20g (4 teaspoons) pure vanilla extract

500g (4 cups) all-purpose flour

100g (⅔ cup) stone-ground whole-grain spelt flour

50g (½ cup) dark cocoa powder, sifted

10g (2 teaspoons) baking powder

10g (2 teaspoons) baking soda

10g (2 teaspoons) freshly ground black pepper

5g (1 teaspoon) fine sea salt

100g (¾ cup) cocoa nibs

For decorating

150g (1 cup) dairy-free dark chocolate, chopped

Zest of 1 orange, dehydrated

50g (⅓ cup + 1 tablespoon) cocoa nibs

7g (1 teaspoon) flaky sea salt

1. Arrange the oven racks in the upper and lower thirds of the oven and preheat to 340°F (170°C). Line 2 large baking sheets with parchment paper or silicone baking mats.

2. Trim the ends off the oranges, cut them into quarters, and remove any seeds. Place the oranges in a food processor and pulse until a rough purée forms, 1 minute. Having some small pieces of zest is fine. Set aside.

3. In the bowl of a stand mixer fitted with the paddle, cream together the butter, cane sugar, and coconut sugar on medium speed until well incorporated and paler, 3 to 4 minutes. Stop the mixer and scrape down the sides and bottom of the bowl with a rubber spatula as needed to help everything fully combine.

4. Add the oat milk, vanilla, all-purpose flour, spelt flour, cocoa powder, baking powder, baking soda, pepper, fine salt, and cocoa nibs. Gently mix on low speed just until a thick batter forms. Don't overmix or the cookies will be tough and chewy.

5. Have a small bowl of water ready. Dip a small spoon or 2.5 oz (70g) ice cream scoop into the water to prevent sticking, then drop 16 to 18 even-sized scoops of the batter onto the lined baking sheets, leaving 2 inches (5cm) between them. (Alternatively, use a scale to weigh 100g/3.5 oz portions of dough to ensure consistency. Shape the batter into balls and place on the lined baking sheet. Lightly press the tops of the cookies with the back of a spoon until ½ inch/1cm thick.)

6. Bake the cookies for 10 to 12 minutes. You want them slightly underbaked, with an almost brownie texture. The cookies will continue baking after they're removed from the oven. If you are not using a convection oven, you may need to rotate the cookies halfway through. Avoid overbaking, or the cookies will dry out. Gently transfer the cookies to a cooling rack to cool completely.

7. To decorate the cooled cookies, melt the dark chocolate over a double boiler and drizzle it over each cookie, then sprinkle with dehydrated orange zest, cocoa nibs, and flaky sea salt.

8. Store the cookies in an airtight container in the fridge for up to 2 days.

Fig, Almond, and Anise Cookies

Makes 12 cookies

For our honeymoon, Natasha and I ventured to Banff, Alberta, home of the Wild Flour Bakery. While they are not a plant-based bakery per se, they did have the most incredible vegan fig and anise cookies. We couldn't get enough of them! This recipe is an homage to that cookie.

The flavour and texture combination of the aromatic anise seeds, sweet, slightly floral, and chewy dried figs, and the nutty almond crunch is so moreish, you will be coming back for a second, then a third . . .

25g (3½ tablespoons) ground flaxseed

65g (¼ cup) unsweetened soy milk

350g (1½ cups) cold vegan butter

350g (1¾ cups) demerara sugar

20g (1½ tablespoons) pure vanilla extract

175g (1½ cups) all-purpose flour, divided

175g (1¾ cups) stone-ground whole wheat flour, divided

20g (¼ cup) anise seeds

10g (2 teaspoons) baking powder

5g (1 teaspoon) fine sea salt

150g (1 cup) sliced natural almonds

180g (1 cup + 2 tablespoons) chopped dried Mission figs

For decorating

120g (⅓ cup) sliced natural almonds

6 dried Mission figs, stems trimmed, figs cut in half lengthwise

1. To make your flax egg, whisk together the flaxseed and soy milk in a small bowl until a smooth paste forms. If there are any lumps, push a small rubber spatula against the side of the bowl to break them up. Let sit for 10 minutes.

2. In the bowl of a stand mixer fitted with the paddle, cream together the butter and demerara sugar on medium speed until it is smooth and paler, 4 to 5 minutes. Add the vanilla and flax egg and beat for 1 minute.

3. Add about half of the all-purpose flour, about half of the whole wheat flour, the anise seeds, baking powder, and salt. Mix until just incorporated. Add the remaining all-purpose flour and whole wheat flour and mix until just combined. Add the almonds and figs and mix until everything is combined. Cover the bowl and chill in the fridge for at least 4 hours or overnight. This will firm up the dough and make weighing and shaping easier and less messy.

4. Line 2 large baking sheets with parchment paper or silicone baking mats. Use your hands to form the chilled dough into 3-inch (8cm) balls (100g/3.5 oz each) and slightly flatten them. Arrange 6 cookies on each lined baking sheet, evenly spaced to allow for spreading. Lightly cover the baking sheet with plastic wrap and chill in the fridge for at least 1 hour or overnight before baking.

5. When ready to bake the cookies, arrange the oven racks in the upper and lower thirds of the oven and preheat to 350°F (175°C).

6. To decorate the cookies, place the sliced almonds in a bowl. Drop each cookie into the bowl to coat all over with almonds. Return it to the baking sheet and top with a fig half. Bake the cookies until they are golden brown on top, 10 to 12 minutes. If you are not using a convection oven, you may need to rotate the cookies halfway through.

7. Store the cookies in an airtight container in a cool, dry place for up to 3 days

Ginger and Molasses Cookies

Makes 14 cookies

Warming, sweet, crunchy, chewy, and moreish, these cookies are a favourite of ours when the weather starts to turn in the autumn. I think it's the delicious complex flavour that comes from the molasses—a syrup derived from brown sugar that is used in making rum.

As soon as I tasted Seed to Culture's locally grown organic ginger, I wanted to use it in my bakes. I thought a ginger cookie was the best way to celebrate this amazing plant. You can absolutely use store-bought ground ginger, but you really must try making your own. It's a revelation! The flavour is floral and familiar but has so many levels. See the Note for how to dehydrate fresh ginger and blend into a powder.

note: To make your own ground ginger, set a dehydrator to 140°F (60°C). If your fresh ginger has a thin skin, there is no need to peel it, but if the skin is thick, then peel it first. Finely chop the ginger, or grate on the large holes of a box grater. Spread the grated ginger on a dehydrator tray lined with parchment paper or a silicone baking mat. Dehydrate for 24 hours, until the ginger is completely dry. Alternatively, place the grated ginger on a baking sheet and dehydrate in the oven on the lowest setting possible for 1 to 2 hours, until completely dry. Blend the dehydrated ginger on high speed in a spice grinder or liquidizer to a fine powder. Store the ground ginger in an airtight container in the freezer for up to 3 months to keep it fresh. Use in any recipes where ground ginger is called for.

340g (1½ cups + 1 tablespoon) cold vegan butter
250g (1¼ cups loosely packed) brown sugar
150g (½ cup) blackstrap molasses
125g (½ cup) pure maple syrup
20g (1½ tablespoons) pure vanilla extract
585g (4¼ cups) all-purpose flour
20g (1 tablespoon) baking soda

25g (5 tablespoons) ground ginger
 (or 100g/3.5 oz/1 cup dehydrated ginger, ground)
15g (2 tablespoons) ground cinnamon
7g (3 teaspoons) ground nutmeg
5g (1 teaspoon) fine sea salt
100g (½ cup) raw cane sugar, for rolling

1. In the bowl of a stand mixer fitted with the paddle, cream together the butter and brown sugar on medium speed until smooth, 2 to 3 minutes.
2. Add the molasses, maple syrup, and vanilla and beat on medium-low speed until fully combined. Stop the mixer and scrape down the sides and bottom of the bowl with a rubber spatula as needed to ensure thorough mixing.
3. In a large bowl, sift together the flour, baking soda, ginger, cinnamon, nutmeg, and salt. Whisk to combine.
4. Add half of the dry ingredients to the wet ingredients and mix on low speed to combine. Add the remaining dry ingredients and mix on low speed until fully incorporated, 1 to 2 minutes. Stop the mixer and scrape down the bottom and sides of the bowl with a rubber spatula as needed to fully mix all the ingredients. Cover the bowl and chill in the fridge for 1 hour. This will firm up the dough and make weighing and shaping easier and less messy.
5. Line 2 large baking sheets with parchment paper or silicone baking mats. Have a small bowl of water ready. Divide the dough evenly into 14 balls (about 110g/3.9 oz each). Roll each ball in your palms to achieve a smooth finish, using a little water on your hands to prevent sticking. Slightly flatten the balls into discs about 1 inch (2.5cm) thick.
6. Arrange the cookies on the lined baking sheets and chill in the fridge for at least 1 hour but ideally overnight. (Unbaked cookies can be stored in an airtight container in the fridge for up to 3 days before baking or in the freezer for up to 1 month. If frozen, defrost the cookies in the fridge for 8 to 10 hours or overnight before baking.)

continued . . .

7. When ready to bake, arrange the oven racks in the upper and lower thirds of the oven and preheat to 340°F (170°C).

8. Place the cane sugar in a medium bowl and roll the cookies in the sugar. Return the coated cookies to the baking sheet, leaving 2 inches (5cm) between them to allow for spreading. Bake the cookies until they are cracking and dark brown on top, 14 to 16 minutes. If you are not using a convection oven, you may need to rotate the cookies halfway through. Allow the cookies to cool completely on the baking sheets.

9. These cookies are best enjoyed on the day of baking but can be stored in an airtight container in a cool, dry place for up to 3 days.

Peanut Butter and Strawberry Jam Cookies

Makes 20 cookies

One of the first recipes for a peanut butter and jelly sandwich appeared in the *Boston Cooking School Magazine* in 1901. When I was a child, it was my favourite sandwich for my packed lunch. Coincidentally, my mother worked in Boston in the 1970s, and maybe that's where she was inspired to make these sandwiches for her four children years later. As a flavour combination, it's not surprising all ages love this salty, crunchy, sweet, fruity combination, in a sandwich or in these delicious cookies.

Strawberry Jam

300g (2 cups) hulled and diced organic strawberries

30g (2 tablespoons) raw cane sugar

55g (¼ cup) water

Juice of 1 lemon

Cookie Dough

30g (4½ tablespoons) ground flaxseed

80g (⅓ cup) unsweetened oat milk

227g (1 cup) cold vegan butter

100g (½ cup) raw cane sugar

300g (1½ cups packed) light brown sugar

500g (2 cups) organic natural crunchy peanut butter

16g (4 teaspoons) pure vanilla extract

9.6g (2 teaspoons) baking soda

1.3g (¼ teaspoon) fine sea salt (optional)

310g (2½ cups) all-purpose flour

50g (½ cup) fine whole wheat flour

150g (1 cup) unsalted roasted peanuts

Make the strawberry jam

1. Combine the strawberries, cane sugar, water, and lemon juice in a small saucepan. Bring to a simmer over medium-high heat, stirring frequently, until a jam consistency is achieved, 15 minutes. Crush the fruit with a fork to break down any larger pieces. Pour the jam into a small bowl and chill in the fridge for 1 hour. This will make it easier to work with to fill the cookie dough.

Make the cookie dough

2. To make your flax egg, whisk together the flaxseed and oat milk in a medium bowl until a smooth paste forms. If there are any lumps, push a small rubber spatula against the side of the bowl to break them up. Let it sit for 10 minutes to bloom and thicken.

3. In a stand mixer fitted with the paddle, cream together the butter, cane sugar, and brown sugar on medium speed until smooth and paler, 2 to 3 minutes. Scrape the bottom of the bowl with a rubber spatula to make sure the butter is fully incorporated. Add the peanut butter, vanilla, and flax egg and beat on medium speed until smooth, about 2 minutes.

4. Add the baking soda, salt (if using), all-purpose flour, and whole wheat flour. Mix on low speed until just combined. Scrape down the sides and bottom of the bowl with a rubber spatula to ensure the mixture is emulsified. Do not overmix, or the cookies will be tough. Cover and chill in the fridge for 30 minutes. This will firm up the dough and make weighing and shaping easier and less messy.

Shape the cookies

5. Have a small bowl of water ready. Line 2 large baking sheets with parchment paper or silicone baking mats. Using wet hands (the dough is very sticky), shape the dough into 20 balls (100g/3.5 oz each). You can use a medium cookie scoop, but I find using your hands works

continued . . .

better as it compresses the dough more. Arrange the dough balls on the lined baking sheets, leaving 3 inches (8cm) between them. Flatten the balls to ½ inch (1cm) thickness to make filling easier. Return the cookies to the fridge for 10 minutes.

Fill the cookies

6. Remove the strawberry jam and the dough discs from the fridge. Use your hands to mould the dough into a bowl shape large enough to hold 1 teaspoon of jam. Spoon the cold jam into each well, then carefully form the cookie dough around the filling and seal closed. Return the filled cookies to the baking sheets. Return to the fridge to chill for 30 to 45 minutes.

Bake the cookies

7. Meanwhile, arrange the oven racks in the upper and lower thirds of the oven and preheat to 340°F (170°C).

8. Pulse the peanuts in a food processor for a few seconds to break them up, then transfer to a medium bowl.

9. Roll the chilled cookies in the chopped peanuts. Return the coated cookies seam side down to the baking sheets, spacing them 3 inches (8cm) apart to allow for spreading. Bake the cookies until golden brown on the bottom, 13 to 15 minutes. If you are not using a convection oven, you may need to rotate the cookies halfway through. They will be very soft coming out of the oven. Allow the cookies to cool on the baking sheets for 5 to 10 minutes before transferring to a cooling rack to cool completely.

10. Store the cookies in an airtight container in a cool, dry place for up to 3 days.

Scottish Shortbread

Makes 12 cookies

My grandparents were from Scotland, where shortbread is traditionally given at weddings and to the "first footers" of New Year. My grandfather passed on while I was writing this book, and shortbread was the last Christmas gift I ever gave him. Shortbread itself goes back at least to the time of Mary, Queen of Scots, who liked it with caraway seeds in, apparently.

Shortbread is butter-heavy by nature, and it is rare to find plant-based shortbread anywhere, though good-quality vegan butter makes for an excellent cruelty-free version of this classic biscuit. We opt for Earth Balance, as they source from Roundtable on Sustainable Palm Oil organizations, and it is easily available in BC, but there are other palm-free vegan butters out there that you could use instead, such as Naturli' or Miyoko's. The goal is a buttery texture that melts in your mouth but is soft and crumbly at the same time.

This shortbread is best the day it is baked, so I like to cut and bake only as many as I need at one time, and keep the remaining dough refrigerated.

> 500g (2¼ cups) cold vegan butter
> 250g (1½ cups) vegan icing sugar
> 250g (2 cups + 1 tablespoon) cornstarch
> 250g (2 cups) red spring wheat flour or
>   whole wheat flour
> 250g (1½ cups + 1 tablespoon) all-purpose
>   flour, sifted
> 10g (2 teaspoons) fine sea salt

Make the dough

1. In the bowl of a stand mixer fitted with the paddle, cream together the butter and icing sugar on medium speed until smooth and paler, 2 to 3 minutes. Scrape the bottom of the bowl with a rubber spatula to make sure the butter is fully incorporated with the sugar.

2. Add the cornstarch and any flavour additions (see page 225) and beat until combined, 1 minute.

3. In a medium bowl, whisk together the red spring wheat flour, sifted all-purpose flour, and salt. Add half of the dry ingredients to the wet ingredients and stir on low speed for 30 seconds. Add the remaining dry ingredients and stir just until a smooth paste forms. Avoid over-mixing, which will develop the gluten in the flour and result in tough shortbread.

Shape the dough and chill

4. Place the cookie dough in the centre of a piece of parchment paper or plastic wrap. Fold one end of the parchment towards you over the dough. Holding a bench knife nearly parallel to the work surface and angled slightly downward, push towards the dough, forcing it into a log in the parchment. The log should be 3 inches (8cm) in diameter.

5. Place the log in the fridge for at least 8 hours or up to 5 days. If there is space in the fridge, it is best to hang the log to prevent any flat sides. I find this is more achievable if the log is wrapped in plastic rather than parchment paper. Otherwise, roll a kitchen towel around the wrapped log to provide some padding, then lay the log on a shelf.

Bake the cookies

6. About 45 minutes before you plan to bake the cookies, arrange the oven racks in the upper and lower thirds of the oven and preheat to 350°F (175°C). Line 2 large baking sheets with parchment paper or silicone baking mats.

7. Remove the shortbread log from the fridge and unwrap it. Cut the log crosswise on a cutting board into slices about ½ inch (1cm) thick. Arrange the cookies on the lined baking sheets, leaving 2 inches (5cm) between them to allow for even baking. (Typically, these cookies don't spread.)

8. Bake the cookies until lightly golden brown on top, 10 to 12 minutes. If you are not using a convection oven,

continued . . .

you may need to rotate the cookies halfway through. If they have spread a little, while they are still hot, use a cookie cutter to trim the edges. This step isn't necessary but will make the biscuits uniform and tidy.

Allow the shortbread to cool on the baking sheet for 1 hour.

9. Store the shortbread in an airtight container in a cool, dry place for up to 3 days.

Shortbread Flavour Variations

Lemon and Thyme

> Zest of 2 lemons
> Juice of 1 lemon
> 7g (3 tablespoons) fresh thyme leaves,
>   finely chopped

Add the ingredients to the creamed butter and sugar along with the cornstarch.

....

Orange and Poppy Seed

> Zest of 2 oranges
> Juice of 1 orange
> 50g (¼ cup) poppy seeds

Add the ingredients to the creamed butter and sugar along with the cornstarch.

Cardamom and Rose

> Zest and juice of 1 lime
> 5g (1½ teaspoons) ground cardamom
> 5g (1 teaspoon) rose water
> 10g (2 teaspoons) pure vanilla extract

Add the ingredients to the creamed butter and sugar along with the cornstarch.

....

Mint, Matcha, and Chocolate

> 10g (2 teaspoons) mint extract
> 10g (5 teaspoons) matcha powder
>   (the best quality available)
> 100g (¾ cup) chopped dairy-free dark
>   chocolate, melted

In step 1, add the mint extract when creaming the butter and sugar together. Whisk the matcha powder into the dry ingredients in step 3. After the dough is fully mixed at the end of step 3, slowly pour in the melted dark chocolate and very gently incorporate on low speed for 5 to 10 seconds to create a ripple effect. Although this will make the dough slightly messy to roll, it looks beautiful and tastes even better.

Apple Tarte "Tatton"

Makes one 9-inch (23cm) tart, serves 4 to 6

Tarte Tatin is a classic dessert that reminds me of holidays in France as a kid. We grew up on the southeast coast of England, and for my family it was cheaper to holiday in France than England. The weather was usually nicer, so we could spend hours at the pool or the beach. I've always loved food and treasured the opportunity to visit small family-run bistros on our trips abroad. The smell of this dessert takes me back to those fond family trips with my beautiful, crazy family.

You'll need just under half the recipe for the puff pastry. Use the remaining pastry for "sausage" rolls (page 277) or for another creation.

300g Puff Pastry (page 270), made at least 24 hours ahead
1.2kg/2.7 lb apples (Honeycrisp, Ambrosia, Braeburn, or Granny Smith); 10 cups quartered
Juice of 1 lemon
150g (¾ cup) fine raw cane sugar
2 whole star anise
45g (3 tablespoons) cold vegan butter, diced
1.5g (½ teaspoon) ground cinnamon
50g (3 tablespoons + 1 teaspoon) calvados (apple brandy)

For serving
Vanilla dairy-free ice cream or Coconut Yogurt (page 327)

1. Preheat the oven to 410°F (210°C). Line a large baking sheet with parchment paper.
2. On a lightly floured work surface, roll out the puff pastry to a thickness of ¼ inch (5mm). Don't roll it too thin or the juices from the apples will likely run. Using a large plate or a 10-inch (25cm) cake pan as a template, cut out a circle and transfer it to the lined baking sheet. Place it in the fridge, uncovered, until needed.
3. Peel, core, and quarter the apples (if the apples are large, slice each quarter in half, but don't make the slices too thin). Place the apple wedges in a medium bowl and squeeze the lemon juice over them to prevent discoloration.
4. Heat a 9-inch (23cm) cast-iron or other ovenproof skillet over medium heat. Add the sugar and gently shake the pan to evenly distribute it. Do not stir the sugar; allow it to soften and start to turn to a liquid, tipping the pan to help maintain even cooking. Once the sugar is melted and starts to turn a light golden brown, add the star anise and cold butter. Again, carefully swirl the pan around to allow the butter to melt and emulsify with the sugar.
5. Add the cinnamon and calvados, being careful as the caramel may boil a little. As the caramel starts to turn more of an amber colour, carefully arrange the apple wedges snugly in the pan so they overlap slightly in concentric circles, starting from the outside of the pan and working your way in. This will become the top, so take your time to arrange the apple wedges neatly. Reduce the heat to medium-low and gently cook the apples in the caramel until they are beginning to soften, 8 to 10 minutes.
6. Remove the pastry from the fridge and lay it over the apples. Carefully tuck in the edges around the apples. This will form a beautiful crust when turned upside down. Using a fork, prick a few holes in the pastry to allow steam to escape. Transfer the tart to the oven and bake until the pastry is golden brown all over, 35 to 40 minutes.
7. Carefully remove the tart from the oven and place it on the stovetop to cool. I like to leave the tart for at least 20 to 30 minutes before turning it out to allow the caramel to thicken. This also keeps the pastry from going soggy.
8. When you are ready to serve, check that the pastry and apples are not stuck to the pan by running a thin-bladed knife around the edge. Place a large plate upside down over the pan and with a quick movement, invert the tart onto the plate. Serve with a scoop of vanilla dairy-free ice cream or coconut yogurt.
9. The tart is best served the day of baking, but it can be baked 1 day in advance. Allow to cool, then cover and store in the fridge. Reheat the tart in a 300°F (150°C) oven for 20 to 25 minutes before turning it out of the pan.

Cherry and Raspberry Bakewell Tart

Makes one 13 × 9-inch (33 × 23cm) tart, serves 16

Bakewell tart is a childhood favourite of mine that originates from the town of Bakewell in Derbyshire, England. It is a classic tart that has a sweet shortcrust pastry base, a layer of jam in the middle, and a beautiful nutty and aromatic almond sponge called frangipane on top. I've kept this recipe rather traditional but have used a sweet and sour cherry jam with some added raspberries. I often adapt the fruit in this tart depending on what's in season and local. I can recommend trying it with pear, rhubarb, or even gooseberry jam.

Sweet Shortcrust Pastry

110g (½ cup) cold vegan butter, cut into 1-inch (2.5cm) cubes

225g (1¾ cups) pastry flour or all-purpose flour

25g (¼ cup) vegan icing sugar

2g (¼ teaspoon) fine sea salt

25g (2 tablespoons) ice cold water

15g (1 tablespoon) extra-virgin olive oil

Cherry Jam

700g (4¼ cups) fresh or frozen sour cherries

100g (⅔ cup) fresh or frozen raspberries

200g (¾ cup) water

Zest and juice of 1 lemon

100g (½ cup) raw cane sugar

50g (⅓ cup) white chia seeds (optional)

Almond Frangipane

170g (¾ cup) cold vegan butter

170g (¾ cup) raw cane sugar

170g (⅔ cup) natural applesauce (page 251)

90g (⅓ cup) unsweetened soy milk

14g (1 tablespoon) almond extract

5g (1 teaspoon) pure vanilla extract

250g (2¼ cups) ground natural almonds

120g (1 cup) all-purpose flour

20g (2 tablespoons) baking powder

20g (2 tablespoons) cornstarch

100g (1 cup) natural flaked/sliced almonds, for topping

Dairy-free ice cream or yogurt, for serving (optional)

Make the pastry

1. Place the bowl of a food processor in the fridge for 30 minutes before starting. This will help keep everything cold when making the pastry.

2. Place the butter, flour, icing sugar, and salt in the chilled bowl of the food processor and pulse until the mixture has a texture like breadcrumbs, 30 seconds. Add the cold water and olive oil and pulse until a shaggy dough forms. Transfer the dough to an unfloured work surface and finish mixing by hand. Bring the pastry together into a ball with no dry patches.

3. Gently roll the pastry between two 12 × 18-inch (30 × 45cm) pieces of parchment paper into a 7 × 4-inch (18 × 10cm) rectangle. (Rolling the pastry between the parchment avoids using flour or icing sugar, which would change the flavour and texture of the pastry.) Transfer the pastry (between the parchment) to a baking sheet and chill in the fridge for at least 2 hours but ideally overnight. (By partly rolling the dough now, it won't need to be worked as much to get it to the correct dimensions later. The pastry needs to stay as cold as possible to

continued . . .

prevent splitting or shrinking, so flattening the dough now, rather than shaping it into a ball, is helpful.)

4. When you are ready to bake, grease a 13 × 9-inch (33 × 23cm) baking pan or 10-inch (25cm) springform pan with a little neutral vegetable oil, such as canola, and line with parchment paper, allowing excess paper to hang over each side for easy removal.

5. Roll out the chilled pastry between the parchment paper so it's about ¼ inch (5mm) thick and ¼ inch (5mm) larger than the pan on all sides. Remove the parchment, lay the pastry in the prepared pan, and gently press it into the corners and sides.

6. Using a small knife, trim off the excess dough, leaving up to ¹⁄₁₀ inch (2.5mm) on all sides to allow for shrinking during baking. Place the pastry, uncovered, back in the fridge to chill while you make the cherry jam.

7. Preheat the oven to 340°F (170°C).

Make the cherry jam

8. Combine the cherries, raspberries, water, lemon zest and juice, and sugar in a medium saucepan. Bring to a simmer over high heat, then reduce the heat to low and gently simmer, stirring, until the jam has reduced by half and the fruit has softened, 10 minutes. Add the chia seeds (if using), gently stir, and continue cooking for another 5 to 10 minutes, until a thick sauce consistency is reached. Remove from the heat and set aside to cool.

Blind-bake the pastry

9. Remove the chilled pastry from the fridge. Place a sheet of plastic wrap over the pastry with a little excess wrap to hang over the sides. Spread a ½-inch (1cm) layer of baking beans, dried chickpeas, or rice over the plastic. (This will stop the pastry from rising when baked.)

10. Place the pastry in the oven and bake until the edges are light golden brown and there are no raw-looking sections, 15 to 20 minutes.

11. Using the plastic wrap as handles, lift out the baking beans in one go. Return the pastry to the oven and bake for another 5 minutes, until the crust is light golden brown all over. Set aside on the counter.

Make the almond frangipane

12. In the bowl of a stand mixer fitted with the paddle, cream together the butter and sugar on medium speed until combined and paler, 2 to 3 minutes.

13. Add the applesauce, soy milk, almond extract, and vanilla and beat for 1 minute.

14. In a medium bowl, whisk together the ground almonds, flour, baking powder, and cornstarch. Add the dry ingredients to the wet ingredients in 2 additions, beating after each addition until the batter is smooth, 2 minutes.

Assemble and bake the tart

15. Using a small rubber spatula or the back of a spoon, spread the cherry jam evenly over the bottom of the pastry crust.

16. Dot spoonfuls of the almond frangipane randomly all over the jam to achieve an even layer. This way you don't spread the frangipane and mix it with the jam. Sprinkle the almonds evenly over the tart.

17. Bake the tart until the frangipane has nicely risen, golden brown and set in the middle, 25 to 30 minutes. Allow the fragile tart to cool in the pan for at least 30 minutes to set. Gently remove from the pan and transfer to a cooling rack for 1 hour. Slice the tart using a long serrated knife. Serve with a generous helping of dairy-free ice cream or yogurt, if desired.

18. Store the tart in an airtight container in the fridge for up to 5 days.

Meyer Lemon Tart

Makes one 9 or 10-inch (23 or 25cm) tart, serves 8 to 10

My first chef job after leaving culinary college was in the Michelin-starred kitchen of Read's in Faversham, England, which was known for its classic French cuisine with British influence. The lemon tart was a signature dish on the menu that diners would return for again and again. This is my veganized version of that elegant dessert, and a nod to David Pitchford for giving me that incredible opportunity in his prestigious kitchen.

This is a beautiful tart to make all year round. Meyer lemons take it to another level. The Meyer lemon is a sweet, floral, and zesty fruit that is dark yellow or orange in colour and smaller than a lemon. You can find them in stores from mid-November till the end of January.

Most of the time, we replace egg with flax or chia seeds, but the liquid consistency and creamy properties of JUST Egg are perfect for this particular classic. At the bakery, we use a 10¼ × 1-inch (26 × 2.5cm) Matfer Bourgeat Exoglass Tart Ring, but you can use a 9-inch (23cm) round tart pan with a removable bottom.

1 batch Sweet Shortcrust Pastry (page 229),
partly rolled and chilled for at least 1 hour

Lemon Custard

300g (1⅓ cups) vegan heavy cream

Zest of 4 Meyer lemons

30g (3 tablespoons) cornstarch

355g (1 bottle) JUST Egg (vegan liquid egg)

200g (¾ cup) Meyer lemon juice

250g (1¼ cups) fine raw cane sugar

Fresh raspberries and mint sprigs, for serving
(optional)

Make and blind-bake the pastry

1. Preheat the oven to 350°F (175°C).

2. Use a neutral vegetable oil, such as sunflower or canola, to lightly grease a 10-inch (25cm) tart ring or 9-inch (23cm) round tart pan with a removeable bottom. Place it on a rimless baking sheet lined with parchment paper or a silicone baking mat. Set aside.

3. Roll out the chilled pastry between 2 sheets of parchment paper to a circle about 14 inches (35cm) in diameter and ¼ inch (5mm) thick. (Rolling the pastry between the parchment avoids using flour or icing sugar, which would change the flavour and texture of the pastry.) Transfer the pastry (with the parchment) to a baking sheet and place in the fridge to chill for 5 to 10 minutes.

4. Remove the chilled pastry from the fridge and remove the top sheet of parchment. Place your hand under the bottom sheet and, with your fingers spread out, quickly and carefully flip the pastry over the tart ring. Let the pastry drop into the ring, guiding it with your fingers to the edges. Allow the excess pastry to fold over the top of the tart ring. Don't trim the excess. Try to avoid handling the pastry too much and therefore overheating it. If there are any rips or tears, you can make repairs with the extra pastry hanging over the edges. If you have any excess pastry, cover and keep in the fridge for any repairs needed later. Use a fork to gently prick holes all over the pastry. (This is called docking and allows steam to escape during baking, preventing the pastry puffing up.) Return the tart case to the fridge to chill for 15 to 20 minutes. (This will help prevent the pastry from shrinking and cracking during baking.)

5. Line the pastry with a sheet of plastic wrap, leaving some overhang, and gently push it into the ring. Fill the tart with baking beans, dried chickpeas, or rice. (This will weigh the pastry down to keep it flat.) Bake the pastry case until the edges are light golden brown, 15 to 20 minutes. Meanwhile, make the lemon custard.

continued . . .

6. Remove the tart from the oven and carefully lift out the plastic wrap and beans. If there are any holes or tears in the pastry, use the reserved trim to patch them up. There must be no holes in the pastry, or the custard will run straight through it. Place the pastry case back in the oven to bake for a further 5 to 7 minutes, until the base is light golden brown and any repair pastry has had time to bake a little.

7. Remove the pastry case from the oven and reduce the heat to 220°F (105°C).

Make the lemon custard

8. In a medium saucepan, bring the cream and lemon zest to a simmer, then remove from the heat. Take out a small amount of the cream (50g/¼ cup or so) and whisk with the cornstarch in a small bowl to make a paste, then whisk the paste into the warm cream.

9. Place the JUST Egg, lemon juice, and sugar in a medium bowl and whisk together. Pour in half the cream mixture and whisk to combine, then whisk in the remaining cream mixture. Pour the custard into the saucepan and gently cook over medium-low heat, stirring constantly with a rubber spatula, until it is hot and starts to thicken slightly. This should take 5 to 10 minutes. Don't heat the custard too fast or it will scramble. Once it is hot and has a heavy cream consistency, pour it through a fine-mesh strainer into a large measuring cup to make it easier to pour into the baked tart case.

10. Once the oven has come down in temperature, place the tart case (still on the baking sheet) on the middle rack, pull the rack out halfway, then pour the custard into the case. Gently slide the shelf back in. Bake the tart until the custard is just set, with a slight wobble, 50 to 60 minutes. Remove the tart from the oven and let it cool for 20 minutes.

11. Using a serrated knife, carefully trim the excess pastry from the rim, cutting away from the tart so the pastry falls away from the filling. Place the tart in the fridge to chill and set for at least 2 hours or overnight.

12. When the tart has fully chilled, remove the tart ring. Decorate the tart with some fresh raspberries and mint, if using. Store the tart in an airtight container in the fridge for up to 4 days.

New York Baked Vanilla Cheesecake with Elderflower-Poached Rhubarb

Makes one 9-inch (23cm) cheesecake, serves 12

This dessert was inspired by a love of three things: foraging, rhubarb, and developing new vegan recipes. Natasha and I love to explore the forests around Whistler, BC, whenever we can. This is a fun dessert that is full of herbal and tart flavours, creamy texture, and delightful aromas.

Throughout the year, we find an abundance of wild foods that can be married to seasonal produce from local farms, so our baking is heavily influenced by the seasons and this mindset. (Just make sure you know what you are foraging and take only what you can use.)

Elderflower blossom is a magical ingredient that has amazing health properties and a beautiful flavour, and it's in season with rhubarb. I love using ingredients that not only elevate each other but also grow at the same time of the year.

note: *Reserve the scraped vanilla pod and allow it to dry at room temperature overnight. It can be used in crème pâtissière and custards or stored with sugar to make vanilla sugar.*

Elderflower Syrup (Makes 800g/4 cups)

25 elderflower heads in full bloom (reserve some flowers to garnish the jam, if making)

Zest and juice of 3 unwaxed organic lemons

Zest and juice of 1 unwaxed organic orange

1.5L (6 cups) boiling water

1kg (5 cups) raw cane sugar

Poached Rhubarb

400g (2 cups) Elderflower Syrup (recipe above)

100g (¼ cup + 3 tablespoons) water

Zest and juice of 1 lemon

1kg/2.2 lb rhubarb, trimmed (8 cups chopped)

Biscuit Base

250g baked Gingerbread Biscuits (page 299) or Scottish Shortbread (page 223); roll the dough a little thinner and bake for a few more minutes so they are extra crunchy

100g (½ cup) vegan butter

Cheesecake Filling

1kg (4½ cups) plain vegan cream cheese (I recommend Tofutti)

2 vanilla pods, split lengthwise and seeds scraped (see Note; or 28g/2 tablespoons pure vanilla extract)

40g (⅓ cup) cornstarch

470g (2 cups) unsweetened dairy-free cream (I recommend Earth's Own Oat Culinary Cream)

235g (1 cup + 1 tablespoon) raw cane sugar

Zest and juice of 1 lemon

Rhubarb jam (see step 6) or Strawberry Jam (page 219), for serving (optional)

Fresh mint leaves, for serving (optional)

Make the elderflower syrup

1. Inspect the elderflower heads carefully and remove any insects or leaves. Place the blossoms in a deep container and add the lemon zest and orange zest. Pour the boiling water over the blossoms. Cover with a muslin cloth or kitchen towel and leave to steep at room temperature for at least 8 hours or overnight.

2. The following day, strain the liquid through a fine chinois or muslin cloth into a large saucepan. Add the lemon juice, orange juice, and sugar. Bring to a boil, then reduce the heat and simmer for 2 or 3 minutes. Pour the syrup into a 1L (4-cup) container and allow it to cool.

3. Store the syrup in the fridge for up to 2 weeks or freeze it in ice cube trays or airtight containers for up to 3 months.

continued . . .

Make the poached rhubarb

4. Place the elderflower syrup, water, and lemon zest and juice in a large saucepan.

5. Cut the rhubarb stalks down the centre lengthwise, then cut into ½-inch (1cm) squares. You should have 8 cups (2L). Transfer the rhubarb to the saucepan. Slowly bring the liquid to a simmer, then remove from the heat. Allow the rhubarb to sit in the poaching liquid until it reaches the desired texture. If you prefer a little more crunch, remove the fruit from the liquid earlier, or for a more tender texture, leave the rhubarb in the liquid longer. Remove the rhubarb using a slotted spoon, transfer it to a plate, and allow both the rhubarb and the poaching liquid to cool completely.

6. If you want to decorate the cheesecake with some rhubarb jam, take half the poached rhubarb and a little sugar syrup and continue to cook it in a small saucepan over low heat until it has a jam-like consistency. Cool and store in the fridge for up to 3 days.

7. Return the rhubarb to the poaching liquid to maintain a good flavour. Store the poached rhubarb in an airtight container in the fridge for up to 3 days.

Prepare the biscuit base

8. Preheat the oven to 350°F (175°C). Lightly coat a 9-inch (23cm) springform pan with a neutral vegetable oil, such as sunflower or canola, and line the bottom and sides with parchment paper. To make the springform pan watertight, wrap the outside with foil.

9. Place the biscuits in a food processor and pulse until they resemble breadcrumbs. You should have 3 cups (750mL). (Alternatively, place the biscuits in a resealable plastic bag and smash them up with a rolling pin.)

10. Melt the butter in a small saucepan over medium heat. Pour the melted butter into a medium bowl, add the biscuit crumbs, and stir with a wooden spoon or spatula to combine.

11. Scatter the biscuit mixture into the lined springform pan and evenly compress it across the base. The neater, the better, as this will be exposed when cut.

Make the filling and bake the cheesecake

12. In the bowl of a stand mixer fitted with the paddle, beat the cream cheese on medium speed until it is smooth, 2 minutes. Scrape the vanilla seeds into the bowl and beat for 1 more minute.

13. In a small bowl, whisk together the cornstarch and 40g (about 3 tablespoons) of the cream to make a thick, smooth paste. Add this to the cream cheese along with the remaining cream, sugar, and lemon zest and juice.

14. Fit the mixer with the whisk. Whisk the cheesecake mixture on medium speed for 1 minute. Stop the mixer and scrape down the sides and bottom of the bowl with a rubber spatula. Continue whisking for another minute, until smooth.

15. Pour the cheesecake filling over the biscuit base and gently spread it to create a smooth top.

16. Carefully place the cheesecake in a deep roasting pan and place in the oven. Pour hot water into the pan to come about 1½ inches (4cm) up the side of the spring-form pan to create a water bath. Bake the cheesecake until it is light golden brown, 1 hour. The cheesecake will still be runny and very wobbly at this stage. Do not open the oven; turn it off and leave the cheesecake inside for 1 hour. Open the oven door and leave the cheesecake in the oven for another hour (for a total of 3 hours cooking and cooling in the oven). Do not rush the cooling times or the cheesecake will collapse.

17. Lift the cheesecake out of the water bath and remove the foil. Transfer the slightly warm cheesecake, uncovered, to the fridge and chill for at least 8 hours or overnight to fully set.

Decorate the cheesecake

18. One hour before serving, remove the poached rhubarb from the fridge and allow it to come to room temperature.

19. When ready to serve, release the sides of the pan and carefully transfer the cheesecake to a large serving plate. Garnish with some poached rhubarb and a little jam and fresh mint, if using.

20. Store the cheesecake, covered, in the fridge for up to 3 days.

Roasted Peach and Lavender Crème Pâtissière Galette

Serves 8 to 10

This seasonal rustic tart has an incredible flaky, buttery crust filled with a herbaceous crème pâtissière and topped with caramelized roasted peaches. Try this recipe with other stone fruits such as nectarines, apricots, plums, or cherries. The tart can be easily adapted with extra vanilla or different herbs such as thyme or rosemary in the crème pâtissière. Galette translates as "flat cake," but this epic tart is far from that and will impress everyone who tastes it—especially when you say it's vegan!

Galette Pastry

300g (1¾ cups + 2 tablespoons) all-purpose flour

15g (1 tablespoon) raw cane sugar

15g (1 tablespoon) coconut sugar

5g (1 teaspoon) fine sea salt

225g cold vegan butter, diced into ¼-inch (5mm) pieces (I recommend Miyoko's)

150g (⅔ cup) cold water

Lavender Crème Pâtissière

300g (1¼ cups) unsweetened soy milk

5g (1 teaspoon) culinary lavender buds

25g (2 tablespoons) raw cane sugar

A pinch of fine sea salt

5g (1 teaspoon) pure vanilla extract

25g (3 tablespoon + ¾ teaspoon) cornstarch

60g (¼ cup) cold vegan butter, diced into ¼-inch (5mm) pieces

1kg/2.2 lb (6 to 8 medium to large) ripe peaches, pitted and cut into eighths

15g (1 tablespoon) unsweetened soy milk, for glazing

15g (1 tablespoon) coconut sugar, for glazing

Leaves from a few sprigs fresh thyme, more for garnish

25g (4 teaspoons) pure maple syrup

Coconut Yogurt (page 327; optional), for serving

Make the pastry

1. Sift the flour into a large bowl. Add the cane sugar, coconut sugar, and salt and mix together with your hand.

2. Add the diced butter. Using your fingers, break up and squish the butter with the flour until it's just mixed but not fully broken down. Small slivers and pieces of butter result in a flaky pastry. Place the mixture, uncovered, in the fridge to chill for 10 minutes.

3. Reserve 1 tablespoon (15g) of the cold water, then drizzle the remaining water evenly over the flour mixture. Gently fold and mix lightly with your hand or a fork until everything is just incorporated with no dry patches, adding the reserved water if necessary. Do not overmix, or the pastry will not be flaky. Press the pastry into a rectangle about 1 inch (2.5cm) thick and wrap it in plastic wrap. Place the dough in the fridge to chill for 15 minutes.

4. Lightly flour a work surface and the pastry. Roll out the pastry to make a rectangle about 15 × 5 inches (38 × 12cm). Dust off any excess flour from both sides of the pastry. With a short side facing you, roll the pastry up, creating layers of butter like a rough puff pastry. Lightly flour the pastry log on top and gently roll it out to a square about 1½ inches (4cm) thick. Wrap the pastry back up and place it back in the fridge for at least 8 hours or overnight to fully chill.

continued . . .

Make the crème pâtissière

5. Combine the soy milk, lavender buds, sugar, and salt in a small saucepan and bring to a simmer over high heat. As soon as the milk is simmering, remove it from the heat. Stir in the vanilla and allow it to infuse for 10 minutes.

6. Place the cornstarch in a medium bowl. Strain one-quarter of the lavender-infused milk through a fine-mesh sieve over the cornstarch and whisk to make a smooth paste. Strain the rest of the infused milk into the paste and whisk well.

7. Rinse out the saucepan. Pour the milk mixture into the saucepan and bring to a simmer over medium heat, whisking constantly as it heats and thickens, about 2 minutes. Remove from the heat. Add the diced butter and whisk until all the butter is incorporated. Place plastic wrap directly on the surface to prevent a skin forming and set aside to cool.

Assemble and bake the galette

8. Place an oven rack in the upper position of the oven and preheat to 350°F (175°C). Line a large baking sheet with parchment paper or a silicone baking mat.

9. Remove the pastry from the fridge, unwrap, and place on a lightly floured work surface. Lightly dust the top of the pastry with flour and roll it out to a 14-inch (35cm) circle, about ¼ inch (5mm) thick. You can leave the edges as is for a rustic look, or for a cleaner look, place a large bowl or plate over the pastry and trim around it with a small knife to neaten up the circle. Dust off any excess flour from both sides of the pastry. Roll up the pastry using the rolling pin and transfer it to the lined baking sheet.

10. Using a small rubber spatula or spoon, spread the crème pâtissière over the pastry, leaving a 2-inch (5cm) border. Starting at the outer edge of the crème pâtissière, arrange the peach wedges in a circular pattern, working your way inwards and slightly overlapping them to form a flower pattern.

11. Fold the pastry up and slightly over the filling to frame the fruit, pleating and turning the baking sheet as you go. Place the galette in the fridge to chill for 15 minutes.

12. Brush the pastry with soy milk and sprinkle the crust and peaches with the coconut sugar. Bake the galette for 30 minutes. Rotate the baking sheet and bake for another 10 to 15 minutes or until the crust is golden brown. Remove the galette from the oven and garnish with some fresh thyme leaves and a drizzle of maple syrup. Serve immediately on its own or with some coconut yogurt.

Gluten-Free

Cast-Iron Skillet Cornbread

Makes one 10-inch (25cm) cornbread, serves 4 to 6

Cornbread today is widely associated with the southern states of America and often has somewhat of a Mexican influence with jalapeño peppers and corn kernels added to the batter, but it has its roots in the cuisine of Indigenous peoples such as the Hopi and the Cherokee. This golden fluffy, crunchy, full-flavoured Southern-style cornbread can be enjoyed with a sweet or savoury meal. This recipe is so simple to put together, but it must be served straight from the oven. I love it with fresh fruit, dairy-free yogurt, and maple syrup for breakfast, or a spicy BBQ vegetable bean chili, vegan sour cream, and cilantro for dinner.

Cooking cornbread in a roasting-hot skillet adds another dimension of texture and flavour that, in my humble opinion, is the only way to make it. This is known as a *pone* of cornbread in the Appalachian Mountains (from the Algonquin *apan*, or "baked"), not a *loaf*.

note: *For an alternative egg replacer, whisk together 20g (2 tablespoons + ¾ teaspoon) ground flaxseed and 80g (⅓ cup) unsweetened oat milk until a smooth paste forms. Let sit for 10 minutes to bloom and thicken.*

325g (1⅓ cups) unsweetened soy milk or pea milk

15g (1 tablespoon) apple cider vinegar

100g (½ cup) vegan liquid egg, such as JUST Egg (see Note)

50g (¼ cup) pure maple syrup

50g (¼ cup) vegan butter, melted

150g (1 cup) gluten-free all-purpose flour

150g (¾ cup) fine-grind cornmeal

25g (2 tablespoons) raw cane sugar

10g (2 teaspoons) baking powder

5.5g (½ teaspoon) baking soda

5g (1 teaspoon) fine sea salt

25g (2 tablespoons) olive oil or coconut oil

1. About an hour before you plan to make the cornbread, preheat the oven to 400°F (200°C). Allow the oven to preheat for at least 30 minutes, then place a 10-inch (25cm) cast-iron skillet in the oven to preheat for at least another 30 minutes. The skillet needs to be extremely hot when the batter is added to achieve the incredible texture.

2. In a large bowl, stir together the soy milk and apple cider vinegar. Let it sit for at least 5 minutes to sour. Once soured, whisk in the vegan liquid egg, maple syrup, and melted butter.

3. In a medium bowl, whisk together the flour, cornmeal, sugar, baking powder, baking soda, and salt.

4. Whisk the dry ingredients into the wet ingredients. Let sit for 5 minutes to hydrate a little. This will help with the texture and flavour of the finished cornbread, like a pancake batter.

5. Carefully remove the hot skillet from the oven and place it on the stovetop over medium heat. Pour the olive oil into the skillet and gently swirl the oil around so it coats the bottom and sides of the pan. Pour the batter into the hot skillet. Place the skillet back in the oven and bake the cornbread until golden brown on top, 20 to 22 minutes. Remove the skillet from the oven and place it on a cooling rack. Let cool for 15 minutes. Cut the cornbread into wedges and serve from the skillet.

6. Store the cornbread in an airtight container in the fridge for up to 3 days.

The Mountain Loaf (Gluten-Free Bread)

Makes one 1.5kg tin loaf, 15 thin slices

Why do we call this bread "The Mountain Loaf"? Because it is 1.5kg of pure energy. One or two thin slices will sustain your adventures for hours. It's packed with seeds, nuts, and slow-releasing energy ingredients like gluten-free oats and one of our favourites, wild rice. Wild rice is also known as Canadian rice and is grown in Saskatchewan. It is second to oats in protein content per 100 calories. The small amount of maple syrup doesn't sweeten this bread, it just helps balance the flavour and maintains the softness.

   This is a versatile loaf in that you can eat it by the slice, cube it into croutons, or even crumble it over a casserole before baking it. Because it is so dense and heavy, but also delicious and nutritious, you only need the thinnest slice or two to feel satiated.

   50g (¼ cup) wild rice

   75g (1 cup + 2 tablespoons) sliced natural almonds

   100g (¾ cup) sunflower seeds

   50g (½ cup) pumpkin seeds

   300g (3⅓ cups) gluten-free old-fashioned
      rolled oats

   125g (¾ cup) flaxseeds

   25g (2½ cups) white or black chia seeds

   15g (1½ tablespoons) psyllium husk powder

   12g (2 teaspoons) fine sea salt

   40g (2 tablespoons + 2 teaspoons)
      pure maple syrup

   40g (¼ cup) extra-virgin olive oil

   15g (1 tablespoon) organic canola oil

   625g (2⅔ cups) water

Soak the wild rice

1. Pulse the wild rice in a food processor until it is lightly scored and broken up, a few seconds. Transfer to a large glass jar with a lid and fill it with cold filtered water. The rice will soak up a lot of water and bloom, so make sure it's well covered with water and has space to swell. Screw on the lid and leave at room temperature for at least 8 hours or overnight.

Mix the dough and let rest

2. Preheat the oven to 350°F (175°C). Lightly coat a 9 × 5 × 3-inch (23 × 12 × 8cm) loaf tin with olive oil and line the bottom and sides with parchment paper.

3. Scatter the almonds, sunflower seeds, and pumpkin seeds on a baking sheet and lightly toast in the oven until they are golden brown, 5 to 7 minutes. Set aside to cool for 30 minutes.

4. Meanwhile, drain the bloomed wild rice through a sieve. Set the sieve over a bowl to continue draining.

5. In a large bowl, stir together the oats, flaxseeds, chia seeds, psyllium husk powder, and salt. Add the cooled toasted almond and seed mixture, maple syrup, olive oil, canola oil, water, and wild rice. Hold the bowl with one hand and with your other hand, squeeze and combine everything together until it is well mixed and bound together, at least 5 minutes.

6. With wet hands, form the mixture into an oval and drop it into the lined tin. Wet your hand again and compress the mixture to fill all the corners of the tin, then lightly round the top. This bread has no raising agent, so the neater it looks now, the more appealing it will look once it is baked. Cover the tin with plastic wrap and let sit in the fridge for at least 8 or overnight. This rest will help with flavour and, more importantly, texture.

continued . . .

Bake

7. Preheat the oven to 385°F (195°C).

8. Bake the loaf until deep golden brown all over and a probe thermometer inserted into the centre reaches 200°F (93°C), 60 to 70 minutes. Allow the loaf to cool in the tin for 30 minutes. Turn the loaf out onto a cooling rack and let cool completely, or for at least 3 hours, before slicing it. The loaf will crumble apart if it is cut too early.

I like to allow the loaf to cool and then place it in the fridge overnight. It's a long process but worth the wait!

9. Store the loaf, loosely covered, in the fridge for up to 1 week (the toasted seeds will turn bad if left at room temperature). Alternatively, slice the loaf, wrap it in plastic wrap, and freeze for up to 1 month. You can toast it straight from the freezer.

English Flapjacks with Strawberry Jelly

Makes about 10 squares

After digging into the history of English flapjacks, it appears that originally the name was given to a shallow traybake dessert. Over time, it has taken on different forms with additions such as dried fruits or chocolate toppings. It is baked in the oven and not fried on the stovetop. In North America, a flapjack is a sort of pancake (perhaps so-named because of the need to flip, or "flap," it during frying). A good English flapjack should be the perfect balance of crunchy and chewy.

The defining components of an English flapjack are oats and a marvellous buttery sweet honey-like substance called golden syrup. This syrup derives from a treacle-like by-product of sugar refining long used as pig food until, in the late-1800s, it was reformulated for human consumption. You can buy Lyle's Golden Syrup in the original-style tin throughout Canada and the UK, and it is recognized as the world's oldest branded food product. All of this adds to the historical importance of the English flapjack!

We top these English flapjacks with a fruit jelly, which is a positive addition to the centuries-old flapjack. The strawberry topping here is our most popular, though apricot has been a huge hit too. Although a jelly and herb topping is not traditional, many English customers have remarked on how superior this flapjack is compared with the solid tooth-breaking dry mass of sticky oats that they grew up with. You can vary the flavours of the jelly with the seasons, as well as using different nuts, herbs, and edible flowers.

Flapjack Batter

210g (1 cup) vegan butter (such as Earth Balance)

210g (1 cup packed) brown sugar

75g (¼ cup) golden syrup (do not substitute)

320g (4 cups) gluten-free old-fashioned rolled oats

120g (1 cup) sliced natural almonds

125g (¾ cup) dried strawberries, golden raisins, or cranberries

Strawberry Jelly

400g/14 oz (2 cups) fresh strawberries, quartered

60g (¼ cup) water

40g (1¾ cups) raw cane sugar

15g (1 tablespoon) agar-agar powder

For decorating

Fresh strawberries, halved or quartered

Toasted sliced natural almonds

Whole fresh mint leaves

Edible flowers (optional)

Make the flapjack batter and bake

1. Preheat the oven to 325°F (160°C). Lightly coat a 9-inch (23cm) square cake tin with canola oil spray, then line the bottom and sides with parchment paper, with extra hanging over the sides.

2. Gently melt the butter, brown sugar, and golden syrup in a small saucepan over low heat, stirring occasionally, until it all becomes a liquid. Pour the mixture into a medium bowl.

3. Add the oats and gently mix with a rubber spatula or wooden spoon. Add the almonds and dried fruit and mix until incorporated. Scrape the mixture into the lined tin and spread out to cover the base in an even layer. Press down to compact everything.

4. Bake until the flapjack is light golden brown, 25 to 30 minutes. Allow the flapjack to cool completely in the tin. You can place the flapjack in the fridge for 1 to 2 hours before adding the jelly to ensure a clean line between the two layers.

Make the strawberry jelly and finish the flapjack

5. Place the strawberries in a heavy-bottomed medium saucepan. Add the water and sugar and bring to a simmer over a medium heat. Cook the berries gently until tender and the water has reduced, 5 minutes

continued . . .

(your kitchen will smell incredible). Remove from the heat and allow the fruit to cool for 5 minutes.

6. Pour the strawberry compote into a liquidizer or blender and add the agar-agar powder. Blend the compote starting on the lowest speed and increasing to high speed until smooth, 1 minute.

7. Pour the purée back into the saucepan and bring it to a simmer over medium heat. Simmer for 2 minutes, whisking to activate the setting properties of the agar-agar.

8. Immediately pour this delicious jelly all over your flapjack. Tilt the tin so the hot jelly evenly spreads into the corners. Place the tin on a flat surface and allow the jelly to cool and set fully, 10 minutes. Place the flapjack in the fridge for 1 hour, to make cutting even easier and cleaner.

9. Cut the flapjack into squares (use a ruler if you prefer precision). Top each flapjack with strawberries, almonds, mint, and edible flowers, if using.

10. Store the flapjacks in an airtight container in the fridge for up to 3 days.

Sprouted Buckwheat, Raspberry, Red Currant, Chocolate, and Almond Scones

Makes 8 to 10 scones

Although these scones are not your typical ones made with flour, they are perhaps more like their original flat and round Scottish ancestors that were made with oats and griddle-baked. This recipe is a grain-free dessert, as buckwheat is classified as a seed (and therefore gluten-free). Sprouting the buckwheat is optional, but it unlocks more nutrition and makes the buckwheat even better for digestion. However, this recipe works just as well with raw dry buckwheat groats too (use 100g/1 cup).

The chocolate chips can be left out to remove any refined sugar; use a little more fruit instead. You can make a larger batch of applesauce and store in 50g (¼ cup) portions in airtight containers in the freezer for up to 1 month. Thaw as needed for another batch of scones.

We like to pair these scones with a squirt of coconut whipped cream and a lovely cup of tea. They are best eaten fresh from the oven and do not keep as well as other desserts. I recommend freezing the scones before decorating them. If frozen, defrost in the fridge for 3 or 4 hours before serving.

Scones
- 200g (2 cups) sprouted buckwheat groats (see sprouting method, page 73; use 100g/1 cup of raw dry groats to yield 200g/2 cups of sprouts)
- 1 unpeeled Braeburn or Gala apple, cut into ½-inch (1cm) pieces (to make 50g/¼ cup applesauce)
- 120g (1 cup) sliced natural almonds
- 160g (⅔ cup) unsweetened almond milk
- 40g (¼ cup) pure maple syrup
- 250g (1½ cups) dairy-free dark chocolate chips
- 75g (⅓ cup) frozen raspberries
- 75g (⅓ cup) frozen red currants

For decorating
- Sliced natural almonds, half left whole and half chopped
- Dairy-free dark chocolate chips
- Fresh raspberries
- Fresh red currants

Dehydrate the sprouted buckwheat groats (if using sprouted groats)

1. Set a dehydrator to 105°F (40°C). Spread the sprouted buckwheat groats on dehydrator trays lined with parchment paper or silicone baking mats. Dehydrate the sprouts for 12 hours.

Make the applesauce

2. Place the apple pieces in a small saucepan with a little water, cover, and cook over medium heat, stirring every 5 minutes, until mushy, 10 to 15 minutes. Blend into a purée using the single-serve jar of a high-speed blender, then let cool.

Make the scones

3. In a food processor, pulse the raw or dehydrated buckwheat groats into a coarse powder. Empty the powder into a large bowl. Repeat the process with the sliced almonds. Add the almond powder to the groats powder and stir together.

4. Add the applesauce, almond milk, and maple syrup and gently mix with a wooden spoon.

5. Add the chocolate chips, raspberries, and red currants and gently fold them through the mixture until all the ingredients are fully combined. (Using frozen, rather than fresh, berries prevents them being smashed into a purée.) Place the mixture in the fridge for 10 minutes to set up. This will make shaping the scones easier.

continued . . .

6. Meanwhile, preheat the oven to 325°F (160°C). Line a large baking sheet with parchment paper or a silicone baking mat.

7. Have a cup of warm water ready. Dipping a medium ice cream scoop in the warm water between scoops to prevent the mixture from sticking, scoop 8 to 10 portions of scone mix onto the lined baking sheet, leaving 1 to 2 inches (2.5 to 5cm) between them to make it easier to decorate.

8. To decorate the scones, place the chopped almonds in a small bowl. Using a bench knife or spatula, pick up the scones, 1 at a time, and roll the top in the nuts.

Return the scones to the baking sheet. Push a small amount of chocolate chips into the middle of each scone, followed with some fresh berries and some sliced almonds.

9. Bake the scones until the nuts are golden brown, 20 to 22 minutes. The scones will not really grow in size, as there is no raising agent. I like to check the bases of the scones, lifting them with a palette knife, to make sure they are light golden brown.

10. These scones are best eaten fresh but can be stored in an airtight container in the fridge for up to 2 days.

Chocolate Dacquoise Cake with Port-Poached Cherries

Makes one 9-inch (23cm) round cake, serves 10 to 12

Dacquoise is a layered cake made of meringue and buttercream that originates from the town of Dax in southwestern France and was enjoyed by French and English nobility from the seventeenth century.

Paired with some delicious port-poached cherries, this is a very decadent adult cake that has the bonus of being gluten-free. We found that it's even better a few days after baking (if it lasts that long), so it is a great cake if you want to be prepared ahead of an event. Serve with dairy-free ice cream or whipped coconut cream.

Cake

375g (2⅓ cups) dairy-free dark chocolate chips

300g (1¼ cups) aquafaba (liquid from two 14 oz/
400mL cans of chickpeas; see page 333), chilled

3.38g (1 teaspoon) cream of tartar

150g (⅔ cup) vegan icing sugar

150g (¾ cup) fine raw cane sugar

10g (2 teaspoons) pure vanilla extract

175g (1⅓ cups) gluten-free all-purpose flour

100g (1 cup) ground hazelnuts

100g (1 cup) ground almonds

12g (2 teaspoons) baking powder

A pinch of fine sea salt

Poached Cherries

250g (1 cup) port

125g (½ cup) pure maple syrup

125g (½ cup) water

400g (2 cups) pitted dark cherries

12g (1½ tablespoons) cornstarch

For decorating

100g/¼ lb whole cherries (I use a mix of white and
dark cherries)

100g (⅔ cup) toasted and chopped natural hazelnuts

50g (⅓ cup) grated dairy-free dark chocolate

Make the cake

1. Preheat the oven to 340°F (170°C). Lightly coat a 9-inch (23cm) springform pan with canola oil spray, then line the bottom and sides with parchment paper.

2. Place the chocolate chips in a medium bowl and place in the freezer for 30 minutes. This will harden the chocolate before the blending process.

3. In a food processor, blend half of the chocolate until it looks like instant coffee. Empty the chocolate into a small bowl. Repeat to blend the remaining chocolate and empty into the bowl. Set aside.

4. Pour the aquafaba into the bowl of a stand mixer fitted with the whisk. Add the cream of tartar and whisk on high speed until firm peaks form, 2 minutes.

5. In a small bowl, stir together the icing sugar and cane sugar. With the mixer on medium speed, add the sugar mixture in 4 additions, mixing for 2 minutes total.

6. Reduce the speed to low, add the vanilla, and mix for 8 minutes.

7. Meanwhile, in a medium bowl, whisk together the flour, ground hazelnuts, ground almonds, baking powder, and salt.

8. Remove the bowl from the stand mixer and tap the whisk on your hand to remove any excess meringue. (Tapping on your hand rather than the bowl prevents de-aerating the meringue.) Add the chocolate along with the flour mixture in 4 additions, gently but thoroughly folding with a large metal spoon after each addition. (The metal spoon will cut through the meringue more easily than a rubber spatula and mix faster without deflating the mix as much.)

9. Using a rubber spatula, gently scrape the batter into the prepared springform pan and gently level the top with the spatula. Immediately transfer the cake to the oven and bake until a skewer inserted into the centre

continued . . .

of the cake comes out clean, 40 to 45 minutes. Let the cake cool in the pan for 15 to 20 minutes. Remove the ring and transfer the cake to a cooling rack to cool completely.

Meanwhile, poach the cherries

10. Combine the port, maple syrup, and water in a medium saucepan. Bring to a simmer over medium heat. Add the cherries, cover, reduce the heat to low, and gently poach the fruit for 15 minutes, gently stirring every 5 minutes, until the cherries have softened and are cooked. Using a slotted spoon, transfer the cherries to a small bowl.

11. Place the cornstarch in a small bowl. Add 50g (3 tablespoons + 1 teaspoon) of the poaching liquid and whisk to make a slurry. Add the slurry to the saucepan and whisk until smooth. Gently cook over medium-low heat, whisking constantly until it has thickened, 5 minutes. Return the cherries to the thickened liquid, stir, and remove from the heat. Set aside to cool.

Decorate the cake

12. Transfer the cake to a serving plate. Decorate with the poached cherries, fresh cherries, chopped hazelnuts, and grated chocolate.

13. Store the cake in an airtight container at room temperature for up to 3 days. It will improve with age.

Orange, Almond, and Cardamom Cake

Makes one 9-inch (23cm) round cake, serves 8

This light and fluffy cake is the perfect accompaniment for afternoon tea. Many people are free from gluten and animal products for all sorts of reasons and yet find it incredibly difficult to find good-quality tasty baked goods. There are many recipes for gluten-free cakes, but they are usually loaded with eggs.

Whether you are a vegan, celiac, or not, this cake is amazingly delicious! If you are heading to any sort of dinner party and want to bring a dessert, you can be sure this cake will be enjoyed by everybody, and they won't even guess it's gluten-free. It's easy to make, too, since it is an all-in-one recipe, with not many steps and not much to clean up—a win for everyone!

250g/8.8 oz whole orange

100g (½ cup) unsweetened soy milk

150g (¾ cup) raw cane sugar

250g (2¼ cups) ground almonds

85g (½ cup) potato starch

15g (3 teaspoons) baking powder

5g (1 teaspoon) ground cardamom

A pinch of fine sea salt

125g (1¾ cups) sliced natural almonds,
   for decorating

1. Preheat the oven to 340°F (170°C). Lightly coat a 9-inch (23cm) springform pan with canola oil spray, then line the bottom and sides with parchment paper.

2. Trim the ends off the orange, cut it into quarters, and remove any seeds. Blend the orange in a food processor until it is broken up but not a smooth purée, 1 minute. Add the soy milk and sugar and blend for 1 minute. Add the ground almonds, potato starch, baking powder, cardamom, and salt. Blend for another minute, until a smooth batter forms, scraping down the sides of the bowl with a rubber spatula halfway through.

3. Immediately pour the batter into the prepared springform pan. Gently level the top with the spatula. Evenly scatter the sliced almonds over the top. Bake until the cake is golden brown and a skewer inserted in the centre comes out clean, 35 to 40 minutes. Let the cake cool in the pan on a cooling rack for 15 to 20 minutes. Remove the ring and base. Serve the cake warm.

4. Store the cake in an airtight container in the fridge for up to 2 days and reheat before serving.

Double Chocolate and Tahini Brownies

Makes about 10 slices

As a chocolate enthusiast, I love a sticky, gooey, teeth-gripping fudgy brownie. Chocolate paired with the salty umami flavour from sesame and the lightness from the chickpea flour is an epic combination. I tested this recipe with oat, rice, and other gluten-free flours but found the chickpea flour worked the best. If you don't have chickpea flour on hand, gluten-free all-purpose flour also works well.

- 25g (3 tablespoons) white sesame seeds
- 125g (½ cup) vegan butter
- 200g (1⅓ cups) dairy-free dark chocolate chips, divided
- 200g (1 cup) raw cane sugar
- 150g (⅔ cup) coconut sugar
- 120g (¾ cup) chickpea flour
- 60g (½ cup) dark cocoa powder
- 30g (¼ cup) cornstarch
- 5g (1 teaspoon) baking powder
- 5g (1 teaspoon) fine sea salt
- 180g (¾ cup) hot water
- 50g (¼ cup) roasted tahini

1. Preheat the oven to 325°F (160°C). Lightly coat a 9-inch (23cm) square cake or brownie pan with canola oil spray, then line the bottom and sides with parchment paper, with extra hanging over the side.

2. Lightly toast the sesame seeds in a dry skillet over medium heat. (Alternatively, you can toast the sesame seeds on a small baking sheet in the oven for a few minutes.) Set aside to cool.

3. Melt the butter and 150g (1 cup) of the chocolate chips in a large heatproof bowl over a double boiler.

Once the chocolate has melted, remove the bowl from the heat. Add the cane sugar and coconut sugar, then gently stir with a rubber spatula until emulsified. Set aside for the sugars to dissolve gently.

4. In a large bowl, whisk together the chickpea flour, cocoa powder, cornstarch, baking powder, and salt.

5. Add the dry ingredients to the wet ingredients and gently stir with a rubber spatula until no dry lumps remain. Add the hot water and continue stirring until a smooth batter forms, 1 minute. Add the remaining 50g (⅓ cup) chocolate chips and gently stir.

6. Pour the batter into the prepared pan and gently spread it in an even layer using a rubber or offset spatula.

7. Fill a small piping bag fitted with a No. 4 plain tip with the tahini. Starting at the far end of the pan, pipe the tahini across the batter in a zigzag pattern. Using a cocktail stick or skewer, swipe in the opposite direction to form a feathered pattern. (If you don't have a piping bag, spoon the tahini onto the batter using a teaspoon and swirl it into the top of the batter with a cocktail stick or skewer.) Sprinkle evenly with the toasted sesame seeds for extra flavour and texture.

8. Bake until a crust has formed but a skewer inserted into the middle of the brownie is sticky and a little wet, 25 to 30 minutes. You don't want to overbake the brownie, or it will lose its luxurious fudgy texture. Let the brownie cool in the pan on a cooling rack for at least 1 hour or overnight in the fridge before cutting.

9. Store the brownies in an airtight container in the fridge for up to 5 days.

Millet, Peanut Butter, and Chocolate Blondies

Makes about 10 slices

What exactly is a blondie, you might ask? Imagine a brownie, except it is not brown as there is no cocoa powder. It is blond in colour, in this case from the peanut butter. If you have a craving for a Snickers bar, this is a healthier and cruelty-free treat that will satisfy you whether you are gluten-free or not.

You can use chickpea flour instead of millet flour, as well as different nut butters such as almond, cashew, or hazelnut and then top with your chosen chopped nut.

50g (⅓ cup) ground flaxseed
155g (⅔ cup) unsweetened oat milk
125g (½ cup) cold vegan butter
300g (1⅓ cups) raw cane sugar
400g (1½ cups) crunchy peanut butter
10g (2 teaspoons) pure vanilla extract
10g (2 teaspoons) baking powder
3g (½ teaspoon) fine sea salt
180g (1 cup) millet flour
250g (1½ cups) dairy-free dark chocolate chips
100g (⅔ cup) chopped natural peanuts

1. Preheat the oven to 350°F (175°C). Lightly coat a 9-inch (23cm) square cake or brownie pan with canola oil spray, then line the bottom and sides with parchment paper, leaving extra hanging over the sides.

2. To make your flax egg, whisk together the flaxseed and oat milk in a small bowl until a smooth paste forms. If there are any lumps, push a small rubber spatula against the side of the bowl to break them up. Let sit for 10 minutes to bloom and thicken.

3. In a stand mixer fitted with the paddle, beat the butter with the sugar on medium speed until smooth and paler, 5 minutes. Add the peanut butter, vanilla, and flax egg and beat until everything is well incorporated, 2 minutes.

4. Add the baking powder, salt, and millet flour and beat on medium speed until no dry patches remain, 1 minute.

5. Add the chocolate chips and gently incorporate until just mixed.

6. Scrape the batter into the lined pan and spread it evenly with a rubber spatula. Lightly compress the batter. Sprinkle evenly with the peanuts. Bake until the blondie is golden brown, 25 to 30 minutes. Let the blondie cool in the pan on a cooling rack for at least 1 hour or overnight before cutting.

7. Store the blondies in an airtight container in the fridge for up to 5 days. The blondies are best eaten at room temperature.

Hummus Cookies

Makes 16 to 18 cookies

As a vegan, I love anything with chickpeas, but especially hummus. I'd eaten chickpea cookies before creating this recipe, but they are normally made with chocolate or peanut butter. My intention was to use all the same ingredients as hummus (except the garlic!) to make a chewy yet soft full-flavoured gluten-free cookie. These cookies are a very happy surprise to all who try them.

These cookies are best the day they are baked, so I like to bake only as many as I need at one time, and keep the remaining dough refrigerated or frozen.

- 600g (3 cups) cooked chickpeas (300g/1½ cups dried chickpeas soaked overnight, cooked in water, and drained)
- 225g (1 cup) cold vegan butter
- 30g (2 tablespoons + ¾ teaspoon) extra-virgin olive oil
- 450g (2¼ cups) raw cane sugar
- 20g (1½ tablespoons) pure vanilla extract
- 15g (1 tablespoon) apple cider vinegar
- Zest and juice of 2 lemons
- 225g (1 cup) roasted tahini
- 450g (3 cups + 2 tablespoons) chickpea flour
- 8g (1½ teaspoons) baking powder
- 15g (1½ teaspoons) baking soda
- 5g (1 teaspoon) fine sea salt
- 500g (3½ cups) white sesame seeds

1. Place the cooked chickpeas in a food processor and pulse until roughly chopped. Set aside.

2. In the bowl of a stand mixer fitted with the paddle, cream together the butter, olive oil, and sugar on medium speed until smooth and slightly paler, 2 to 3 minutes.

3. Add the vanilla, apple cider vinegar, lemon zest and juice, and tahini. Beat until combined.

4. Add the chopped chickpeas, chickpea flour, baking powder, baking soda, and salt. Mix on low speed until there are no dry patches and a wet dough forms.

5. Scrape the dough into a plastic container with a lid or cover the stand mixer bowl and place it in the fridge. Chill the dough for at least 2 hours but ideally overnight. This will allow the dough to firm up and make shaping a lot easier.

6. Once the dough has chilled, line a large baking sheet with parchment paper or a silicone baking mat.

7. Have a bowl of water ready. Wet your hands and shake off excess water, then scoop the dough and roll neatly into 16 to 18 balls (110g each), placing them on the lined baking sheet. (Alternatively, use a 3.5 oz/100g ice cream scoop.) Lightly flatten each ball to about 1 inch (2.5cm) thickness. Place the tray of cookies in the fridge for 1 hour.

8. Place the sesame seeds in a large bowl. Remove the cookies from the fridge and, 1 at a time, roll them in the seeds until they are generously coated on all sides. Line the baking sheet with a clean sheet of parchment paper or clean silicone baking mat, return the cookies to it, and place the tray in the fridge for another hour. This will help the cookies hold their shape while baking.

9. Position the oven racks in the upper and lower thirds of the oven and preheat to 350°F (175°C). Line another large baking sheet with parchment paper or a silicone baking mat.

10. Divide the chilled cookies between the lined baking sheets, leaving 2 to 3 inches (5 to 8cm) between them. Bake the cookies until they are golden brown on top, 18 to 22 minutes. If you are not using a convection oven, you may need to rotate the cookies halfway through. The baked cookies are very delicate, so allow them to cool for 15 minutes on the baking sheet, then transfer them to a cooling rack to cool completely, 1 hour.

11. Store the cookies in an airtight container at room temperature for up to 3 days. The unbaked seeded cookies can also be stored in an airtight container in the fridge for up to 3 days or in the freezer for up to 2 weeks.

Raspberry and Earl Grey Tea Baked Doughnuts

Makes 12 small doughnuts

I used to be a bit of a purist when it came to doughnuts and would only even consider the deep-fried version. Then I opened the bakery and wanted to experiment with different flours and gluten-free options. I also started looking at different whole foods that could be used as egg replacers. This recipe came about from a staff member baking on her days off and bringing us some gluten-free baked vanilla doughnuts. They were delicious and so soft. I instantly thought how well they would taste with some sort of jam and accompanied with a cup of tea. Then I thought, why not put all those flavours in the doughnut? We bake these fresh, just before opening our bakery doors, and they are very popular.

Doughnuts

250g (1 cup) unsweetened oat milk

7g (1 tablespoon) loose Earl Grey tea leaves

150g (⅔ cup) pure maple syrup

28g (2 tablespoons) pure vanilla extract

250g (2 cups) fresh or frozen raspberries

150g (1 cup) gluten-free old-fashioned rolled oats, blended into a flour

100g (⅔ cup) white chia seeds

15g (3 teaspoons) baking powder

3g (½ teaspoon) fine sea salt

Icing

175g (1⅓ cups) vegan icing sugar

Juice of 1 lemon

For decorating (optional)

100g (¾ cup) dehydrated raspberries

Make the doughnuts

1. Preheat the oven to 350°F (175°C).

2. In a small saucepan, combine the oat milk and tea leaves and bring to a simmer over medium heat. Remove from the heat and allow to steep for 5 minutes. Strain the tea through a fine-mesh sieve into a large bowl. Let cool for 10 minutes, then place in the fridge to chill for 20 minutes.

3. Remove the infused milk from the fridge. Add the maple syrup, vanilla, and raspberries. Lightly whisk to combine.

4. Add the oat flour, chia seeds, baking powder, and salt and whisk until a thick batter forms with no dry spots remaining. Allow the batter to rest so the dry ingredients hydrate, 10 minutes.

5. Fill a piping bag fitted with a No. 6 or 8 plain tip with the batter. Lightly coat two 6-ring doughnut pans with canola oil spray. Working quickly, pipe the batter into the wells of the pans, filling to the rim.

6. Bake until the doughnuts are golden brown and a skewer inserted into the centre of the doughnuts comes out clean, 14 to 16 minutes. Immediately invert the pan over a cooling rack and gently tap to release the doughnuts. Arrange them dome side up and let cool completely, 30 minutes.

Meanwhile, make the icing and finish the doughnuts

7. Sift the icing sugar into a medium bowl. Add the lemon juice and stir with a rubber spatula until the icing is smooth and covers the back of the spatula nicely. If the icing runs off very quickly, add a little more icing sugar, and if the icing is thick and doesn't move, add a little more lemon juice.

8. Fill a piping bag fitted with a No. 3 or 4 plain tip with the icing. Pipe fine lines over the top of the doughnuts in a zigzag pattern. (Alternatively, use a spoon to drizzle the icing over the doughnuts.) Garnish the doughnuts with dehydrated raspberries, if using.

9. These doughnuts are best enjoyed on the day they are made but can stored in an airtight container in the fridge for up to 2 days.

Maplecomb

Makes 500g

This aerated sugary treat has many names all over the world, including sponge toffee, honeycomb, cinder toffee, hokey pokey, fairy food, puff candy, and seafoam candy. This version is made vegan by switching out the traditional honey for maple syrup, corn syrup, or brown rice syrup. Obviously, now that we live in Canada, maple syrup is the number one choice every time when it comes to choosing a liquid sugar!

90g (6 tablespoons) water
150g (⅔ cup) pure maple syrup or light corn syrup
10g (2 teaspoons) pure vanilla extract
500g (2½ cups) raw cane sugar
30g (2 tablespoons) baking soda

1. Lightly grease a 13 × 9 × 2-inch (33 × 23 × 5cm) baking pan with a neutral oil such as sunflower or canola and line the bottom and sides with parchment paper or foil. Lightly grease the top of the parchment paper or foil. (Alternatively, line a large baking sheet with a silicone baking mat.)

2. In a large, deep saucepan, combine the water, maple syrup, vanilla, and sugar. Let sit for 5 minutes to allow the sugar to start dissolving.

3. Bring the mixture to a simmer over medium-high heat, without stirring or shaking. If it starts to boil up the sides of the saucepan, use a small pastry brush dipped in water to wipe down the sides to prevent sugar crystallization. Place a candy thermometer in the saucepan and simmer until the mixture turns golden brown and reaches 300°F (150°C) if using maple syrup, or 335°F (168°C) if using corn syrup. This should take approximately 10 minutes.

4. Remove the saucepan from the heat and, working quickly, add the baking soda and whisk thoroughly to mix everything together, about 5 seconds. The mixture will bubble and expand. Immediately pour the toffee into the prepared pan—do not shake, spread, or flatten the toffee, just let it be. Allow the toffee to cool completely in a dry area before touching it, 1 hour.

5. Break the maplecomb into pieces. Use it to garnish cake or dessert, or dip it into melted dark chocolate and chopped toasted nuts to have as a sweet treat. Store in an airtight container at room temperature for up to 3 days.

Celebration

Puff Pastry

Makes 1.2kg of pastry

This vegan puff pastry has an incredibly flaky texture, light and aerated, with a beautiful clean cultured butter flavour. The recipe took a lot of testing to get there! It's all about the butter you choose and allowing lots of time between the folds. Vegan butter has moved on a lot from the nasty margarine of the 1970s. I highly recommend Miyoko's cultured vegan butter. Naturli' vegan block performs equally well. I have tested this recipe with both brands and have had great results. Avoid using margarine or oil-heavy vegan butters, as they are very difficult to work with and make greasy, heavy pastry.

Making the puff pastry the day before needed ensures that none of the steps are rushed and the pastry has time to fully chill in the fridge overnight. Once the pastry is made, it's time to make the "sausage" rolls on page 277 or the apple tart on page 226.

430g (2 cups) salted or unsalted vegan butter, frozen for at least 1 hour or overnight
510g (4 cups + 2 tablespoons) all-purpose flour
5g (1 teaspoon) fine sea salt salt (optional)
280g (1 cup + 3 tablespoons) ice cold water

1. Grate the frozen butter on the large holes of a box grater onto a plate or into a bowl. Place the grated butter back in the freezer while preparing the other ingredients.
2. In the bowl of a stand mixer fitted with the paddle, combine the flour, salt (if using), and 50g (3 tablespoons + 2 teaspoons) of the frozen grated butter. Mix on low speed until the butter is incorporated and the mixture resembles breadcrumbs, about 2 minutes. Add the ice cold water and mix on low speed until a shaggy dough forms with no dry patches, 1 minute.
3. Remove the dough from the mixer and gently knead it on an unfloured work surface until it becomes smoother. Press the dough into a rough rectangle about 1 inch (2.5cm) thick. Place it in a resealable plastic bag or wrap it in plastic wrap and chill in the fridge for 1 hour.

4. Lightly flour your work surface. Remove the dough from the fridge (keep the bag or plastic to wrap the dough between folds). Roll out the dough into a rectangle approximately 12 × 18 inches (30 × 45cm) with a long side facing you. Scatter 380g (1⅔ cups) of the frozen grated butter over the dough, leaving a 2-inch (5cm) border on all sides.
5. Fold the exposed border over the dough on all sides. Carefully fold the left side of the dough over to the right by a third, and then again by another third. It should resemble a book about 5 × 8 inches (12 × 20cm).
6. Lightly flour the work surface and the dough. Turn the dough so a long side is facing you. Gently roll out the dough to a 12 × 18-inch (30 × 45cm) rectangle. Do not be too heavy-handed, as the butter must stay inside the dough. If the dough starts to stick, lightly flour the work surface and the dough. Do a second fold, starting on the left and folding the dough to the right by a third and again to the right by a third. Place the dough back in the bag or plastic wrap and chill in the fridge for 1 hour.
7. Remove the dough from the fridge. Lightly flour the work surface and the dough. With a long side facing you, gently roll out the dough into an 8 × 20-inch (20 × 50cm) rectangle.
8. Fold the dough like a book: starting on the left side, fold the dough to the middle. Then fold the right side to the middle. Fold one half over the other, like closing a book, to form a 5 × 8-inch (12 × 20cm) rectangle (see photos). This is called a *book fold*. You have just folded the dough 4 times and created lots of beautiful layers with the butter captured between each one, called *lamination*. Wrap the dough back up in the plastic and place it back in the fridge for 30 minutes.
9. Repeat steps 7 and 8 two more times, chilling the dough for at least 30 minutes between folds.
10. After the final book fold, wrap the dough very well with your reserved plastic wrap and chill it overnight before using it. The puff pastry can also be frozen for up to 1 month. Defrost in the fridge overnight before using.

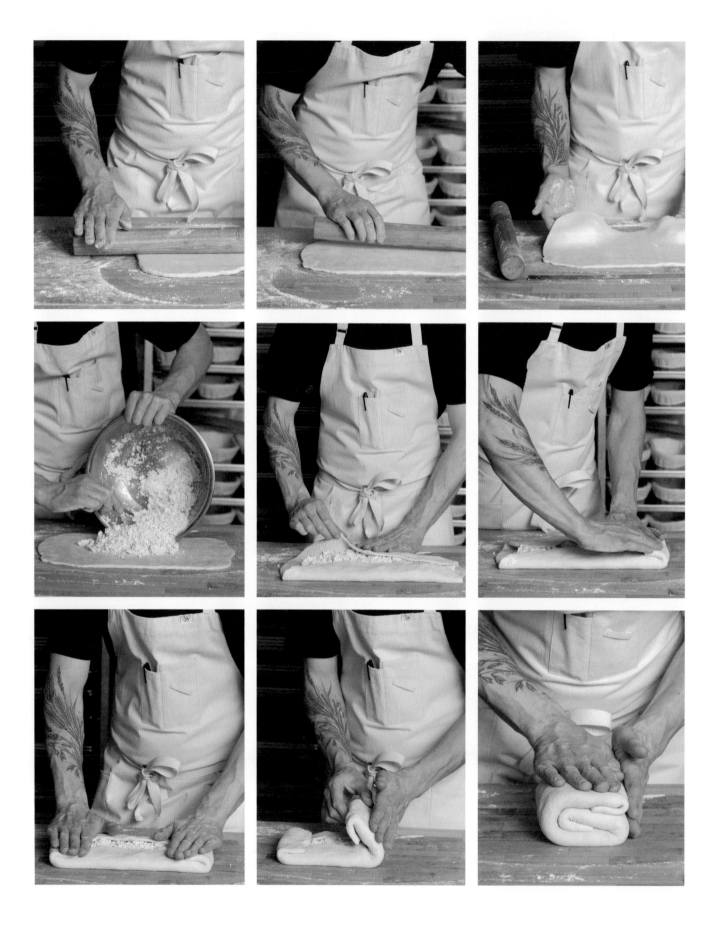

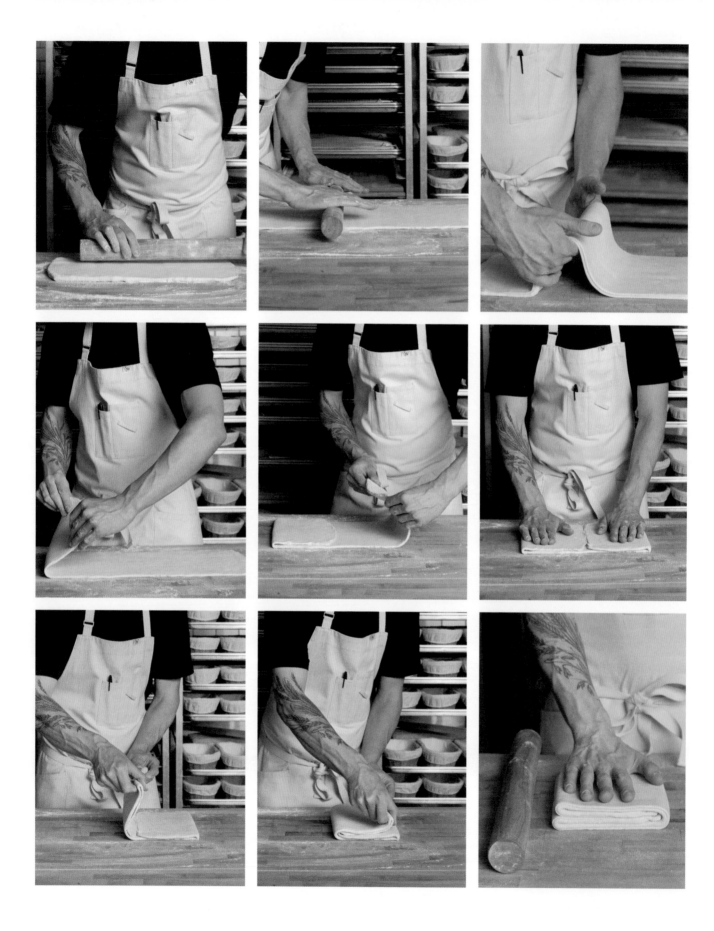

Lentil, Mushroom, and Herb "Sausage" Rolls

Makes 6 large or 12 small pastries

There is a well-known chain of bakeries in the UK called Greggs, which garnered much media attention when it launched its incredibly popular vegan sausage roll for Veganuary in 2019. I have never been able to try one of these celebrated sausage rolls, so I decided to make my own instead. Greggs use the branded Quorn vegetarian mince filling in theirs, but being a chef, I just had to make my own filling from scratch, with lentils and umami-bomb mushrooms. Serve these rolls as party canapés, ideally on the day they are baked, with some homemade chutney, tomato ketchup, or mustard.

1 batch Puff Pastry (page 270), made at least
   24 hours ahead

Filling

200g (1 cup) dried green or Puy lentils
   (400g/2½ cups cooked)
500g (2¼ cups) vegetable stock
200g (2¼ cups) cremini mushrooms, washed
175g (2 cups) mixed mushrooms (such as oyster,
   brown shimeji, maitake, and enoki)
13g (1 tablespoon) olive oil
1 medium red onion, finely chopped
3 large garlic cloves, puréed
50g (⅓ cup) pine nuts, chopped
50g (½ cup) walnuts, chopped
30g (1 tablespoon) brown miso paste
15g (1 tablespoon) vegan Worcestershire sauce
15g (1 tablespoon) prepared English mustard
8.5g (1 tablespoon) ground flaxseed
5g (2 teaspoons) porcini powder
5g (3 sprigs) chopped fresh sage
5g (2 sprigs) chopped fresh rosemary
5g (3 sprigs) chopped fresh thyme
5g (1 teaspoon) smoked salt
2.5g (½ teaspoon) black pepper
Leaves from a large handful of fresh flat-leaf
   parsley, finely chopped

"Egg" Wash

50g (¼ cup) unsweetened soy milk
5g (1 teaspoon) pure maple syrup

50g sesame seeds, for sprinkling

1. Check the lentils for sticks and stones. Place the lentils in a fine-mesh sieve, and rinse them thoroughly under cold running water. Transfer them to a small saucepan and add the vegetable stock. Bring to a boil, then reduce the heat to low and simmer until they are tender, 15 to 20 minutes. Strain the lentils, reserving the cooking liquid, and set both aside.

2. Working in batches, in a food processor, pulse the cremini mushrooms and the mixed mushrooms until finely chopped. Set aside.

3. Heat the olive oil in a large saucepan or casserole pot over low heat. Once the oil is warmed, add the red onions and cook, stirring every minute or so, until they are softened and translucent, 7 to 8 minutes. Add the garlic and cook, stirring, until it is softened and fragrant, 1 minute.

4. Add the mushrooms and increase the heat to medium. Continue cooking until the mushroom liquid has reduced, 2 to 3 minutes. Add 150g (⅔ cup) of the lentil cooking liquid, pine nuts, walnuts, miso, Worcestershire sauce, mustard, flaxseed, porcini powder, sage, rosemary, thyme, smoked salt, and pepper. Continue cooking until the liquid has thickened and reduced, 3 to 4 minutes.

5. Add the drained lentils and parsley and mix thoroughly. Remove from the heat and allow the mixture to cool for 5 minutes.

6. Transfer half of the mixture to the food processor and pulse it to a sausage texture. Stir this back into the pan. Transfer the mixture to an airtight container and place it in the fridge to chill for at least 1 hour or overnight.

continued . . .

7. Line a baking sheet with parchment paper and place another sheet of parchment paper on a work surface. Shape the mushroom and lentil mixture into two even sausage-sized logs, approximately 12 inches (30cm) long. Place the sausages on the lined baking sheet and return them to the fridge while you roll out the puff pastry.

8. Roll out the puff pastry on a lightly floured work surface to a 12 × 16-inch (30 × 40cm) rectangle, ¼ inch (5mm) thick. Cut the pastry in half lengthwise to make 2 smaller rectangles, each 12 × 8 inches (30 × 20cm).

9. To make the "egg" wash, in a small bowl, whisk together the soy milk and maple syrup.

10. Remove the lentil sausages from the fridge. Lay a sausage on each pastry rectangle, just off the centre. Lightly brush the "egg" wash around the pastry to help seal the edges. Fold the pastry up and over the sausage, and crimp the edges together with a fork. (The rolls are not actually rolled.) Lightly brush the top of the pastries

with the "egg" wash and sprinkle with the sesame seeds. Transfer the rolls to the lined baking sheet and chill in the fridge for 30 minutes.

11. Meanwhile, preheat the oven to 425°F (220°C).

12. Transfer the sausage rolls to a cutting board. Using a large knife, cut each roll into six 2-inch (5cm) or three 4-inch (10cm) pieces. Arrange the cut rolls on the lined baking sheet, leaving 2 inches (5cm) between them.

13. Bake the sausage rolls until they are golden brown, 30 to 35 minutes. Transfer them to a cooling rack (to avoid greasy bottoms) to cool for 5 minutes before serving. Using a serrated knife, cut the sausage rolls into smaller bite-size pieces.

14. Store the sausage rolls in an airtight container in the fridge for up to 3 days or in the freezer for up to 2 weeks. Thaw in the fridge and reheat in a 375°F (190°C) oven for 20 minutes.

Hot Cross Buns

Makes 18 buns (150g each)

Easter is, of course, a Christian tradition, a time when Jesus was said to have died on the cross and been resurrected two days after his burial. Hot cross buns are spiced sweet buns with dried fruits such as raisins inside and were traditionally made without dairy products, which people gave up for the forty-day period of abstinence named Lent. They have been eaten during Lent, and especially on Good Friday, for centuries. The cross is said to represent that which Jesus was crucified upon, and the spices symbolize those used to embalm Christ's body.

These hot cross buns are great freshly baked, but also delicious sliced in half and toasted on both sides until golden brown the day after. Packed with aromatic spices and dried and fresh fruit, they are easy to put together, and the bake will fill your home with the most amazing aromas. Whether you are religious or not, hot cross buns are a real treat.

Levain

1½ batches Levain (page 29)

Bun Dough

1 medium orange

150g black raisins

50g ground flaxseed

600g unsweetened oat milk

300g active levain (6 to 8 hours after feeding)
   (or 25g fresh baker's yeast)

125g pure maple syrup

500g red spring wheat or stone-ground whole
   wheat flour

500g bread flour

150g cold vegan butter

5g ground allspice

5g ground cinnamon

5g freshly grated nutmeg

5g ground ginger

25g fine sea salt

250g Braeburn or Gala apple, diced into ¼-inch
   (5mm) pieces

150g dried apricots, diced into ¼-inch (5mm) pieces

Cross Mixture

150g (⅔ cup) water

25g (⅓ cup) canola or vegetable oil

150g (1¼ cups) all-purpose flour

2.5g (½ teaspoon) baking powder

2.5g (½ teaspoon) raw cane sugar

2.5g (½ teaspoon) fine sea salt

"Egg" Wash

40g (¼ cup) unsweetened soy milk

5g (1 teaspoon) pure maple syrup

5g (1 teaspoon) organic canola oil

Maple Glaze

150g (½ cup) pure maple syrup

150g (¾ cup) raw cane sugar

150g (¾ cup) water

Prepare the levain

1. Prepare the levain as directed on pages 29 to 30 in the Sourdough Starter Guide. Feed the active starter early in the morning (by 7 a.m.) the day you plan to mix the dough so that it is active and tripled in size after 4 to 6 hours. Alternatively, prepare the levain with a less active starter—approximately 10 percent inoculation (10g) calculated to the total weight of flours—the night before (by 10 p.m.) so it's ready in the morning, 8 to 10 hours later.

Prepare ingredients for the dough

2. Trim the ends off the orange, cut it into quarters, and remove any seeds. Place the orange in a small saucepan, cover with water, and simmer for 45 minutes. Drain the

continued . . .

oranges and transfer to a high-speed blender. Blend on high speed to a smooth purée. Measure 150g of the purée, transfer to a small bowl, and set aside to cool. (Save any remaining purée for another use.)

3. Place the raisins in a small bowl, cover with boiling water, stir, and let sit for 30 minutes. This will allow the raisins to swell, become juicy, and not take any additional moisture from the dough. Drain the raisins and set aside in the bowl.

4. To make your flax egg, whisk together the flaxseed and oat milk in a small bowl until a smooth paste forms. If there are any lumps, push a small rubber spatula against the side of the bowl to break them up. Let sit for 10 minutes to bloom and thicken.

Mix

5. In the bowl of a stand mixer fitted with the dough hook, combine the flax egg, reserved orange purée, active levain, maple syrup, spring wheat flour, bread flour, butter, allspice, cinnamon, nutmeg, and ginger. Mix on medium-low speed until a shaggy dough forms with no dry patches, 5 minutes. Cover the dough with a kitchen towel or loose-fitting lid and allow it to rest for 10 minutes.

6. Add the salt and start kneading on low speed, then gradually increase the speed to high. Knead until the dough looks smooth and pulls away from the sides of the bowl, 6 to 8 minutes. Turn the mixer off and allow the dough to rest for 5 minutes. Perform the windowpane test to check if the dough is sufficiently mixed and developed: Pull away a small piece of dough and stretch it between your fingers to create a "window." If you can see light without tearing the dough, enough gluten has developed and the dough is strong. If the dough rips quite easily, continue kneading for 1 or 2 minutes longer, then repeat the windowpane test.

7. Add the apple, apricots, and softened raisins to the dough. Mix on medium-low speed until combined, 2 minutes.

8. Lightly oil a large bowl or container that is three or four times the size of the dough. Remove the dough from the mixer bowl and form it into a ball or droplet shape. Drop the dough smooth side up into the oiled bowl and cover with a kitchen towel or loose-fitting lid. Let the dough sit in a warm (72 to 75°F/22 to 24°C), draft-free place for 30 minutes.

9. After the resting period, give the dough one set of stretch-and-folds as directed on pages 33 to 34. Cover the dough and allow to bulk ferment at room temperature until it has doubled in size, 2 to 3 hours. (If you are using fresh baker's yeast, the dough will ferment a lot quicker, so it will only need to rest for 1 hour.) Cover the dough with a loose-fitting lid or plate and place in the fridge to cold proof overnight, 16 to 18 hours.

Shape and proof

10. Line 2 large baking sheets with parchment paper. (You will need to preheat another 2 large baking sheets in step 13. If you don't have 4 large baking sheets, arrange the buns on a parchment-lined large cutting board or simply on parchment on the work surface.) Remove the dough from the fridge and transfer it to a lightly floured work surface. Using a bench knife or chef's knife, divide the dough into 18 equal-size pieces (150g each) and shape them into balls. It's best to weigh the buns for even baking and appearance.

11. Working with 1 ball at a time, flatten it into a disc. Working from 12 o'clock, pull the dough into the centre. Keep going all the way round the disc. This shaping technique is used to strengthen the dough before its final shape. Turn the ball over and slightly cup your hands and form the dough into a ball shape (see pages 106 to 107 for shaping photos).

12. Arrange the shaped buns on the lined baking sheets, leaving 1 inch (2.5cm) between them. As the buns proof and double in size, they will connect. Loosely cover the buns with a sheet of plastic wrap or a kitchen towel and allow to proof in a warm (72 to 75°F/22 to 24°C), draft-free place until they have doubled in size, 2 to 3 hours. Every 20 to 30 minutes, check that the cover is not sticking, loosening it if necessary to allow some space. Once the buns have doubled in size, gently press the top of a bun with your finger; if your finger leaves a slight indent, the buns are ready to be baked.

13. About an hour before the buns have finished proofing, arrange the oven racks in the upper and lower thirds of the oven and place a large baking sheet on each rack. Preheat the oven to 385°F (195°C).

Prepare the cross mixture

14. In a medium bowl, combine the water, canola oil, all-purpose flour, baking powder, sugar, and salt. Whisk together until a smooth paste forms with no dry patches. Do not overmix or the paste will develop gluten too much and make piping more difficult. Cover and set aside to relax for 20 to 30 minutes.

15. Transfer the cross mixture to a piping bag fitted with a No. 6 plain tip.

"Egg" wash and bake

16. If you only have two baking sheets, only "egg" wash and pipe crosses on the buns you are baking first. Repeat once the first lot of buns baked and removed from the oven.

In a small bowl, whisk together the soy milk, maple syrup, and canola oil. Gently brush the "egg" wash onto the top and sides of each bun. Pipe a line of cross mixture along each row of buns, then pipe lines in the other direction to make crosses. Immediately slide the buns on their parchment onto the preheated baking sheets. Bake the hot cross buns until they are golden brown, 18 to 20 minutes. If you are not using a convection oven, you may need to rotate the buns halfway through. Transfer the buns to a cooling rack and let cool for at least 10 minutes before glazing.

Make the maple glaze and finish the buns

17. In a small saucepan, combine the maple syrup, sugar, and water. Bring to a boil and reduce the liquid until tacky between your fingertips, but do not over-reduce or it will crystallize. Using a pastry brush, glaze the buns with at least two coatings. This will add a little more sweetness and a great texture to the buns and make them shine.

18. Enjoy these hot cross buns freshly baked or, if they last long enough, store them in an airtight container at room temperature for up to 3 days. If stored, slice the buns in half and toast.

Carrot Hot Cross Buns

Makes 18 buns (150g each)

This fun variation of the classic hot cross bun was inspired by the start of local spring carrots and wanting to cater to the anti-raisin folk too, as well as a little nod to all the springtime bunnies who love carrots. Replacing half of the soy milk with carrot juice produces a beautiful golden dough, and the flavour and texture are heightened with poached diced carrot and spices like cardamom and anise. This combination will create many intoxicating aromas throughout your home and bring your neighbours calling. These carrot buns really come into their own when served with the orange-infused vegan butter.

Levain

    1½ batches Levain (page 29)

Bun Dough

    1 medium orange

    200g carrot, diced into ¼-inch (5mm) pieces

    400g freshly pressed carrot juice

    50g ground flaxseed

    300g unsweetened soy milk

    300g active levain (6 to 8 hours after feeding) (or 25g fresh baker's yeast)

    125g pure maple syrup

    500g red spring wheat or stone-ground whole wheat flour

    500g bread flour

    150g cold vegan butter

    5g ground allspice

    5g ground cinnamon

    5g ground cardamom

    5g ground ginger

    5g anise seeds

    25g fine sea salt

    250g Braeburn or Gala apple, diced into ¼-inch (5mm) pieces

Orange Butter

    1 large carrot (125g), peeled and thinly sliced

    Zest and juice of 1 orange, plus more zest to taste

    150g (¼ cup) soft vegan butter (such as Earth Balance)

Cross Mixture

    150g (⅔ cup) water or carrot juice

    25g (⅓ cup) canola or vegetable oil

    150g (1¼ cups) all-purpose flour

    2.5g (½ teaspoon) baking powder

    2.5g (½ teaspoon) raw cane sugar

    2.5g (½ teaspoon) salt

"Egg" wash

    40g (¼ cup) unsweetened soy milk

    5g (1 teaspoon) pure maple syrup

    5g (1 teaspoon) organic canola oil

Maple Glaze

    150g (½ cup) pure maple syrup

    150g (¾ cup) raw cane sugar

    150g (¾ cup) water

    1 cracked cardamom pod

    5g (1 teaspoon) pure vanilla extract

Prepare the levain

1. Prepare the levain as directed on pages 29 to 30 in the Sourdough Starter Guide. Feed the active starter early in the morning (by 7 a.m.) the day you plan to mix the dough so that it is active and tripled in size after 4 to 6 hours. Alternatively, prepare the levain with a less active starter—approximately 10 percent inoculation (10g) calculated to the total weight of flours—the night before (by 10 p.m.) so it's ready in the morning, 8 to 10 hours later.

continued . . .

Prepare ingredients for the dough

2. Trim the ends off the orange, cut it into quarters, and remove any seeds. Place the orange in a small saucepan, cover with water, and simmer for 45 minutes. Drain the orange and transfer to a high-speed blender. Blend on high speed to a smooth purée. Measure 150g of the purée, transfer to a small bowl, and set aside to cool. (Save any remaining purée for another use.)

3. Combine the diced carrot and the carrot juice in a small saucepan. Bring to a simmer over medium heat, then remove from the heat. Allow the carrot to continue cooking in the hot carrot juice until softened, 10 minutes. Strain the carrot and place in a small bowl. Measure 300g of the carrot juice into a separate small bowl. (Any remaining carrot juice can be used in the cross mixture to replace some of the water.)

4. To make your flax egg, whisk together the flaxseed and soy milk in a small bowl until a smooth paste forms. If there are any lumps, push a small rubber spatula against the side of the bowl to break them up. Let sit for 10 minutes to bloom and thicken.

Mix

5. In the bowl of a stand mixer fitted with the dough hook, combine the flax egg, reserved orange purée, carrot juice, active levain, maple syrup, spring wheat flour, bread flour, butter, allspice, cinnamon, cardamom, ginger, and anise seeds. Mix on medium-low speed until a shaggy dough forms with no dry patches, 5 minutes. Cover the dough with a kitchen towel or loose-fitting lid and allow it rest for 10 minutes.

6. Add the salt and start kneading on low speed, then gradually increase the speed to high. Knead until the dough looks smooth and pulls away from the sides of the bowl, 6 to 8 minutes. Turn the mixer off and allow the dough to rest for a few minutes. Perform the windowpane test to check if the dough is sufficiently mixed and developed: Pull away a small piece of dough and stretch it between your fingers to create a "window." If you can see light without tearing the dough, enough gluten has developed and the dough is strong. If the dough rips quite easily, continue

kneading for 1 or 2 minutes longer, then repeat the windowpane test.

7. Add the apple and poached carrot to the dough. Mix on medium-low speed until combined, 2 minutes.

8. Lightly oil a large bowl or container that is three or four times the size of the dough. Remove the dough from the mixer bowl and form it into a ball or droplet shape. Drop the dough smooth side up into the oiled bowl and cover it with a kitchen towel or loose-fitting lid. Let the dough sit in a warm (72 to 75°F/22 to 24°C), draft-free place for 30 minutes.

9. After the resting period, give the dough one set of stretch-and-folds as directed on pages 33 to 34. Cover the dough and allow it to bulk ferment at room temperature until it has doubled in size, 2 to 3 hours. (If you are using baker's yeast, the dough will ferment a lot quicker, so it will only need to rest 1 hour at room temperature.) Cover the dough with a loose-fitting lid or plate and place in the fridge to cold proof overnight, 16 to 18 hours.

Make the orange butter

10. Combine the sliced carrot and orange zest and juice in a small saucepan. Simmer until the carrot is very soft, 10 to 15 minutes.

11. Strain the cooking liquid (reserving the carrot), return it to the saucepan, and reduce it until it has slightly thickened.

12. Blend the carrot and reduced cooking liquid in a high-speed blender until smooth. It should weigh approximately 75g. Transfer the mixture to a small bowl and refrigerate until cold, 1 hour.

13. In a small bowl, using a rubber spatula, mix the purée with the soft butter until smooth. Add extra orange zest to taste. Store the orange butter in an airtight container in the fridge until ready to spread on the hot cross buns.

Shape and proof

14. Line 2 large baking sheets with parchment paper. (You will need to preheat another 2 large baking sheets in step 17. If you don't have 4 large baking sheets, arrange the buns on a parchment-lined large cutting board or simply on parchment on the work surface.)

Remove the dough from the fridge and transfer it to a lightly floured work surface. Using a bench knife or chef's knife, divide the dough into 18 equal-size pieces (150g each) and shape them into balls. It is best to weigh the buns for even baking and appearance.

15. Working with 1 ball at a time, flatten it into a disc. Working from 12 o'clock, pull the dough into the centre. Keep going all the way around the disc. This shaping technique is used to strengthen the dough before its final shape. Turn the ball over and slightly cup your hands and form the dough into a ball shape (see pages 106 to 107 for shaping photos).

16. Arrange the shaped buns on the lined baking sheets, leaving 1 inch (2.5cm) between them. As the buns proof and double in size, they will connect. Loosely cover the buns with a sheet of plastic wrap or a kitchen towel and allow to proof in a warm (72 to 75°F/22 to 24°C), draft-free place until they have doubled in size, 2 to 3 hours. Every 20 to 30 minutes, check that the cover is not sticking, loosening it if necessary to allow some space. Once the buns have doubled in size, gently press the top of a bun with your finger; if your finger leaves a slight indent, the buns are ready to be baked.

17. About an hour before the buns have finished proofing, arrange the oven racks in the upper and lower thirds of the oven and place a large baking sheet on each rack. Preheat the oven to 385°F (195°C).

Prepare the cross mixture

18. In a medium bowl, combine the water (or water and any leftover carrot juice), canola oil, all-purpose flour, baking powder, sugar, and salt. Whisk together until a smooth paste forms with no dry patches. Do not overmix or the paste will develop gluten too much and make piping more difficult. Cover and set aside to relax for 20 to 30 minutes.

19. Transfer the cross mixture to a piping bag fitted with a No. 6 plain tip.

"Egg" wash and bake

20. If you only have two baking sheets, only "egg" wash and pipe crosses on the buns you are baking first. Repeat once the first lot of buns are baked and removed from the oven.

In a small bowl, whisk together the soy milk, maple syrup, and canola oil. Gently brush the "egg" wash onto the top and sides of each bun. Pipe a line of cross mixture along each row of buns, then pipe lines in the other direction to make crosses. Immediately slide the buns on their parchment onto the preheated baking sheets. Bake the hot cross buns until they are golden brown, 18 to 20 minutes. If you are not using a convection oven, you may need to rotate the buns halfway through. Transfer the buns to a cooling rack and let cool for at least 10 minutes before glazing.

Make the maple glaze and finish the buns

21. In a small saucepan, combine the maple syrup, sugar, water, cardamom, and vanilla. Bring to a boil and reduce the liquid until tacky between your fingertips, but do not over-reduce or it will crystallize. Using a pastry brush, glaze the buns with at least two coats. This will add a little more sweetness and a great texture to the buns and make them shine.

22. Enjoy these hot cross buns freshly baked and spread with the orange butter. If they last long enough, store them in an airtight container at room temperature for up to 3 days. If stored, slice the buns in half and toast.

Maple, Macadamia, and Rye Biscotti

Makes about 14 biscotti

This dangerously moreish classic Italian twice-baked biscuit is perfect for dunking in coffee. Biscotti are usually made with all-purpose flour, sugar, eggs, and almonds or pine nuts, but here I've replaced most of those. Applesauce, with its ability to bind ingredients and its moist texture, is a great substitute for eggs. I also switched out some sugar for maple syrup, and use some rye flour and the king of nuts, macadamia, which has a similar texture to pine nuts and a great crunch like almonds. Extra-virgin coconut oil gives the biscotti a subtle buttery coconut note.

Because biscotti are twice-baked, they're drier, and so they're best dunked in a beverage. Dessert wine is the typical choice in Italy, and coffee is more common outside of Italy. This dryness means they have a long shelf life and therefore make excellent gifts, especially around Christmas.

2 medium unpeeled apples such as Braeburn
    or Gala, cut into ½-inch (1cm) pieces
    (to make 85g/⅓ cup applesauce)
75g (⅓ cup) extra-virgin coconut oil, melted
60g (4 tablespoons) pure maple syrup
10g (2⅓ teaspoon) pure vanilla extract
3g (⅔ teaspoon) almond extract
180g (1½ cups) all-purpose flour
60g (⅔ cup) stone-ground whole-grain rye flour
100g (½ cup) raw cane sugar, plus more for
    sprinkling
7g (1½ teaspoons) baking powder
3g (1 teaspoon) fine sea salt
150g (1¼ cups) chopped natural macadamia nuts

1. Place the apple pieces in a small saucepan with a little water, cover, and cook over medium-low heat, stirring every 5 minutes, until mushy, 10 to 15 minutes. Blend into a purée using the single-serve jar of a high-speed blender. Transfer to a large bowl and set aside to cool at room temperature, 30 minutes. (It is important not to use chilled applesauce as it will solidify the coconut oil.)

2. Meanwhile, preheat the oven to 340°F (170°C). Line a large baking sheet with parchment paper or a silicone baking mat.

3. To the cooled applesauce, add the melted coconut oil, maple syrup, vanilla, and almond extract. Whisk together.

4. Sift the all-purpose flour into a large bowl. Add the rye flour, sugar, baking powder, and salt. Whisk together.

5. Add the dry ingredients to the wet ingredients in 2 additions, gently mixing until a shaggy dough forms. Add the macadamia nuts and mix until just incorporated.

6. Turn the dough out onto the lined baking sheet. Using slightly wet hands, form the dough into a 3 × 7-inch (8 × 18cm) rectangle about ½ inch (1cm) thick. Lightly sprinkle with sugar. Bake until golden brown, 18 to 20 minutes. Remove from the oven and reduce the temperature to 325°F (160°C). Let the log cool on the baking sheet for 10 minutes.

7. Using a sharp bread or chef's knife, slice the log crosswise into ½-inch (1cm) pieces. Transfer the biscotti back onto the baking sheet, keeping them standing up, with space in between for even baking. Return the biscotti to the oven and bake until they are golden brown on all their sides, 20 to 30 minutes. Play around with timing of the second bake if you prefer a softer or crunchier biscuit. They will keep for longer if baked for about 30 minutes. The biscotti may feel slightly soft when removed from the oven, but they will dry out as they cool. Let the biscotti cool on the baking sheet for 10 minutes. Carefully transfer to a cooling rack and let cool completely.

8. The biscotti are best served with freshly made coffee and are great for dunking. Store them in an airtight container at room temperature for up to 5 days.

Celebration Chocolate Cake with Double Chocolate Buttercream

Makes one 9-inch (23cm) round 2-layer cake, serves 12 to 14

Here is *the* chocolate cake for a special celebration and any chocolate lover. Indulgent and rich, this cake comes with a warning: Don't let your eyes be bigger than your belly! I'm talking from experience. You don't want to end up like Bruce Bogtrotter—you know, the kid from Roald Dahl's *Matilda*. This cake tends to get better day by day after it is baked, so it is best to bake it a day ahead of serving.

Sponge

240g (1 cup) unsweetened soy milk

15g (1 tablespoon) apple cider vinegar

210g (1½ cups) all-purpose flour

110g (1 cup) dark cocoa powder

12.5g (2½ teaspoons) baking powder

8g (1½ teaspoons) baking soda

335g (1½ cups) fine raw cane sugar

65g (½ cup) stone-ground whole-grain spelt flour

2.5g (½ teaspoon) fine sea salt

180g (¾ cup) natural applesauce (page 251)

120g (½ cup) espresso or French press coffee, cooled

120g (½ cup) extra-virgin coconut oil, melted

15g (3 teaspoons) pure vanilla extract

Double Chocolate Buttercream

225g (1 cup) cold vegan butter

300g (2¼ cups) vegan icing sugar

80g (¾ cup) cocoa powder, sifted

80 to 100g (⅓ to ½ cup) unsweetened oat milk

5g (1 teaspoon) pure vanilla extract

100g (½ cup) chopped dairy-free dark chocolate, melted

For decorating

Maplecomb (page 266)

Fresh seasonal berries (strawberries, raspberries, blueberries, blackberries, or elderberries)

Dairy-free vanilla ice cream, for serving (optional)

Make the sponge layers

1. Preheat the oven to 350°F (175°C). Lightly coat two 9-inch (23cm) springform pans with canola oil spray and line the bottom and sides with parchment paper.

2. To make your buttermilk, in a medium bowl, stir together the soy milk and apple cider vinegar. Let sit for at least 5 minutes to sour. The milk will curdle.

3. Meanwhile, sift the all-purpose flour, cocoa powder, baking powder, and baking soda into a large bowl. Add the cane sugar, spelt flour, and salt and whisk to combine.

4. To the buttermilk, add the applesauce, cooled coffee, coconut oil, and vanilla. Whisk to combine.

5. Make a well in the middle of the dry ingredients. Pour the wet ingredients into the well and, using a rubber spatula, gently stir together using a figure-eight movement until the batter is just mixed and there are no dry patches or lumps. (This motion will help to combine all the ingredients without developing too much gluten, so preventing a tough cake.) Place the prepared springform pans, 1 at a time, on a digital scale and evenly divide the batter, approximately 700g per pan.

6. Bake the cakes until a skewer inserted in the centre of the cakes comes out clean, 30 to 35 minutes. Allow the cakes to cool in their pans for 15 to 20 minutes. Carefully remove the rings and transfer the cakes to a cooling rack to cool for at least 1 hour before icing.

continued . . .

Make the double chocolate buttercream

7. Place the butter in the bowl of a stand mixer fitted with the paddle (or in a large bowl if using a hand-held electric mixer) and beat on medium speed until it is soft and paler, 2 to 3 minutes.

8. Sift the icing sugar into the bowl and continue beating until the sugar has dissolved and the mixture is smooth, 1 to 2 minutes. Add the cocoa powder, oat milk, vanilla, and melted chocolate. Continue beating on medium speed until smooth. If the buttercream is a little thick, add a splash more oat milk and mix through.

Decorate the cake

9. If the cakes are a little domed, you can trim the tops with a long serrated knife. Place 1 sponge layer trimmed side up on a cutting board or cake board lined with parchment paper. This will help when rotating the cake

to decorate and with transferring the finished cake to a serving plate. Spoon a third of the buttercream (approximately 260g) over the cake and use a palette knife to spread it evenly all the way to the edges. Place the second cake layer on top, trimmed side down so the flattest side becomes the top. Cover the top and sides of the cake with an even layer of the remaining buttercream and smooth it with a palette knife.

10. Either lift the cake a little and slide away the parchment paper or carefully transfer it to a serving plate using 2 large palette knives. Finish the cake by arranging chunks of maplecomb and some fresh seasonal berries on top. Serve with a scoop of vanilla ice cream, if desired.

11. Store the cake in an airtight container in the fridge for up to 5 days.

Whole Wheat Pecan and Maple Pie

Makes one 10-inch (25cm) pie, serves 12

When I think of pecan pie, I think of the classic North American tart that is packed with nuts and sugar and eaten in the fall, around Thanksgiving. My variation of this festive delicacy takes inspiration from the classic British treacle tart, which is made with Lyle's Golden Syrup and breadcrumbs. As a sourdough baker this was the perfect opportunity to incorporate elements from both tarts. For the crumbs, I highly recommend using 100% Rye Sourdough (page 92) for its delicious malty and earthy flavours, but any sourdough will do for an inclusion of at least 25 percent in the pastry crust. The whole wheat pastry is very malleable and is lovely to work with. Giving a nod to our home turf, I added Canadian organic pure maple syrup along with golden syrup and molasses for more layers of sweetness and caramel tones.

Sweet Shortcrust Pastry

110g (½ cup) cold vegan butter, cut into
    1-inch (2.5cm) cubes
225g (1¾ cups) whole wheat pastry flour
25g (¼ cup) vegan icing sugar
2g (¼ teaspoon) fine sea salt
25g (2 tablespoons) ice cold water
15g (1 tablespoon) extra-virgin olive oil

Filling

150g (⅔ cup) vegan liquid egg (such as JUST Egg)
30g (¼ cup) cornstarch
50g (¼ cup) vegan butter, melted
200g (¾ cup) pure maple syrup
200g (½ cup) golden syrup
50g (2 tablespoons) blackstrap molasses
25g (2 tablespoons) pure vanilla extract
100g (¾ cup) sourdough breadcrumbs
    (I recommend 100% rye)
5g (2 teaspoons) ground cinnamon
2.5g (½ teaspoon) fine sea salt
250g (2 cups + 2 tablespoons) natural pecan pieces
    or chopped pecans

100g (¾ cup) natural pecan halves, for decorating

Make and blind-bake the pastry

1. Place the bowl of a food processor in the fridge for 30 minutes before starting. This will help keep everything cold when making the pastry.

2. Place the butter, whole wheat pastry flour, icing sugar, and salt in the chilled bowl of the food processor and pulse until combined, about 1 minute. Add the cold water and olive oil and pulse until a shaggy dough forms. Transfer the dough to an unfloured work surface and finish mixing by hand. Bring the pastry together into a ball with no dry patches.

3. Gently roll the pastry between two 12 × 18-inch (30 × 45cm) pieces of parchment paper into a 5-inch (12cm) disc. (Rolling the pastry between the paper avoids using flour or icing sugar, which would change the flavour and texture of the pastry.) Transfer the pastry (between the parchment) to a baking sheet and chill in the fridge for at least 2 hours but ideally overnight. (By partly rolling the dough now, it won't need to be worked as much to get it to the correct dimensions later. The

continued . . .

pastry needs to stay as cold as possible to prevent splitting or shrinking, so flattening the dough now, rather than shaping it into a ball, is helpful.)

4. When you are ready to bake, place a 10-inch (25cm) non-stick tart ring on a baking sheet lined with parchment paper or a silicone baking mat. (Alternatively, you can use a 10-inch/25cm round tart pan with a removeable bottom and lightly rub butter on the bottom and sides.)

5. Roll out the chilled pastry between the parchment paper into a 12-inch (30cm) circle, about ¼ inch (5mm) thick. Place the pastry back into the fridge and chill for at least 30 minutes.

6. Working quickly and confidently, remove the top sheet of parchment paper. Gently flip the pastry over the tart ring (or tart pan) and carefully ease and press it into the corners. Return the pastry to the fridge and chill for 30 minutes.

7. Meanwhile, preheat the oven to 340°F (170°C).

8. Using a small knife, trim off the excess dough, leaving ½ inch (1cm) on the sides to allow for shrinking during baking. Keep the trim, covered and in the fridge, in case you need to make repairs later.

9. Lightly prick holes all across the surface of the pastry with a fork. (This is called docking and allows steam to escape during baking, preventing the pastry from puffing up.) Line the pastry with a sheet of plastic wrap, leaving some overhang, and fill with baking beans, dried chickpeas, or rice. (This will weigh the pastry down to keep it flat.)

10. Bake the pastry case until the edges are golden brown, 20 to 25 minutes. Remove the tart from the oven and carefully lift out the plastic wrap and beans. If there are any holes or tears in the pastry, use the reserved trim to patch them up. There must be no holes in the pastry, or the filling will run straight through it. Return the pastry case to the oven to bake until the base is light golden brown and any "repair" pastry has had a chance to bake a little, 5 to 7 minutes. Remove the baked tart case from the oven and set aside while you prepare the filling.

Make the filling and bake the pie

11. In a large bowl, whisk together the vegan liquid egg and cornstarch until smooth. Add the butter, maple syrup, golden syrup, molasses, vanilla, breadcrumbs, cinnamon, and salt and whisk until smooth. Add the 250g (2 cups + 2 tablespoons) pecan pieces and mix with a rubber spatula.

12. Pour the filling into the baked tart case and gently spread it to an even layer. Decorate the top with the 100g (¾ cup) pecan halves. Carefully transfer the pie to the oven and bake until the filling is golden brown and just set when jiggled, 30 to 35 minutes. Remove the tart from the oven and let cool on the baking sheet for 30 minutes.

13. Using a serrated knife, carefully trim the excess pastry from the rim, cutting away from the tart to prevent the pastry crumbling onto the filling. Remove the tart ring.

14. Enjoy the pecan pie warm from the oven. Once it has fully cooled, store the pie in an airtight container in the fridge for up to 3 days.

Spiced Fruit and Nut Festive Sourdough

Makes two 9 × 5 × 4-inch (23 × 12 × 10cm) Pullman loaves

This celebration loaf can be easily adapted with different dried fruits, nuts, and spices to suit your tastes and preference. I've also made variations using mandarins, clementines, and satsumas. I love baking this loaf, as it makes our home smell incredible for the whole day. If you're trying to sell your home, bake this loaf on the morning of some viewings and thank me later!

A Pullman tin is basically a pan loaf with a lid, which results in a perfectly square slice, ideal for sandwiches in lunch boxes and toast made in toasters.

Levain

1 batch Levain (page 29)

Dough

100g whole natural hazelnuts

100g cooked chestnuts, roughly chopped

100g natural pecans, pieces or roughly chopped

10g ground cinnamon

5g ground ginger

2.5g ground nutmeg

2.5g ground cloves

Zest and juice of 1 large orange

100g dried figs, stems trimmed, figs halved
  or quartered

100g black raisins

100g dried cranberries

600g warm water (75 to 78°F/24 to 26°C)
  (85% hydration)

420g bread flour

210g stone-ground whole wheat flour

70g stone-ground whole-grain rye flour

50g pure maple syrup

175g active levain (100% hydration)

15g fine sea salt

Prepare the levain

1. Prepare the levain as directed on pages 29 to 30 in the Sourdough Starter Guide. Feed the active starter early in the morning (by 7 a.m.) the day you plan to mix the dough so that it is active and tripled in size after 4 to 6 hours. Alternatively, prepare the levain with a less active starter—approximately 10 percent inoculation (10g) calculated to the total weight of flours—the night before (by 10 p.m.) so it's ready in the morning, 8 to 10 hours later.

Prepare the inclusions

2. A couple of hours after mixing the levain, preheat the oven to 340°F (170°C). Scatter the hazelnuts on a small baking sheet and lightly toast them in the oven until they are golden brown, 5 minutes. Allow them to cool a little, then put the nuts in a kitchen towel and gently rub off the skins. Discard most of the skins. In the cloth, break up the nuts a little. Transfer the broken nuts to a small bowl. Add the chestnuts and pecans. Set aside.

3. Brush off any hazelnut skin from the baking sheet. Sprinkle the cinnamon, ginger, nutmeg, and cloves on the sheet and toast in the oven until fragrant, 2 to 3 minutes. Set aside.

4. Place the orange zest and juice in a small bowl. Add the figs, raisins, and cranberries. Stir to coat the dried fruit in the orange marinade, then let sit for 30 minutes.

Autolyse and mix

5. This dough is easily mixed by hand in a large bowl or with a stand mixer fitted with the dough hook on medium speed. Pour the warm water into the bowl. Add the bread flour, whole wheat flour, rye flour, toasted spice mixture, and maple syrup. Mix until a shaggy dough forms with no dry patches, 2 to 3 minutes. Cover the bowl with a kitchen towel or loose-fitting lid and let the dough rest in a warm (72 to 75°F/22 to 24°C), draft-free place for 30 minutes (autolyse). There will be no change in the dough's appearance. *continued . . .*

6. After the resting period, add the active levain to the dough and mix for 1 to 2 minutes. Cover the bowl and let sit for 10 minutes.

7. Add the salt and knead the dough using the Rubaud method as directed on page 33 (see photos on page 32) at a medium-high pace, until it is smoother in appearance, feels more active, and has a little more elasticity, 6 to 8 minutes. (If using a stand mixer, knead the dough on medium-low speed.) The dough should pull away from the sides of the bowl. Allow the dough to rest in the bowl for 2 minutes.

8. Add all the fruits and nuts, including any unabsorbed orange juice, and knead the dough with your hand (or with the stand mixer on medium-low speed) until everything is combined and evenly distributed, 1 minute.

Bulk ferment

9. Place the dough in a lightly oiled bowl or container that is four times the size of the dough and cover with a loose-fitting lid or kitchen towel. Place the dough in a warm (72 to 75°F/22 to 24°C), draft-free place. A constant temperature will ensure a consistent fermentation. Set a timer for 30 minutes.

10. When the timer goes off, perform the first set of stretch-and-folds as directed on pages 33 to 34. Again, set the timer for 30 minutes. Repeat the sets of stretch-and-folds another three or four times over a 2-hour period, depending on how the dough feels (for a total of 3 hours of timed stretch-and-folds). Once the dough feels tighter, is doming, and has good strength, cover with a kitchen towel or loose-fitting lid and allow it to rest for 60 to 90 minutes in a warm (72 to 75°F/22 to 24°C), draft-free place until it has increased in volume by approximately 50 percent.

Pre-shape and proof

11. Gently remove the dough from the container and transfer it to an unfloured work surface. Using a bench knife, cut the dough into 2 equal pieces (1kg each).

Working with 1 piece at a time, gently pre-shape the dough into a round ball. Loosely cover the dough with a kitchen towel and let it bench rest for 30 to 40 minutes.

Final shape and overnight cold proof

12. Lightly oil two 9 × 5 × 4-inch (23 × 12 × 10cm) Pullman loaf tins—don't forget the inside of the lid—and line the bottoms with parchment paper. This will help to prevent the bottom of the bread from overcolouring from the natural sugars.

13. Shape each loaf into a simple rectangle as shown on page 44. Very lightly flour the dough and carefully place it seam side down in the prepared tins. Cover with the lids and allow the loaves to proof at room temperature until they have started to increase in volume and dome a little, anywhere between 30 minutes and 2 hours (depending on the warmth of your kitchen).

14. Gently re-cover the tins of dough with their lids and place the loaves in the fridge to cold proof overnight, 12 to 18 hours.

Bake

15. The following day, check the loaves to see how much they have risen. I like to make sure they have risen to the top of the tins. Let the loaves come to room temperature, at least 1 to 2 hours. This is necessary because of the high quantity of inclusions (fruit and nuts).

16. When the loaves are almost at room temperature, preheat the oven to 375°F (190°C).

17. Bake the loaves with the lids on for 30 minutes. Lower the oven temperature to 350°F (175°C) and continue baking the bread until it is dark golden brown, another 20 minutes. Remove the tins from the oven, take the lids off (to maintain a crispy crust), and place the tins on a cooling rack for 5 minutes. Turn the loaves out of the tins and allow the bread to cool for at least 1 hour before slicing it.

18. See Storing Bread (page 51).

Gingerbread Biscuits

Makes about 2 dozen 3-inch (8cm) biscuits, or the base for 2 cheesecakes

Gingerbread has a fascinating history, apparently dating from the ancient Greeks and into the medieval era and beyond: Queen Elizabeth I would offer gingerbread to her courtiers, and the fairy tale of Hansel and Gretel has since popularized gingerbread houses at Christmastime.

These festive spicy biscuits are delicious when they are still warm from the oven, or cooled and beautifully decorated with royal icing, or used as a base for a cheese-cake. I like these biscuits to pack a punch of flavour, but if you are more sensitive to spices, the amounts can be halved—it won't affect the baking of the biscuits.

Biscuits

300g (2½ cups) all-purpose flour

80g (½ cup) stone-ground whole-grain spelt flour

3g (½ teaspoon) fine sea salt (optional)

10 to 12g (4 to 5 teaspoons) ground ginger (depending how spicy you want them)

10g (4 teaspoons) ground cinnamon

2.2g (1 teaspoon) ground nutmeg

2g (1 teaspoon) ground allspice

10g (1 teaspoon) baking soda

150g (⅔ cup) vegan butter (such as Miyoko's)

120g (⅔ cup packed) brown sugar

100g (¼ cup) golden syrup

50g (2 tablespoons) black treacle

Royal Icing (optional)

300g (2⅓ cups) vegan icing sugar, sifted

30g (2 tablespoons) aquafaba (liquid from canned chickpeas)

15g (1 tablespoon) lemon juice

Make the biscuits

1. Place the all-purpose flour, spelt flour, and salt (if using) in a large bowl and whisk together.

2. Measure the ginger, cinnamon, nutmeg, allspice, and baking soda into a small bowl and whisk together.

3. Place the butter, brown sugar, golden syrup, and treacle in a medium saucepan and gently melt over low heat, stirring occasionally, until the sugar has just dissolved, 2 minutes.

4. Add the spice mixture and whisk for 10 seconds, then remove from the heat. Add the flour mixture and, using a wooden spoon or rubber spatula, mix until a smooth cookie dough forms with no dry patches.

5. Wrap the warm dough in plastic wrap and flatten into a rectangle about ½ inch (1cm) thick. Transfer the dough to the fridge to chill for at least 1 hour.

6. Meanwhile, preheat the oven to 350°F (175°C). Line a large baking sheet with parchment paper or a silicone baking mat.

7. Unwrap the chilled dough. Roll out the dough between 2 sheets of parchment paper to approximately ¼-inch (5mm) thickness. Cut out shapes using your choice of cookie cutter and transfer to the lined baking sheet, evenly spacing them. The size of the biscuits does not matter too much, as long as the thickness is consistent. Gather any trim and re-roll to cut out more biscuits. Chill the biscuits in the fridge for 15 minutes.

8. Bake the biscuits for 8 to 12 minutes, depending whether you prefer soft or crunchy cookies. Transfer the biscuits to a cooling rack and let cool for at least 1 hour before decorating. (Alternatively, let the biscuits cool for just 20 minutes if not icing.)

Make the royal icing (if using) and decorate

9. Place the icing sugar, aquafaba, and lemon juice in a medium bowl and mix together until smooth and the icing coats the back of a spoon. Transfer the royal icing to a piping bag fitted with a small round plain tip. Get creative and decorate the biscuits any way you like.

10. Store the gingerbread biscuits in an airtight container in a cool, dry place for up to 3 days.

Mince Pies

Makes 20 deep pies

Festive pies packed with boozy macerated fruit and spices—Christmas in a mouthful! Originally these pies contained minced meat such as mutton or beef and the pastry was made with suet, but nowadays those ingredients have been replaced by more fruit and, in this recipe, some nuts). Start macerating your fruit at least two weeks before baking, but your mincemeat will taste even better if started a few months or even a year ahead! If macerating the fruit mix longer than a month, store it in a cool place or the fridge and every month, stir in a little extra sherry or brandy. This will improve the flavour and maintain the shelf life.

Fruit Mince

Zest and juice of 1 lemon

Zest and juice of 1 orange

200g coarsely grated unpeeled apple (about 2 medium apples, such as Braeburn or Gala)

200g (1¼ cups) currants

200g (1¼ cups) black raisins

100g (⅔ cup) golden raisins

100g (¾ cup) dried cherries

100g (½ cup) dried apricots, quartered

100g (¾ cup) dried cranberries

100g (½ cup) dry sherry

100g (½ cup) brandy

250g (1 cup) hard apple cider

10g (4 teaspoons) ground cinnamon

10g (1 tablespoon) ground allspice

10g (1 tablespoon) ground ginger

5g (2 teaspoons) ground nutmeg

200g (2¾ cups) blanched almonds, slivered

150g (⅔ cup) coconut sugar

Sweet Shortcrust Pastry

440g (2 cups) cold vegan butter, cut into 1-inch (2.5cm) cubes

900g (1¾ cups) pastry flour or all-purpose flour

100g (1 cup) vegan icing sugar

8g (1 teaspoon) fine sea salt

100g (½ cup) ice cold water

60g (¼ cup) extra-virgin olive oil

"Egg" Wash

40g (¼ cup) unsweetened soy milk

5g (1 teaspoon) pure maple syrup

5g (1 teaspoon) organic canola oil

Raw cane sugar, for sprinkling

Prepare the fruit mince

1. Place the lemon zest and juice, orange zest and juice, apple, currants, black raisins, golden raisins, cherries, apricots, cranberries, sherry, brandy, and apple cider in a large container with a lid.

2. Thoroughly clean your hands, then mix and squeeze the fruit with the liquids to assist with the maceration process. Flatten the mixture and cover with the lid. Leave it to macerate at room temperature for 1 week, mixing and squeezing every couple of days.

3. After the week-long maceration period, place the cinnamon, allspice, ginger, and nutmeg in a dry small skillet. Heat over medium heat until lightly toasted and aromatic, 2 minutes. Remove from the heat and let cool.

4. Add the toasted spices, almonds, and coconut sugar to the fruit and mix together thoroughly. Store the mixture in a cool place to mature and develop for at least 1 month.

Make the pastry

5. The day before or early in the morning of the day you plan to bake the mince pies, place the bowl of a food processor in the fridge to chill for 30 minutes.

continued . . .

6. Place the butter, pastry flour, icing sugar, and salt in the chilled bowl of the food processor and pulse until combined, about 1 minute. Add the cold water and olive oil and pulse until a shaggy dough forms.

7. Transfer the dough to an unfloured work surface and finish mixing by hand. Bring the pastry together into a ball with no dry patches.

8. Lightly flour your work surface. Using a bench knife, divide the pastry into two 800g portions. Press or roll the pastry into 2 rectangles approximately 1 inch (2.5cm) thick. Wrap the pastry in plastic wrap and chill in the fridge for at least 4 hours but ideally overnight.

Assemble and fill the pies

9. When ready to assemble the pies, lightly grease two 12-cup muffin tins (20 moulds) with vegan butter.

10. Working with 1 portion of pastry at a time, gently roll it out into a larger rectangle between 2 sheets of parchment paper until about 1/10 inch (2.5mm) thick. Transfer it to the fridge and repeat with the second portion of pastry. Chill the rolled pastry for at least 15 minutes.

11. Take out the first sheet of pastry from the fridge and remove the top sheet of parchment. Using a 3-inch (8cm) round pastry cutter, cut out 20 discs. Place the top sheet of parchment paper back on and return the pastry rounds to the fridge. There is no need to cover them. Repeat with the second sheet of pastry (these will form the tops). If you have any trim, you can cut festive decorations such as stars or holly leaves.

12. Remove the first 20 discs from the fridge. Carefully line the moulds, using your thumb to gently push the pastry into the bottom and sides. The pastry should completely line the muffin cup, all the way to the rim.

13. Evenly divide the fruit mince among the 20 shells, approximately 75 to 80g per pie. Pack the mixture in tight enough that there are no air pockets and the fruit is slightly domed.

"Egg" wash, let the pastry set, and bake the pies

14. In a small bowl, whisk together the soy milk, maple syrup, and canola oil. Lightly brush the rim of the pies with the "egg" wash and place the remaining 20 pastry discs on top. Gently squeeze the edges to seal.

15. Lightly brush the tops with some more "egg" wash. Top with any pastry decorations and brush those too. Sprinkle with a little cane sugar. Place the pies in the fridge to chill for at least 30 minutes and up to a couple of days to allow the pastry time to set. This will help prevent shrinkage during baking.

16. About 1 hour before you plan to bake the pies, arrange the oven racks in the upper and lower thirds of the oven and preheat to 350°F (175°C).

17. Reduce the oven temperature to 325°F (160°C) and bake the pies until they are golden brown, 15 to 17 minutes. Rotate the pies halfway through baking. Remove the pies from the oven and let them sit in the tins for 10 minutes, then carefully remove them and transfer to a cooling rack. These festive treats are best enjoyed warm from the oven, maybe with some dairy-free cream or ice cream.

18. Store the pies in an airtight container in the fridge for up to 5 days.

Zero-Waste

Panzanella Salad

Serves 4

Panzanella is a well-known Italian salad in which bread is the key ingredient. Usually recipes call for stale bread, but my recipe is best with one- or two-day-old sourdough bread that still has some freshness and texture. Use organic local tomatoes at the peak of the season where you live to make this beautiful summer salad.

The bread is lightly charred (toasted) in a cast-iron skillet so it sucks up the heirloom tomato juice vinaigrette. The idea of including purslane came from talking with my friends Christoph and Jill, who own an incredible organic vegetable farm in Lillooet called Seed to Culture, an heirloom vegetable paradise that you never want to leave! Purslane has an almost sea vegetable texture, slightly salty and sour but also crunchy and robust enough to hold its own in a salad like this. Paired with some incredible basil and fennel blossom, this salad will brighten up any lunch or dinner.

Salad

500g/1.2 lb vine-ripened heirloom tomatoes (mixed colours and sizes)

5g (1 teaspoon) fine sea salt

250g (2 cups) day-old sourdough bread with crust torn into ½ to 1-inch (1 to 2.5cm) pieces

20g (1½ tablespoons) extra-virgin olive oil

50g (½ cup) drained capers

100g (2 cups) purslane

25g (½ cup) fresh sweet basil and/or Thai basil leaves

10g (3 tablespoons) fennel blossoms

Dressing

5g (1 teaspoon) chopped garlic

30g (2 tablespoons) champagne vinegar

5g (1 teaspoon) Dijon mustard

1g (¼ teaspoon) cracked black pepper

105g (½ cup) extra-virgin olive oil

Make the salad

1. Preheat the oven to 375°F (190°C).

2. Cut the tomatoes into wedges and slices of different sizes to add extra texture and visual appeal. Place the tomatoes in a colander set over a large bowl. Sprinkle with the salt and gently mix with your hand or a spoon. Set the tomatoes aside for 15 to 20 minutes to macerate.

3. Place the torn sourdough in a separate large bowl. Drizzle with the olive oil and toss the bread to coat.

4. Heat a large cast-iron skillet over medium heat until hot. Add the bread to the hot pan and shake so it settles into an even layer. Transfer the skillet to the oven and bake for 10 minutes, until the croutons are lightly toasted and golden brown around some edges. If they need a little more colour, turn them with a spoon and continue baking for another 5 minutes. Set the croutons aside.

Make the dressing and finish the salad

5. To the bowl the bread was in, add the garlic, champagne vinegar, mustard, and pepper. The tomatoes will have macerated a little by now and expelled some beautiful tomato juice into the bowl under the colander. Pour this tomato juice into the dressing and whisk everything together. Continue to whisk while slowly pouring in the olive oil until emulsified and thickened.

6. In a separate large bowl, combine the toasted croutons, capers, purslane, and three-quarters of the tomatoes. Lightly toss with some of the dressing. Transfer the salad to a serving bowl. Garnish with the remaining tomatoes, basil, and fennel blossoms.

Herb Stuffing with Red Onion and Pine Nuts

Serves 6 to 8

This recipe is a great way to use up older bread that has gone a little dry. Though stuffing is often associated with festive holidays, I personally would eat a variation of stuffing year-round! The fresh herbs, pine nuts, and grated apples add loads of flavour, moisture, and texture. I also like to use a mix of bread, such as my 100% Rye Sourdough with Toasted Seeds and Flakes (page 95) along with some Country Sourdough (page 55) end pieces. This recipe can also be made with gluten-free bread, by reducing the breadcrumb weight to 300g.

25g (2 tablespoons) vegan butter

100g (½ cup) extra-virgin olive oil

350g (2⅔ cups) finely chopped red onions
   (2 medium onions)

25g (3 tablespoons) puréed garlic (4 to 5 cloves)

20g (4 tablespoons) finely chopped fresh sage

5g (1½ tablespoons) finely chopped fresh thyme

5g (1½ tablespoons) finely chopped fresh rosemary

400g (3⅓ cups) sourdough breadcrumbs
   (I used a blend of seeded rye and whole wheat)

150g (1 cup + 2 tablespoons) pine nuts

20g (½ cup) finely chopped fresh chives

20g (⅓ cup) finely chopped fresh flat-leaf parsley

200g coarsely grated unpeeled apples
   (2 medium apples, such as Braeburn or Gala)

15g (1 tablespoon) English or French mustard

100g (½ cup) vegetable stock

5g (1 teaspoon) fine sea salt

2.5g (½ teaspoon) cracked black pepper

1. Preheat the oven to 350°F (175°C).

2. Melt the butter with the olive oil in a medium saucepan over low heat. Once the butter begins to bubble and brown a little, add the red onions and cook, stirring frequently, until soft and translucent, 10 minutes.

3. Add the puréed garlic and cook for 1 to 2 minutes. Add the sage, thyme, and rosemary and cook for another minute. Transfer to a large bowl.

4. Add the breadcrumbs, pine nuts, chives, parsley, grated apple, mustard, vegetable stock, salt, and pepper and stir together well. Taste the stuffing for seasoning, adding more salt and pepper to taste.

5. Spoon the stuffing into a 9 × 13-inch (23 × 33cm) baking dish lined with parchment paper and gently press it down with the spatula to compress (Alternatively, roll the stuffing into balls.) Cover the dish with foil and bake the stuffing for 35 to 40 minutes. Remove the foil and continue baking for another 15 to 20 minutes until the top is crunchy and golden brown. This stuffing is best served straight from the oven.

6. Cover and store the cooled stuffing in the fridge for up to 3 days. Reheat the stuffing thoroughly for at least 20 minutes in a 400°F (200°C) oven.

Liège Waffles

Makes 14 to 16 waffles

The Liège waffle is a yeasted waffle that is thicker, richer, and chewier than the Brussels, or Belgian, waffle that is leavened with baking powder. The dough can be made the day before serving, so the waffles can be enjoyed for breakfast or brunch with minimal effort. Pearl sugar is a European decorative sugar in which the sugar crystals are compressed into nibs. Mixed through the dough, these caramelize and add a beautiful crunchy exterior with a pop of sweetness inside. It can be a little difficult to find in stores in Canada, so look for it online.

200g (¾ cup) vegan liquid egg (such as JUST Egg)

200g (⅔ cup) sourdough discard (90% to 100% hydration, 50:50 bread flour and whole wheat flour)

70g (4 tablespoons) pure maple syrup

7g (2 teaspoons) pure vanilla extract

480g (4 cups) all-purpose flour

2.5g (½ teaspoon) fine sea salt

60g (4 tablespoons) cold vegan butter (I use Miyoko's), diced

120g (1 cup) pearl sugar

For serving (optional)

Fresh berries

Fruit compote

Dairy-free yogurt

Pure maple syrup

Chocolate spread

Toasted nuts

Mix the dough and bulk ferment

1. In the bowl of a stand mixer fitted with the dough hook, combine the liquid vegan egg, sourdough discard, maple syrup, vanilla, flour, and salt. Knead on medium-low speed for 5 minutes.

2. With the mixer running, gradually add the butter, a little at a time, and knead on medium-low speed for 5 minutes, until the butter is fully incorporated into the dough. Increase the speed to medium and continue kneading for 5 to 10 minutes, until the dough is smooth and shiny and pulls away from the sides of the bowl.

3. Lightly oil a container that is three times the size of the dough. Form the dough into a ball and place it seam side down in the container and cover tightly with a lid. Let the dough rise in a warm (72 to 75°F/22 to 24°C), draft-free place until it has increased in volume by approximately 20 percent, 2 to 3 hours. The dough will not double in volume, but there should be some noticeable activity. Place the dough in the fridge to ferment overnight, 12 to 18 hours.

Shape the dough and make the waffles

4. The following day, remove the dough from the fridge and let it come up to room temperature for 1 hour. Transfer the dough to a large bowl. Using one hand to hold the bowl, use your other hand to knead the pearl sugar through the dough until it is evenly distributed.

5. Preheat a waffle iron on medium heat. Spray the iron with a neutral oil such as sunflower or vegetable oil.

6. Divide the dough into equal-size portions (65 to 80g/ 2 to 3 oz each) and shape into balls. I recommend weighing each dough ball to help with consistent cooking times.

7. Place 2 dough balls (or 4 if your iron will allow) on the hot waffle iron, close the lid, and cook until the waffles are golden brown, 4 to 5 minutes. Transfer the cooked waffles to a cooling rack. (Do not keep them warm in the oven, as they will dry out.) Repeat to cook the remaining waffles, using a wet kitchen towel to clean the waffle iron thoroughly between batches, as the pearl sugar will burn and ruin the next batch of waffles.

8. Once all the waffles are cooked, reheat under the broiler and serve with toppings of your choice.

9. Store any remaining waffles in an airtight container in the fridge for up to 3 days.

Sourdough Crumpets

Makes 4 or 5 crumpets

A perfect way to start the day is with a warm sourdough crumpet! A crumpet is a bit like an English muffin, but with more holes for butter and jam to seep into. Here is a quick and easy recipe that's made with 100 percent sourdough discard, thus avoiding food waste. I usually feed my starter every 12 hours. In the morning I take what I need for the starter feed and place the remaining 300g in a separate bowl. This is usually pretty much all my discard. See page 25 for how to grow a sourdough starter from scratch.

I highly recommend buying at least four non-stick ring moulds, 3.5 inches (9cm) in diameter and 1.25 inches (3cm) tall, for making crumpets. However, you could use greased round cookie cutters instead. Apparently, if making the crumpets ahead of time, you should only cook them on one side. We always eat them all in one go, so I've never had a chance to try this out! These are delicious with vegan butter and maple syrup or jam.

300g (1 cup + 1½ tablespoons) sourdough discard (90% to 100% hydration, 50:50 bread flour and whole wheat flour)

50g (3 tablespoons + 1 teaspoon) unsweetened oat milk

5g (1 teaspoon) raw cane sugar

1.25g (¼ teaspoon) fine sea salt

1.25g (½ teaspoon) baking powder

1.2g (¼ teaspoon) baking soda

25g (2 tablespoons) extra-virgin coconut oil

For serving

Vegan butter

Jam or pure maple syrup

1. Place the sourdough discard and oat milk in a medium bowl and mix with a rubber spatula until combined. Set aside to rest, uncovered, for 5 minutes.

2. Meanwhile, lightly spray the inside of four 3.5 × 1.25-inch (9 × 3cm) ring moulds with coconut oil spray. Lightly spray a large non-stick skillet, place the rings in the skillet, and heat over medium-low heat. (If the pan is too hot, the crumpets will overcolour on the bottom before the batter is cooked through.)

3. Stir the sugar and salt into the starter mixture. Using a small fine-mesh sieve (such as a tea strainer), sift the baking powder and baking soda into the batter. Stir the thick batter well to combine everything.

4. Use a large spoon to carefully drop the mixture into the preheated rings until three-quarters full, to allow room for rising. The batter should now be very active. Set a time for 5 minutes. When the timer goes off, if the crumpets still look a little runny on top, cook for another 3 minutes. Don't rush this stage. Once the crumpets are nicely set and golden brown on the bottom, use a wide offset spatula to carefully flip them (with the ring moulds). Add a little coconut oil to the pan if needed and continue cooking for another 5 to 7 minutes, until golden brown on the bottom. Remove from the pan, gently push the crumpets out of their ring moulds, and place them on a cooling rack. Repeat with any remaining batter. (If there is only a small amount of batter left, it makes a beautiful crêpe-style pancake.)

5. Once all the crumpets are cooked and cooled, reheat them under the broiler or in the toaster.

6. The crumpets are best eaten the day they are made but can be made in advance and stored in an airtight container in the fridge for up to 2 days. Toast the crumpets before serving.

Za'atar Lavosh Crackers

Makes 8 large crackers

Lavosh (or lavash) crackers originate from the Middle East and are common in Armenian and Iranian cuisine. A cracker bread, or paraki, lavosh is a very thin unleavened bread that is dried to be eaten later. Traditionally they are shaped using a hay-filled pillow to stretch the dough and are cooked in a tandoor-style oven. The bread is often topped with sesame or poppy seeds, adding a nutty flavour. In this recipe the topping is herby, tangy za'atar. The fresh herbs in the dough add a herbaceous flavour.

Cracker Dough

140g (⅔ cup) water, at room temperature (75°F/24°C)

100g (¾ cup) active levain (page 29) or sourdough discard

125g (1 cup) all-purpose flour more for dusting

125g (1 cup) stone-ground whole wheat flour

25g (¼ cup) rye flour

30g (¼ cup) extra-virgin olive oil

5g (1½ tablespoons) finely chopped fresh rosemary

5g (1½ tablespoons) finely chopped fresh thyme

5g (1 teaspoon) fine sea salt

Za'atar Mix

9g (1 tablespoon) sesame seeds

6g (1 tablespoon) dried thyme

2g (1 teaspoon) dried oregano

2g (1 teaspoon) dried marjoram

3g (1 teaspoon) ground sumac

To finish (optional)

Extra-virgin olive oil

Flaky sea salt

Make, shape, and ferment the dough overnight

1. This dough is easily mixed by hand in a large bowl or with a stand mixer fitted with the paddle on low speed. Pour the water into the bowl. Add the active levain, all-purpose flour, whole wheat flour, rye flour, olive oil, rosemary, thyme, and salt. Mix until a smooth dough forms, 2 to 3 minutes.

2. On a lightly floured work surface, shape the dough into a ball. Place the dough in a large container, cover with a tight-fitting lid, and let rest at room temperature for 1 hour to start to activate a little. Transfer to the fridge to ferment overnight, 12 to 18 hours.

Roll the dough

3. The following day, when you are ready to make the crackers, arrange the oven racks in the upper and lower thirds of the oven and preheat to 350°F (175°C). Line 4 large baking sheets with parchment paper or silicone baking mats. (If you are using 2 baking sheets, roll out all the dough. Set aside 2 sheets of rolled dough on parchment paper ready to be baked after the first batch is out of the oven.)

Set up your pasta machine. (Alternatively, you can roll the dough with a rolling pin.)

4. Lightly flour a work surface with all-purpose flour, place the dough on it, and lightly flour the top of the dough. Gently roll the dough into a rectangle approximately 6 × 8 inches (15 × 20cm) and 1 inch (2.5cm) thick. Using a chef's knife, cut the dough lengthwise into 4 long strips. Roll each strip by hand to about ½ inch (1.25cm) thickness.

5. If using a pasta machine, set it to the thickest setting and lightly flour it. Working with 1 strip of dough at a time, lightly flour both sides, then feed the dough through the machine once to ¼ inch (5mm) thickness. (There is no need to cover the other dough strips while rolling; a slightly drier dough will be easier to handle.)

continued . . .

Lay the dough flat with a long side facing you and fold both short sides in to meet in the centre. Then fold the strip in half to form a rectangle. (This folding will improve the texture of the cracker and trap small air pockets that will puff during baking.) Feed the dough through the machine on the same setting. Repeat the folding, then feed the dough through the machine two or three times on the same setting. Continue to feed the dough through the pasta machine on progressively thinner settings, a few times on each setting, down to the second-thinnest or thinnest setting, until the dough is 1/16 inch (1.5mm) thick. Place the rolled dough on a lined baking sheet and repeat with the remaining dough strips.

or

If rolling by hand, working with 1 strip of dough at a time (leaving the remaining strips uncovered), use a rolling pin to roll out the dough until it is 1/16 inch (1.5mm) thick. Pause occasionally, letting the dough rest for a minute before rolling again. This way you will achieve a thinner cracker. Place the rolled dough on a lined baking sheet and repeat with the remaining dough strips.

Make the za'atar mix, finish, and bake the crackers

6. In a small bowl, stir together the sesame seeds, thyme, oregano, marjoram, and sumac.

7. Fill a spray bottle with water. Lightly spray the crackers all over with water. Sprinkle the za'atar mix evenly over the crackers. If desired, drizzle a little olive oil over top and finish with a pinch of flaky sea salt to elevate the flavours. Bake the crackers until they are golden brown and crispy, 10 to 12 minutes, rotating the pans halfway through if needed for even colour. Remove the crackers from the oven and allow them to cool completely on the baking sheets. (If using 2 baking sheets, bake the second batch.) Once cooled, break them into large shards.

8. Store the crackers in an airtight container in a cool, dry place for up to 3 days.

Fermented Rye Crackers with Seeds

Makes 8 large crackers

A great way to use up excess starter from feedings is to make these incredibly thin, crisp, and moreish sour crackers. A topping of mixed seeds adds another level of flavour and texture. I like to add nigella seeds, also known as kalonji, which are frequently used in Indian, Middle Eastern, and North African cuisine. A kind of black cumin, they are pungent and offer an incredible onion flavour. The starter and dough are prepared the day before baking, so plan accordingly.

Rye Starter

300g (3 cups) stone-ground whole-grain rye flour

300g (1¼ cups) warm water (72 to 75°F/22 to 24°C)

100g (⅓ cup + ½ tablespoon) active rye starter, wheat starter, or sourdough discard

Seeds

100g (¾ cup) pumpkin seeds

100g (¾ cup) sunflower seeds

25g (3 tablespoons) nigella seeds

25g (3 tablespoons) white or blue poppy seeds

25g (2 tablespoons + 2 teaspoons) flaxseeds

Prepare the rye starter (if not using a wheat starter or discard)

1. The morning of the day before you plan to bake the crackers, make a 100 percent rye starter: Split your wheat starter (see Note on page 92) in half. Reserving half for your regular feed schedule, in a medium bowl feed the other half with 100g warm water (75 to 78°F/ 24 to 26°C), 100g rye flour, and 25g sourdough culture. Stir together, transfer to a clean jar or other container, and cover with a loose-fitting lid. Let rest in a warm (72 to 75°F/22 to 24°C), draft-free place for 12 hours.

Prepare the cracker dough

2. Stir together the rye flour, warm water, and active rye starter or discard in a medium bowl. Transfer the dough to a 2-quart (2L) container and cover with a loose-fitting lid. Let rest in a warm (72 to 75°F/22 to 24°C), draft-free place for 12 hours.

Prepare the seeds and bake the crackers

3. When you are ready to bake the crackers, arrange the oven racks in the upper and lower thirds of the oven and preheat to 375°F (190°C).

4. In a food processor, combine the pumpkin seeds, sunflower seeds, nigella seeds, poppy seeds, and flaxseeds. Pulse them for a few seconds to break up the larger seeds. (Alternatively, break up the seeds with a mortar and pestle.) Set aside.

5. Line 4 large baking sheets with parchment paper. (If you don't have 4 baking sheets, spread 2 sheets of dough at a time. When the first batch goes in the oven, spread the rest of the mix and let sit, uncovered, at room temperature until ready to bake.)

6. Remove 1 sheet of parchment from a baking sheet and lay it on your work surface. Using a large offset spatula, spread a quarter of the cracker dough as thinly as possible, moving the spatula from one side of the sheet to the other, until you have covered the whole sheet. The dough should be approximately 1/16 inch (1.5mm) thick. Scrape off any thicker parts of dough and return it to the bowl. Return the parchment to the baking sheet. Repeat to spread the remaining dough on the remaining 3 parchment sheets. Sprinkle the seed mix evenly and generously over the dough.

7. Bake the crackers until light golden brown and dry all over, 18 to 22 minutes. The bake time will depend on how thinly the crackers were spread. Remove the crackers from the oven. Slide the parchment paper off the sheet and transfer to a work surface or rack and allow the crackers to cool completely. (If using 2 sheet pans, bake the second batch). Once cooled, snap them into large shards.

8. Store the crackers in an airtight container in a cool, dry place for up to 3 days.

Discard Sourdough Pancakes (Crêpes)

Makes 5 or 6 pancakes

In North America, pancakes are thick and fluffy. This recipe makes what in England we call pancakes. They are closer to French crêpes, but slightly thicker and smaller. The banana is used for flavour and as the egg replacer. This batter can be made the night before and stored in the fridge for a healthier and more fermented pancake batter. The recipe can easily be doubled or tripled for larger families, groups of friends, or events.

note: *For a savoury serving option, omit the coconut sugar and replace the banana with 20g (2 tablespoons) ground flaxseed. Add some finely chopped fresh herbs (dill, parsley, or cilantro) and a puréed garlic clove. The pancakes could be filled with a ragout of creamy mushrooms, or some crushed roasted spiced sweet potato and green onions, or your favourite taco fillings. Experiment and have fun—this is a base recipe that can be adapted for any mealtime.*

1 ripe banana

300g (1¼ cups) unsweetened oat milk

100g (⅓ cup) coconut yogurt

15g (1 tablespoon) coconut sugar

A pinch of fine sea salt

200g (⅔ cup) sourdough discard

5g (1 teaspoon) baking powder

75g (½ cup) potato starch (or 25g/¼ cup cornstarch)

75g (⅔ cup) all-purpose flour

75g (½ cup) stone-ground whole wheat flour or
    spelt flour

50g (¼ cup) extra-virgin coconut oil, for frying

Sweet serving suggestions (see Note for savoury options)

Lemon juice and sugar

Fresh berries, dairy-free yogurt, and toasted nuts

Caramelized bananas, coconut yogurt, and pure
    maple syrup

1. Preheat the oven to 300°F (150°C).

2. In a large bowl, mash the banana with a fork until puréed. Add the oat milk, yogurt, coconut sugar, salt, and sourdough discard. Whisk together to form a batter.

3. Sift in the baking powder, potato starch, and all-purpose flour. Add the whole wheat flour and whisk for 1 minute, until a smooth batter forms. Cover the bowl with a kitchen towel or loose-fitting lid and let rest at room temperature for at least 30 minutes. This will allow the flours to hydrate and the sourdough to begin to activate and develop some sour flavours. The longer the batter sits and ferments, the better the flavour. You can even store the batter in the fridge for the following day, though you might need to thin it with a little plant milk before using.

4. Heat a medium non-stick skillet over medium heat for 1 minute. Add 5g (1 teaspoon) of coconut oil to the hot pan and allow it to melt and heat up. Pour a ladleful (5 oz) of batter into the centre of the skillet and tilt the pan in a circular motion so the batter covers the bottom of the pan. (If you prefer a thinner crêpe-style pancake, whisk an extra 50 to 100g/3 to 6 tablespoons of oat milk into your batter.) Fry the pancake until lots of bubbles form on the top and the bottom is golden brown, 1 to 2 minutes. Add a little more coconut oil to the pan if it looks dry and allow it to melt, then flip the pancake and cook until the other side is golden brown, another 1 to 2 minutes. I like to flip the pancake back one more time to crisp up the first side. Transfer the pancake to a baking sheet, cover with foil, and keep warm in the oven while you cook the remaining pancakes.

5. Any unused batter can be stored in the fridge, loosely covered to allow the gases to release, for up to 24 hours.

Roasted Potato Frittata

Makes one 10-inch (25cm) frittata, serves 6

This recipe was inspired by an amazing old Scottish cookbook called *The Scots Kitchen: Its Traditions and Lore with Old-Time Recipes*, first published in 1929. It was a gift to me from some very close friends in Edinburgh. There's a recipe for potato scones, a very simple recipe using mashed potatoes, flour, and butter. This recipe is a little thicker than the traditional thinly rolled scones mentioned in that time-honoured cookbook, so I feel it is better described as a frittata than a scone. Low and slow is the key when cooking this frittata, to achieve a soft interior with a crispy exterior. Next time you make roasted potatoes for dinner, reserve a few and you'll be able to knock out this simple recipe for breakfast or lunch. My serving suggestion is Spring Pea, Arugula and Herb Spread (page 351), Cultured Cashew, Pine Nut, and Lemon Ricotta (page 348), and salad greens.

375g/13 oz peeled and roasted skin-on potatoes, any waxy potatoes such as German Butterball, Yukon Gold, or Anya (about 3 cups crushed)

100g (½ cup) sourdough discard

200g (¾ cup) unsweetened oat milk

50g (⅓ cup) stone-ground whole wheat flour

6g (1 teaspoon) baking powder

3g (½ teaspoon) fine sea salt

A pinch of cracked black pepper

15g (1 tablespoon) vegan butter

5g (1 teaspoon) extra-virgin olive oil

1. In a medium bowl, lightly crush the roasted potatoes with a fork. Some larger pieces of potato are fine. Add the sourdough discard, oat milk, whole wheat flour, baking powder, salt, and pepper and gently stir together with a rubber spatula until just mixed.

2. Heat a medium non-stick skillet over medium-low heat. Add the butter and olive oil. Once the butter starts to bubble, tip the pan in a circular motion to cover the bottom of the pan.

3. Position an oven rack on the top shelf and preheat the broiler.

4. Pour the frittata mixture into the pan and use the spatula to spread it evenly. Cook the frittata, checking the colour of the bottom by gently lifting it with the spatula. When it's nicely golden brown on the bottom, after about 10 minutes, place the frittata under the broiler for 2 minutes to cook the top a little. This will make flipping the frittata a lot easier. Once the top has set somewhat and is starting to colour, remove the frittata from the oven and use a wide spatula to carefully flip it over.

5. Return the pan to the stovetop and continue to cook the frittata over medium-low heat for another 10 minutes. Once it is golden brown on both sides, carefully slide the frittata onto a cutting board. Allow the frittata to cool for a few minutes, then cut it into wedges and serve immediately.

Raspberry and Hazelnut Bread Pudding with Banana and Coconut Custard

Serves 6

Centuries old, bread pudding is one of our favourite zero-waste recipes. It's best made with stale crusty end pieces of bread and overripe bananas, which naturally thicken and sweeten the custard. This is a very economical and filling dessert for any family, and you can use whatever you have on hand for ingredients. I've even made bread pudding with day-old cinnamon buns and brioche, which is quite luxurious! This recipe can be easily adapted with different fruit and nuts and works well with chunks of dark chocolate. Prepare the pudding ahead of time so the stale bread has time to soak up some of the custard and fruit juices.

400g/14 oz bananas, preferably overripe

1 can (13.5 oz/400mL) full-fat coconut milk

100g (⅓ cup) unsweetened oat milk

25g (2 tablespoons) coconut sugar (optional)

25g (3 tablespoons) ground flaxseed

2 vanilla pods, split lengthwise and seeds scraped, pod reserved (or 28g/2 tablespoons pure vanilla extract)

300g (2½ cups) stale sourdough end pieces (leave the crust on), cut into ½-inch (1cm) cubes

350g (3 cups) frozen raspberries or berries of choice

100g (¾ cup) whole skin-on natural hazelnuts

50g (½ cup) old-fashioned rolled oats

Dairy-free vanilla ice cream, for serving

1. Place an oven rack in the bottom position of the oven and preheat to 350°F (175°C).

2. In a high-speed blender, combine the bananas, coconut milk, oat milk, coconut sugar, and flaxseed. Blend on high speed until well combined, 2 minutes. Add the vanilla seeds and blend for 1 minute.

3. Pour one-third of the custard into a 13 × 9-inch (33 × 23cm) baking dish. Evenly scatter half the bread cubes over the custard. If you have used a fresh vanilla pod, lay the scraped pod on top of the bread so the flavour permeates through the pudding as it bakes. Scatter over half of the raspberries, followed by another third of the custard, the remaining bread cubes, and the remaining raspberries. Finish with the remaining custard.

4. Gently press everything down with a spatula so the sourdough soaks up some of the custard and berry flavours. Set aside for at least 30 and up to 1 hour to allow the bread to soak well. There is no need to cover.

5. Meanwhile, place the hazelnuts in a food processor and pulse for a few seconds to break them up a little. (Alternatively, roughly chop the nuts with a knife.)

6. Scatter the oats and chopped nuts over the pudding. Place the baking dish on a baking sheet to catch any spills. Bake the bread pudding until it is golden brown on top and the liquid is bubbling, 45 minutes. Serve the warm bread pudding with vanilla ice cream.

7. Once the pudding is completely cool, cover, and store in the fridge for up to 3 days.

French Meringues with Seasonal Berries and Coconut Yogurt

Serves 8 to 10

The main difference between French and Italian meringue is when the sugar is added. In French meringue, sugar is added to the egg white or its substitute during the whipping stage. It can be baked plain or used as a base for macarons and other desserts. It is not very stable, so it needs be baked as soon as it's prepared, or it runs the risk of separating. Baked French meringue is more tender, light, and fragile than Italian meringue, which is made by adding a hot sugar syrup at the whipping stage. The hot syrup partially cooks the egg whites or aquafaba, making it stable enough that it does not need to be baked (see Italian Meringue, page 329).

This dessert is my version of the British classic Eton Mess, which was first served in the 1930s at Eton College, where many royals and aristocrats have been educated. The original version did not contain meringue, which is a shame, as meringue adds the perfect texture. I strongly recommend using a dehydrator over an oven, as I have had more consistent results.

French Meringues (makes 30 to 40 individual meringues)

250g (1 cup + 1 tablespoon) aquafaba (liquid from two 14 oz/400mL cans of chickpeas; see page 333), well chilled

3.5g (1 teaspoon) cream of tartar

5g (1 teaspoon) pure vanilla extract

125g (½ cup) superfine (caster) or raw cane sugar

125g (1 cup) vegan icing sugar

Coconut Yogurt

1 can (13.5 oz/400mL) full-fat coconut milk, chilled

2 vegan probiotic capsules (not solid pills)

5g (1 teaspoon) pure vanilla extract (optional)

5g (1 teaspoon) pure maple syrup (optional)

For assembly

Fresh strawberries, raspberries, and blueberries or poached rhubarb

Freeze-dried raspberries

Fresh wild foraged flowers such as strawberry, salmonberry, and/or elderflower

Fresh mint leaves, baby basil, and/or red-vein sorrel

Make the meringues

1. Set a dehydrator to 175°F (80°C).

2. In the bowl of a stand mixer fitted with the whisk (or in a large bowl if using a hand-held electric mixer), whip the aquafaba on medium speed until it is frothy. The bowl must be very clean and dry. Any fat residue can inhibit the aeration and quality of the meringue. Add the cream of tartar and whisk until foamy and starting to peak, 2 to 3 minutes. While whisking, add the vanilla, then gradually add the superfine sugar and the icing sugar. Reduce the speed to medium-low and continue whisking until thick, smooth, and firm peaks form, 12 to 15 minutes.

3. Transfer the meringue mixture into a piping bag (your choice of tip; you can also use a tablespoon if you are not worried about finesse). Pipe drops, 1 inch (2.5cm) in diameter and height, onto a sheet of parchment paper. Lay the parchment with the meringues on the dehydrator trays. Dehydrate for 3 to 5 hours, depending on the size of the meringues and how you like them—still a little chewy or fully dry. (Alternatively, slide the parchment onto a large baking sheet and dehydrate the meringues in the oven set to the lowest temperature possible for 2 to 3 hours.)

4. Store the meringues in an airtight container at room temperature for up to 5 days.

continued . . .

Make the coconut yogurt

5. Shake the can of chilled coconut milk, then pour it into a very clean medium bowl. Whisk the coconut milk until very smooth.

6. Using a funnel if you have one to avoid getting any drips down the sides of the jar, carefully pour the coconut milk into a 750mL or 1L (3 or 4-cup) sterilized jar. Empty the contents of the probiotic capsules into the coconut milk and thoroughly stir with a clean wooden or plastic spatula. Do not use a metal spoon, as it can react with the probiotic powder. Once the powder is fully mixed in, cover the jar with a piece of muslin cloth or a very thin kitchen towel and secure with a rubber band. Leave the yogurt to activate at room temperature for 24 to 48 hours, depending how warm the room is. Taste the yogurt with a clean wooden spoon throughout the process to check the thickness and taste. Leaving for 48 hours gives the yogurt a nice tanginess that balances well with the sweetness from meringues.

7. Once you are happy with the yogurt, stir in the vanilla and maple syrup (if using). Cover with a tight-fitting lid and refrigerate for up to 7 days. Do not use if the smell is off-putting or there is mould.

Assembly

8. Spoon the delicious tangy, thick coconut yogurt into a large glass serving bowl or individual dessert bowls. (Glass shows off the vibrancy of the fruit, but it is not essential.) Scatter some quartered and halved strawberries, raspberries, and blueberries over the yogurt. Arrange pieces of meringue over the berries, and finish with your chosen garnish.

Italian Meringue

Makes about 450g (2 cups) meringue

This vegan Italian meringue is very versatile, so it can be used in many recipes—such as our Meyer Lemon Tart on page 231. Though it uses aquafaba in place of egg whites, the technique is the traditional one for making meringue, and the result is the same. The egg industry is generally merciless when it comes to the welfare of chickens and their chicks, so it is a great relief to finally have an accessible cruelty-free egg substitute in aquafaba, which is a fancy name for chickpea cooking liquid.

60g (¼ cup) water

200g (1 cup) superfine (caster) sugar

200g (¾ cup + 1 tablespoon) aquafaba (liquid from 1½ (14 oz/400mL each) cans of chickpeas; see page 333), well chilled

1g (¼ teaspoon) cream of tartar

5g (1 teaspoon) pure vanilla extract

1. In a small saucepan, combine the water and sugar and let sit for a few minutes so the sugar can dissolve and form a paste. Bring to a boil over medium-high heat, without stirring. If the mixture starts to boil up the sides of the saucepan, use a small pastry brush dipped in water to wipe down the sides to prevent sugar crystallization. Place a candy thermometer in the saucepan and simmer until it reads 240°F (116°C), 8 to 10 minutes.

2. As soon as the sugar begins to simmer, combine the aquafaba and cream of tartar in the bowl of a stand mixer fitted with the whisk (or a large bowl if using a hand-held electric mixer). The bowl must be very clean and dry. Any fat residue can inhibit the aeration and quality of the meringue. Whisk on medium-high speed until firm peaks form, 8 to 10 minutes.

3. Add the vanilla and reduce the speed to medium. Once the sugar syrup reaches 240°F (116°C), slowly pour a steady stream of the syrup into the whipped aquafaba, doing your best to keep it away from the whisk and stopping the mixer occasionally to allow the mixture to combine. Once all the syrup is incorporated, continue whisking the meringue for another 5 minutes. It will be smooth and glossier in appearance but still have firm peaks.

4. The meringue is best used straight away but can be stored for up to 24 hours in an airtight container in the fridge.

Dips, Spreads, and Accompaniments

Chickpea Hummus

Makes about 2 to 2.5kg (about 5 lb)

I much prefer using dried chickpeas instead of canned when making hummus, as they yield a fresher taste and more nutrients, plus the cooking liquid can be turned into the egg white substitute called aquafaba (see Note). If you are short on time, though, there is no problem using canned organic chickpeas; reserve the aquafaba for other uses. This recipe can be cut in half to make a smaller batch if desired.

note: *To make aquafaba, return 12 cups (3L) of the cooking liquid to the saucepan, bring to a boil, then reduce the heat to medium and simmer until reduced to a syrupy consistency weighing 300g, 15 to 20 minutes. Reducing the aquafaba intensifies its protein content and strength, giving it the viscosity of egg whites, so it can be used in many recipes that call for egg whites. Store aquafaba in an airtight container in the fridge for up to 5 days or pour tablespoons into ice cube trays and freeze for up to 1 month. Use in recipes such as French Meringues (page 327), Italian Meringue (page 329), Double Chocolate and Tahini Brownies (page 258), or Orange, Cardamom, and Olive Oil Brioche (page 139).*

    300g (1½ cups) dried chickpeas (or three 14 oz/
        400mL cans chickpeas)
    12 cups (3L) cold water, for cooking the chickpeas
    200g (1 cup) roasted tahini, divided
    10g (5 teaspoons) lemon zest, divided
    100g (½ cup) lemon juice, divided
    40g chopped garlic (2 to 4 cloves), divided
    10g (1¾ teaspoons) fine sea salt, divided
    4 to 6½ cups (1 to 1.5L) water at room temperature,
        divided

Garnishes

    50g (⅓ cup) white sesame seeds
    25g (2 tablespoons) extra-virgin olive oil

1. The night before, rinse the dried chickpeas in cold water, then place them in a large bowl or other container and pour in cold water to cover by at least 2 inches (5cm). Cover and let sit on the counter for about 12 hours. The chickpeas will expand and soften.

2. Drain the chickpeas and transfer them to a large saucepan. Add the cold water and bring to a boil, then reduce the heat to low and simmer, partially covered, and cook until the chickpeas are soft and very tender, about 45 minutes, periodically skimming off and discarding the white foam that forms on top. Remove from the heat and drain (reserve the cooking water to make aquafaba; see Note). Reserve a small amount of whole chickpeas for garnish.

3. Preheat the oven to 350°F (175°C). Scatter the sesame seeds on a small baking sheet and lightly toast them in the oven until they are golden brown, 5 to 6 minutes. Set aside to cool.

4. Place half of the warm chickpeas in a food processor and blend to a smooth paste, 2 to 3 minutes.

5. Add half each of the tahini, lemon zest, lemon juice, garlic, and salt and continue blending for another few minutes until smooth. With the machine running, slowly add half the room-temperature water and blend for 4 to 5 minutes, until the hummus is velvety smooth. Taste the hummus and add more salt if needed. Scrape the hummus into a large bowl.

6. Repeat with the remaining half of the ingredients. Add the hummus to the first batch and stir to combine.

7. Spoon some of the hummus into a serving bowl and garnish with the reserved chickpeas, a drizzle of olive oil, and the toasted sesame seeds.

8. Store the remaining hummus in an airtight container in the fridge for up to 5 days. Best brought to room temperature before serving.

Barbecued Red Pepper and Almond Romesco Sauce

Makes about 700g (3 cups) sauce

Romesco sauce originates from the Spanish region of Catalonia, where fishermen would make the sauce to be eaten with fish. Traditional recipes include roasted tomatoes, almonds, pine nuts or hazelnuts, olive oil, and ñora peppers, and are thickened with either flour or stale bread. My recipe uses a barbecue to cook the vegetables, which is inspired from another Catalonian cooking technique of grilling vegetables over an open fire. This adds the beautiful charred flavour that reminds me of summer. The ñora peppers, traditionally used to make paprika and chorizo, add depth of flavour, and sourdough bread adds another texture.

Serve with charred sourdough, fresh tomatoes, vegan cheese, fresh herbs, and salad; use as a side to your summer barbecue of grilled local vegetables; or use as a marinade for tofu.

200g (2 cups) whole natural almonds,
    plus 25g (¼ cup) for garnish

1 large head of garlic

500g/1 lb sweet red peppers

200g/7 oz vine-ripened tomatoes of any variety

100g (½ cup) extra-virgin olive oil, divided

50g (¼ cup) torn sourdough (leave the crust on)

30g dried ñora or ancho chilies (about 4 chilies),
    stem and seeds discarded

20g (1 tablespoon + 1 teaspoon) sherry vinegar
    or red wine vinegar

Juice of 1 lemon

5g (3 teaspoons) red chili flakes

5g (1 teaspoon) fine sea salt

2.5g (1 teaspoon) freshly cracked black pepper

1. Preheat the grill to medium-high. Preheat the oven to 350°F (175°C).

2. Scatter the almonds on a small baking sheet and lightly toast them in the oven until they are golden brown, 5 to 7 minutes. (Alternatively, you can toast the nuts in a small skillet on the barbecue.)

3. Peel the outer layers from the garlic head, then slice ¼ to ½ inch (5mm to 1cm) off the top. Place the prepared garlic head on a sheet of foil, drizzle with a little of the olive oil, and sprinkle with salt, then wrap it up to make a parcel. Place the garlic parcel on one side of the grill and slowly cook, with the lid closed, turning the parcel occasionally, until the garlic is golden and soft, 45 to 60 minutes. Remove from the grill and allow the garlic to cool in the foil.

4. While the garlic is cooking, place the sweet peppers and tomatoes in a large bowl. Lightly coat with ½ tablespoon of the olive oil, lightly season with salt, and toss to coat evenly. Grill the vegetables slowly until softened and charred all over, 5 to 10 minutes for the tomatoes and 10 to 20 minutes for the peppers. Do not rush the cooking; "low and slow" will give more flavour. Transfer the charred tomatoes to a plate and set aside to cool slightly. Transfer the charred peppers to the bowl, cover, and let the peppers steam for 20 minutes. (The steam will make them easier to peel.)

5. Peel the charred peppers and discard the seeds.

6. Unwrap the garlic and separate the cloves. Squeeze the cloves into the bowl of a food processor. Add the charred tomatoes, charred sweet peppers, toasted almonds, and torn bread. Blend for 1 minute. Add the dried chilies, remaining olive oil (6 to 7 tablespoons), sherry vinegar, lemon juice, red chili flakes, salt, and black pepper. Blend until smooth. Add more olive oil and salt to taste.

7. Store the romesco sauce in airtight containers in the fridge for up to 5 days or freeze for up to 1 month. If frozen, defrost in the fridge overnight before using.

Charred Eggplant Baba Ghanoush

Makes about 1kg (4 cups)

This dip is another Middle Eastern creamy appetizer that packs in the flavour to accompany breads, such as pita. Traditionally the skin is taken off the eggplant, but we like to char the skin to add more smoky aromas and flavours. Roasted eggplant on top adds more texture to the dip. It's a nice alternative to hummus or can be eaten alongside salads and falafels.

Cloves from 1 head of garlic, peeled

100g (½ cup) light olive oil

1.5 kg Italian eggplant (3 medium eggplants)

100g (½ cup) tahini

40g (3 tablespoons) lemon juice

10g (1¾ teaspoons) fine sea salt

Garnishes

1 medium Italian eggplant

5g (1 teaspoon) fine sea salt

50g (⅓ cup) sesame seeds

Leaves from 1 bunch fresh flat-leaf parsley, chopped

Pita Bread (page 117), for serving

Char the eggplant

1. Place the garlic cloves in a small saucepan and cover with the olive oil. Gently cook, stirring frequently, over low heat until the garlic is soft with little or no colour, 30 to 45 minutes. Remove the pan from the heat and leave the garlic in the oil to cool completely; this will help infuse the oil with lots of flavour.

2. Meanwhile, heat a dry large cast-iron pot over medium heat. Place the 3 eggplants in the pot, cover, and set a timer for 10 minutes. When the timer goes off, use tongs to gently lift the eggplants to check they are charred on the bottom. If they are, turn over the eggplants. Again, set the timer for 10 minutes and repeat. The aim is to char the eggplants on all sides. As the eggplants cook, they will expel liquid and collapse. Turning the eggplants twice during the cooking should be enough to char all the skin. Once the eggplants are fully charred and look shrivelled, remove the pot from the heat and let the eggplants cool with the lid on for 30 minutes. Keeping the eggplant covered while they are cooling contains the smoke and allows the smoky flavours to infuse.

Prepare the garnishes and roast the eggplant

3. Preheat the oven to 350°F (175°C).

4. Chop the garnish eggplant into 1-inch (2.5cm) pieces and place them in a medium bowl. Lightly season with the salt. Set aside for 10 minutes.

5. Place the sesame seeds on a small baking sheet and lightly toast them in the oven until golden brown, 5 to 6 minutes. Transfer to a small bowl. Return the baking sheet to the oven.

6. Drizzle 1 tablespoon of the reserved garlic oil over the eggplant and mix well. Spread the eggplant on the hot baking sheet and bake until fully soft, 20 to 30 minutes. Set aside until ready to serve.

continued . . .

Finish the baba ghanoush

7. Strain the confited garlic, reserving the cloves and oil separately.

8. Remove the stems from the charred eggplants and discard. I love to leave the charred skin on, as it adds a delicious flavour and beautiful colour, but feel free to scoop out the flesh and discard the skin if you prefer. Place the eggplants in a high-speed blender along with the garlic cloves, tahini, lemon juice, and salt. Reserve the eggplant juices in the pot to add to the blender if you need it. Start blending on a low speed and gradually increase to high speed, blending until smooth, 2 minutes. Taste the dip and add more salt, lemon, and/or tahini to taste, or thin with the reserved eggplant juices if desired.

9. The dip can be stored in an airtight container in the fridge for up to 2 days. Blend before using.

10. To serve, bring the dip to room temperature. Scrape the dip into a serving bowl and garnish with the roasted eggplant cubes, a little garlic oil, the toasted sesame seeds, and parsley. Serve with pita bread.

Roasted Butternut Squash Dip with Pumpkin Seed and Walnut Dukkah

Makes about 800g (3⅓ cups) dip

A creamy roasted squash dip topped with crunchy aromatic dukkah (or duqqa), an Egyptian nut, seed, and spice blend, will elevate any vegan deli board or sandwich. Try it with Za'atar Lavosh Crackers (page 315) or on a wedge of sourdough bread with salad. The dukkah can be varied by switching out the walnuts for hazelnuts, pine nuts, or almonds.

Roasted Butternut Squash Dip

1.5kg/3.3 lb butternut squash, peeled, seeds removed, flesh diced into 1-inch (2.5cm) pieces (1.2kg/2.7 lb prepared squash)

2 sprigs fresh rosemary

6 sprigs fresh thyme

15g peeled and smashed garlic cloves (2 large cloves)

10g (1¾ teaspoons) fine sea salt

25g (2 tablespoons) extra-virgin olive oil, plus more for garnish

150g (½ cup + 3 tablespoons) water, divided

100g (½ cup) tahini

Zest and juice of 1 lemon

Pumpkin Seed and Walnut Dukkah

5g (1 teaspoon) coriander seeds

5g (1 teaspoon) cumin seeds

5g (1 teaspoon) fennel seeds

5g (1 teaspoon) smoked paprika

1.5g (¼ teaspoon) cayenne pepper

100g (¾ cup) natural walnut halves

150g (1¼ cups) pumpkin seeds

50g (¼ cup) white sesame seeds

50g (¼ cup) black sesame seeds

Za'atar Lavosh Crackers (page 315), for serving

Roast the squash

1. Preheat the oven to 350°F (175°C).

2. On a large baking sheet, lay 2 large sheets of foil parallel to each other with a slight overlap (enough to make a parcel that will contain all the squash). Pile the prepared squash on the foil. Add the rosemary, thyme, garlic, salt, olive oil, and 100g (¼ cup + 3 tablespoons) of the water. Mix everything together with your hands to coat the squash. Fold over the excess foil to make a parcel, crimping the edges to seal. (The water will create steam during the first half of cooking so the squash stays soft, and the olive oil will help with the roasting in the second half of cooking.) Roast the squash for 30 minutes. Carefully open the parcel, watching out for the steam. Gently stir everything with a wooden spoon or spatula, then rewrap the parcel and continue roasting for another 20 to 30 minutes, until the squash is soft and cooked through. Allow to cool in the foil for 10 minutes. Leave the oven on.

Make the pumpkin seed and walnut dukkah

3. Combine the coriander seeds, cumin seeds, fennel seeds, paprika, and cayenne in a small blender or spice grinder and pulse until the seeds are cracked and broken down but not quite a powder. Tip the spice mixture onto a small baking sheet. Add the walnuts, pumpkin seeds, and white and black sesame seeds and mix with your hands to evenly coat the nuts and seeds.

4. Bake for 5 minutes, until everything is aromatic, lightly toasted, and golden brown. Set aside to cool.

5. Transfer the cooled dukkah to a food processor and pulse for a few seconds to break up the nuts and seeds a little. The dukkah can be stored in an airtight container at room temperature for up to 3 days.

continued . . .

Blend the roasted butternut squash dip

6. Once the squash mixture has slightly cooled, unwrap the foil parcel and discard the herb sprigs. Transfer the squash and garlic to a food processor. Add the tahini, lemon zest and juice, and the remaining 50g (¼ cup) water. Blend until smooth and creamy, 3 to 4 minutes. Stop the processor and scrape down the sides of the bowl halfway through. Taste and add more salt if needed and more water if it looks a little thick. As the dip cools, it will thicken slightly from the tahini.

7. The dip can be stored in an airtight container in the fridge for up to 3 days.

8. To serve, bring the dip to room temperature. Spoon into a flat serving bowl or wide glass jar. Garnish with a little olive oil and liberally scatter the dukkah over top. Serve with za'atar lavosh crackers.

Macadamia Feta

Makes about 500g (2 cups)

I developed this vegan feta to recreate the crumbly, rich, and creamy textures and flavours of sheep and goat feta cheese using macadamia nuts. Macadamia feta can be used in lots of recipes. It's especially good in my Macadamia Feta and Herb Scones (page 205), or enjoyed on pizzas, salads, and pastas. The process takes at least four days, so plan accordingly.

Feta

150g (1¼ cups) natural macadamia nuts

550g (2¼ cups) filtered water, divided

Zest of 2 lemons

50g (¼ cup) lemon juice

5g garlic (2 cloves)

20g (3½ tablespoons) nutritional yeast

2.5g (½ teaspoon) fine sea salt

5g (2 tablespoons) agar-agar flakes or powder

Brine

1kg (4¼ cups) filtered water

50g (¼ cup) fine sea salt

Prepare the feta

1. Place the macadamia nuts in a 1L (4-cup) glass jar or other container. Add 300g (1¼ cups) of the filtered water. Cover and let soak in the fridge overnight.

2. The next morning, prepare a rectangular plastic or glass container with a lid, approximately 5½ × 3½ × 1½ inches (14 × 9 × 4cm) to set the feta in. Lightly spray or wipe the inside with extra-virgin olive oil, then line it with a sheet of plastic wrap, pressing into all the corners and stretching out as many creases as possible.

3. Drain the nuts and transfer to a high-speed blender. Add the remaining 250g (1 cup) filtered water, lemon zest, lemon juice, garlic, nutritional yeast, and salt. Blend on low speed for 30 seconds, then slowly increase to high speed, blending until the creamy mixture is smooth and beginning to heat, 2 to 3 minutes

4. Add the agar-agar. Blend, starting on low speed and slowly increasing to high, for about 4 minutes to activate the setting properties of the agar-agar. The cream will be very hot. Pour the cream mixture into the prepared container and let cool for 15 minutes. Cover the container with the lid and place in the fridge to set overnight.

Meanwhile, prepare the brine

5. In a medium saucepan, bring the 1kg (4¼ cups) filtered water to a boil, then add the salt. Remove from the heat and set aside to cool. Pour the cooled brine into a container large enough to fit the slab of feta, cover, and set aside in the fridge overnight.

Brine the feta

6. The next morning, remove the feta from the fridge. Using the plastic wrap as handles, gently lift the set feta from the container and transfer it to the chilled brine container (ensuring that the feta is submerged in the brine). Cover and return to the fridge for at least 2 days and up to 5 days, depending how firm or salty you like your feta.

7. Once the feta is brined to your liking, gently remove it from the brine (discarding the brine) and store it in an airtight container in the fridge for up to 10 days.

Carrot Lox (Vegan "Smoked Salmon")

Makes 4 to 6 servings

Carrot lox is a beautiful savoury brunch that can be prepared in no time the day before it is needed, even while you're preparing your dinner. I like to cook the carrots whole to retain the natural flavours and colours of this humble vegetable. I created this recipe because I had a craving for a delicious bagel topping that was packed with flavours, including umami, smoke, and a slight sweetness. I suggest serving this with toasted sourdough Seeded Bagels (page 115), vegan cream cheese, capers, sliced cornichons, black pepper, chopped parsley and dill, finished with a squeeze of lemon.

250g (1 cup) tamari

250g (1 cup) water

100g (⅓ cup) vegan fish sauce

50g (¼ cup) caper brine

30g (2 tablespoons) liquid smoke

50g (¼ cup) raw cane sugar

500g/1 lb medium or large unpeeled carrots
    (5 to 6 cups uncooked ribbons)

10g/3 dried shiitake mushrooms

15g/2 sheets kombu seaweed

1. Preheat the oven to 350°F (175°C).

2. In a medium rectangular non-metallic baking dish, combine the tamari, water, fish sauce, caper brine, and liquid smoke. Stir in the sugar until dissolved, then set the poaching liquid aside.

3. Wash the carrots and trim both ends. Leave the skin on to preserve the beautiful orange colour after poaching. Add the carrots to the poaching liquid. Add the shiitake mushrooms. Lay the kombu on top and around the carrots. Place a sheet of parchment paper over the carrots, followed by a sheet of foil folded around the edges. This will help maintain a nice even cooking temperature and will prevent dry spots or major evaporation.

4. Bake until the carrots are tender when poked with a sharp skewer or small knife, 50 to 60 minutes. Remove from the oven, uncover the carrots, and allow to cool completely.

5. Transfer the cooled carrots and poaching liquid to a container with a lid and store in the fridge to marinate overnight. The carrots are easier to cut when cold.

6. When you are ready to serve your carrot lox, remove the carrots from the liquid and peel the skin off. Using a mandoline or vegetable peeler, peel the carrots into long ribbons that resemble slices of smoked salmon.

7. Store the whole carrots in their liquid in the fridge for up to 5 days. Store the ribbons separately in the fridge for up to 2 days.

Wild Nettle and Roasted Pistachio Pesto

Makes about 1kg (4¼ cups) pesto

Young nettles are in abundance in British Columbia from April into early summer. They mark the start of the foraging season for us. This perennial plant, also known as the stinging nettle, is easy to harvest if you have some thick gloves. It's best to take the top four leaves, as they are the youngest parts of the plant and therefore the most flavoursome and nutritious. Foraging nettles in this way also allows the plant to continue to grow. Always check with a professional forager or guidebook before foraging in the wild.

Nettles have many medicinal properties and can be dried and steeped for tea, syrup, tincture, or oil. Natasha loves to make nettle tea and nettle soup, another great accompaniment to sourdough bread! Nettles are very tasty and high in vitamins, minerals, and protein. As they are practically free if foraged, you can justify spending a little extra on quality pistachios. The pesto can be used in many baking recipes, simply spread on a slice of sourdough with some cherry tomatoes and spring salad greens, or used on a sourdough pizza.

A great addition to this recipe is spruce tips, which are also in season at the same time of year. They can be harvested easily by gently pulling the tips from the end of the branch. Simply add a small handful to the saucepan when blanching the nettles, or use them raw when blending the pesto. Spruce tips have a lime-like flavour, so you might reduce or even leave out the lemon.

400g (14 cups) raw nettle leaves
200g (1⅓ cups) roasted pistachios
20g (2 tablespoons) chopped garlic
Zest and juice of 1 lemon
25g (¼ cup) nutritional yeast
10g (1¾ teaspoons) fine sea salt
5g (2 teaspoons) freshly cracked black pepper
300g (1⅓ cups) extra-virgin olive oil

1. Prepare a large bowl of ice water. Bring a large pot of water to a boil. Add the nettle leaves and submerge them using a long spoon. Mix them around for 30 seconds, then drain the nettles through a colander. Immediately plunge the hot leaves into the ice bath to chill, locking in the colour (chlorophyll) and flavour. Stir the leaves around. You may need to drain the bowl and refill with more cold water and ice to chill the leaves as quickly as possible.

2. Once the leaves are cold, drain them in the colander and squeeze out any excess water. Blot the leaves between paper towel to remove any additional water.

3. Transfer the nettles to a food processor and add the pistachios and garlic. Pulse for 1 minute to break them up a little. Add the lemon zest and juice, nutritional yeast, salt, and pepper. Blend for 1 minute, then stop the processor and scrape down the sides of the bowl. Continue to blend while streaming in the olive oil for another minute until everything is chopped and mixed. If you prefer a thinner pesto, add up to another 50g (3 tablespoons) of olive oil. Taste the pesto and adjust the seasoning if needed.

4. Store the pesto in a couple of jars in the fridge for up to 5 days or in smaller airtight containers in the freezer for up to 1 month. If frozen, defrost the pesto in the fridge overnight before using.

Cultured Cashew, Pine Nut, and Lemon Ricotta

Makes about 300g (1¼ cups) ricotta

I love the sour, tart flavours of cheese but don't want to consume dairy or overly processed vegan cheese options. I came up with this ricotta recipe because I love making sourdough pizzas at home most Sunday evenings and wanted an easy cheese to use. The consistency is firm but not solid and it has a texture akin to creamy curds. Because it's cultured, this ricotta has a beautiful natural sour undertone, like a good yogurt. Nutritional yeast adds a great kick of cheesiness plus nutrients such as B-complex vitamins, and some are fortified with vitamin B12.

We love this generously spooned on some charred sourdough bread with some Spring Pea, Arugula, and Herb Spread (page 351), young pea shoots, and toasted nuts.

100g (⅔ cup) cashew nuts

100g (⅔ cup) pine nuts

1 vegan probiotic capsule (not solid pill)

100g (¼ cup) filtered water

Zest and juice of ½ lemon (5g zest and 10g juice)

15g (¼ cup) nutritional yeast

2.5g (1 teaspoon) puréed garlic (1 clove)

5g (1 teaspoon) fine sea salt

2g (½ teaspoon) freshly cracked black pepper

1. Place the cashews and pine nuts in a large glass jar or other container cover with 500g (2 cups) water, and let soak in the fridge overnight.

2. The following day, drain and rinse the nuts. Place the nuts in a high-speed blender. Empty the contents of the probiotic capsule over the nuts. Pour in the filtered water and blend until smooth, using the tamper to push nut chunks down. The mixture will be thick; avoid heating it too much.

3. Scrape the cream into a wide, shallow container so it is approximately 1 inch (2.5cm) thick. Press a sheet of plastic wrap directly on the surface to prevent a skin forming.

4. Set a dehydrator to 105°F (41°C). Place the covered cream in the dehydrator and dehydrate for 20 to 24 hours. Alternatively, leave the covered cream on the counter at room temperature for 36 hours. The texture should be rather firm, like medium tofu.

5. In a small bowl, combine the lemon zest and juice, nutritional yeast, garlic, salt, and pepper. Stir thoroughly, then add the cultured cream and fold it all together. Taste for seasoning, and maybe add more garlic or lemon. Be aware that the lemon juice will thin the ricotta.

6. Transfer the ricotta to a glass jar or other container and chill for at least 1 hour before serving. Store, covered, in the fridge for up to 3 days.

Spring Pea, Arugula, and Herb Spread

Makes about 850g (6 cups) spread

There's nothing better than podding fresh peas. It's one of those jobs that takes twice as long as it should, as you eat half of what you need. Once you're done, don't throw out the pods—they are so versatile and contain plenty of flavour, nutrients, and fibre. They can be run through a juicer and used in this recipe instead of the extra-virgin olive oil if you're looking for an oil-free variation. The juice can also be used in salad dressings or sauces. Another option is to blanch the pods the same way as the peas in this recipe and blend them to a purée. The purée should be chilled quickly once blended to preserve the colour. It is important to add the salt after the water boils, to prevent the chromium oxide coating on stainless steel pans being damaged by chlorine and chloride salts.

This is a beautiful, light, herbaceous spread that captures long, sunny, active days. Enjoy this spread on toast with some Cultured Cashew, Pine Nut, and Lemon Ricotta (page 348) and fresh salad leaves, or as an addition to your sourdough pizza.

7.5g (1½ teaspoons) fine sea salt, plus 10g (1½ tablespoons) for blanching
500g (3½ cups) fresh or frozen peas
150g (7½ cups) arugula
20g (¾ cup) fresh mint leaves
40g (2 cups) fresh basil leaves
20g (½ cup) fresh chives, thinly sliced
Zest and juice of 1 lime
15g (2 cloves) garlic, mashed to a purée
25g (⅓ cup) nutritional yeast
100g (½ cup) extra-virgin olive oil
2.5g (½ teaspoon) freshly ground black pepper

1. Fill a medium bowl with ice water.
2. Half-fill a medium saucepan with water and bring to a boil. One the water is boiling, add the 10g (1½ tablespoons) salt. Add the peas and blanch for 2 minutes. Drain the peas and immediately transfer them to the ice water to cool for 5 minutes. This will stop the cooking and help retain the beautiful green colour (chlorophyll). Drain the peas again and set aside.
3. Place the arugula in a food processor and pulse to chop a little, 30 seconds. Add the mint, basil, chives, lime zest and juice, garlic, and nutritional yeast. Blend for 1 minute, until roughly chopped. Stop the processor a couple of times to scrape down the sides of the bowl.
4. Add the olive oil, the remaining 7.5g (1½ teaspoons) salt, and pepper and blend for another minute, until everything is mixed.
5. Add the peas and pulse until crushed but not puréed. Taste the spread and adjust the seasoning as needed.
6. Transfer the spread to an airtight container and refrigerate for at least 1 hour to help develop more flavour. Store it in the fridge for up to 3 days.

Roasted Beetroot, Toasted Sunflower Seed, and Nasturtium Pâté

Makes about 1kg (4 cups) pâté

It's all well and good making delicious sourdough, but you need to have something to put on it. Pâté is so versatile—you can adorn a cheese board, fill a sandwich, stuff vegetables, or dress a salad with it.

I have a particular weakness for mustard and will incorporate it into any meal I can, and I seek that pepperiness in other foods too. Nasturtiums certainly hit the mark! While Natasha likes to have attractive flowers in the garden, I prefer focusing on growing food, so nasturtiums are a win-win for us. They thrive in poorer soil without the need of fertilizer. The edible flowers smell nice, attract pollinators, act as a trap to prevent pests attacking your prized fruit and vegetable patch, and beautify any salad. And here is a recipe for using the leaves.

Serve this pâté with thinly sliced sourdough. It makes a great filling in a sandwich with pickles, sprouts, salad, and Macadamia Feta (page 343).

1kg/2.2 lb purple or rainbow beets

75g (⅓ cup) extra-virgin olive oil, divided

250g (1 cup) water, divided

1 head of garlic

1 sprig fresh rosemary

1 small bunch fresh thyme

20g (1½ tablespoons) salt, divided

25g (2 tablespoons) apple cider vinegar

25g (2 tablespoons) raw cane sugar

175g (6 cups) fresh nasturtium leaves, a few (15g/½ cup) reserved for garnish

450g (3⅓ cups) sunflower seeds

5g (2 teaspoons) black pepper

Garnishes

Reserved toasted sunflower seeds (from above)

1 or 2 small rainbow beets, shaved

Nasturtium flowers and reserved leaves (see above)

5g (1 teaspoon) extra-virgin olive oil

1. Preheat the oven to 400°F (200°C).

2. Wash the beets thoroughly and trim both ends. I don't usually peel the beets, as the skin is full of flavour and nutrients, but feel free to do so if you prefer. Cut the beets into 2-inch (5cm) pieces and place them in a medium baking dish.

3. Pour 25g (2 tablespoons) of the olive oil and 100g (⅓ cup) of the water over the beets. Cut the head of garlic in half crosswise and nestle the garlic halves cut side up among the beets. Add the rosemary and thyme. Season everything with half of the salt. Cover with a lid or foil and roast for 30 minutes. Add the apple cider vinegar and sugar and give everything a stir. Cover again and continue roasting for another 30 minutes, until the beets are soft when poked with a sharp knife.

continued . . .

Remove the beets from the oven and set aside, covered. Reduce the oven temperature to 350°F (175°C).

4. Fill a large bowl with ice water. Bring a large pot of water to a boil. Add the nasturtium leaves and submerge them using a long spoon. Mix them around for 30 seconds, then drain the leaves through a colander. Immediately plunge the leaves into the ice bath for 1 minute, until they are cold. Drain them in the colander and squeeze out any excess water. Set aside the blanched leaves.

5. Spread the sunflower seeds on a large baking sheet and toast them in the oven until golden brown, 8 to 10 minutes. Reserve 50g (½ cup) of the toasted seeds for the garnish. Set aside the remaining seeds.

6. Uncover the cooked beets and discard the herb sprigs. Squeeze the beautifully soft garlic cloves into a food processor. Add the beets along with any cooking juices,

the remaining 150g (⅔ cup) of water, the toasted sunflower seeds, and 160g (5 cups) of the nasturtium leaves. (Depending on the size of your food processor, you may need to blend in two batches.) Process until smooth. With the machine running, slowly stream in the remaining 50g (¼ cup) of olive oil until the pâté is emulsified. Taste the pâté and adjust the seasoning if necessary. Thin with a little water or olive oil if desired. The freshness of the beets will dictate how much liquid is needed.

7. The pâté can be stored in an airtight container in the fridge for up to 5 days.

8. To serve, bring the pâté to room temperature. Spoon into a serving bowl and garnish with the shaved raw beet, the reserved toasted sunflower seeds, nasturtium flowers, and the reserved nasturtium leaves. Drizzle with a little extra olive oil if desired.

Smoky and Spicy Baked Beans

Makes 4 to 6 servings

Baked beans was a dish discovered by colonists in North America, with its roots in Indigenous cuisine much like cornbread, and since then baked beans have become so ingrained in British and North American cuisine. Homemade baked beans are so easy, and much better than the store-bought ones, which are steamed, not even baked at all. Baked beans, in my opinion, must be baked, and the great thing is that they don't require much attention as they are slow-cooking in the oven. You can adjust the flavourings in this recipe to your taste and personal preference, but I find it has a lovely balance between sweet, spicy, and smoky. Beans on toast is a great British classic for any mealtime. I like to serve the beans with a chunk of sourdough toast and some sautéed brown mushrooms, or on a tasty baked potato.

I usually make these beans the day before I need them so they can sit in the fridge overnight. The flavour the following day is even better.

500g (2¾ cups) dried organic white beans (or 1kg/2.2 lb canned organic white beans, drained and rinsed; I like using navy or cannellini beans)

500g/1 lb red, yellow, or white onions, finely chopped (2 or 3 large onions)

25g (2 tablespoons) extra-virgin olive oil

20g (3½ teaspoons) fine sea salt

100g (10 tablespoons) garlic powder

50g (½ cup) onion powder

50g (7 tablespoons) smoked paprika

25g (¼ cup) ground coriander

5g (a pinch) cayenne pepper powder

50g (¼ cup loosely packed) brown sugar or coconut sugar

125g (½ cup) apple cider vinegar

1kg/2.5 lb chopped fresh or canned chopped organic tomatoes

100g (⅓ cup) gochujang (Korean red chili paste; optional)

50g (¼ cup) liquid smoke

1. If using canned beans, skip to step 3. Wash the dried beans under cold running water, then drain them and place in a large container. Add cold water to cover the beans by 2 inches (5cm), then cover and let soak in the fridge for 24 hours to soften.

2. Drain the beans and place them in a large pot with 3kg (3 L) of water. I add lots of water up front so I don't have to add more halfway through the cooking. Bring to a boil over high heat, then lower the heat to medium-low and simmer, covered, until the beans are tender, 60 to 90 minutes. Drain the beans and set aside.

3. Preheat the oven to 400°F (200°C).

4. In a 13 × 9-inch (33 × 23cm) baking or casserole dish, mix the onions with the olive oil and salt. Bake for 10 minutes, then stir the onions and continue baking for another 10 minutes.

continued . . .

5. Meanwhile, mix the garlic powder, onion powder, paprika, coriander, and cayenne in a small bowl. In a separate small bowl, whisk together the brown sugar and apple cider vinegar.

6. Once the onions are translucent and nicely cooked, stir in the spice mixture. Return the onions to the oven and bake for 3 minutes. This toasts the spices and helps release natural oils, adding lots more flavour to the onions.

7. Remove the spiced onions from the oven. Stir in the sugar and vinegar mixture, then add the tomatoes and gochujang, if using. If using canned tomatoes, rinse the cans with a little water and add that water to the pan. Mix well. Return to the oven and bake, uncovered, for 30 minutes.

8. Remove the pan from the oven and stir. The sauce should have reduced by a third to a half. Stir in the beans. Return to the oven and bake for another 30 minutes.

9. Stir the beans and bake for another 15 to 30 minutes, until the desired consistency is reached. Remove the beans from the oven and stir in the liquid smoke. Taste for seasoning, adding a little more salt if needed. Serve immediately, or allow the baked beans to fully cool and store, covered, in the fridge overnight.

10. Store the beans in an airtight container in the fridge for up to 5 days or freeze them for up to 3 months.

Acknowledgements

M any people have contributed to this incredible journey that has led me to write my book. I would like to offer gratitude and thanks to . . .

Natasha, my beautiful wife, for putting up with my chef and baker careers, all the long hours, for nourishing me with your whole-foods plant-based cooking and raw vegan food, for being the chief taster, my business partner, and my co-writer, and for your honest feedback and ideas. I couldn't have done any of this without you. I love you so much.

My family, my grandfather John Dickie—a fellow author and veteran journalist who passed on while I was writing this—my mother and father, Lorna and Peter Tatton, Oli, Ali, and Heather, for your encouragement and listening ears through all my struggles. You are all so dear to me.

Tina James, our yoga teacher and very good friend, possibly our biggest fan since the inception of BReD in Whistler, who taught us to smile in the face of adversity. You're family to us.

Our key team members, past and present, Flynn Daley, Jana Mihalikova, and Stéphanie Rochon, for believing in and executing our bakery vision.

Our suppliers Anita's Organic Mill, for all the Canadian grains that we bake with. Our local organic farmers Christoph Miles and Jill Miners, and Anna and Jeanette Helmer, who work tirelessly to grow the best produce in BC. Your farms are magical places!

Janis Nicolay, our photographer, for your cool, collected, humble attitude, and professionalism. I love working with you.

Andrea Magyar, our editor at Penguin Canada, for seeking us out and giving us this dream opportunity.

Jeffery Laine at Asterix Studios, our graphic designer, for understanding our brand and ethos and translating that into our identity and always having our back and supporting us along the way.

The vegan business community, especially Katrina Fox, Kathleen Gage, David Pannell, and Lisa Fox, for taking action to bring forth a vegan world, empowering us and other vegan businesses around the globe to get the message out.

The vegan culinary trailblazers who helped shape my food and continue to inspire me: Matthew Kenney, Richard Makin of School Night Vegan, Doug Evans, Joanne Molinaro of The Korean Vegan, Liz Miu, George Lee of Chez Jorge, and Erin Ireland. You've all been moving the needle on plant-forward eating and the world is a better place for it.

All the incredible bakers who taught me so much by sharing their recipes and techniques with the world, I regard you all so highly, my sourdough brothers and sisters: Richard Bertinet, Chad Robertson, Jennifer Latham, Richard Hart, Daniel Larsson, Dan Riesenberger, Maurizio Leo, Monika Walecka, Vanessa Kimbell, Adam Pagor, Alex Phaneuf, and Or Amsalam. You inspire me to keep pushing on from bake to bake.

The restaurateurs and chefs who nurtured me in fine-dining cuisine, David Pitchford, Chris Wicks, Nick Cassettari, and Eric Griffith. You pushed me hard and instilled discipline and high standards in me.

Janaki Larsen, for creating beautiful ceramics to showcase my creations.

Our Whistler community, for encouraging us to open a bakery on the unceded territory of the Squamish Nation and Lil'wat Nation, and all our visitors from near and far who have supported us along the way. We owe you everything.

And finally, every vegan out there, for living a compassionate lifestyle, eliminating animals from the food supply chain, and inspiring others through your actions, if nothing else. You are our people.

Index